# Beyond the Tower

## Concepts and Models
## for Service-Learning
## in **Philosophy**

C. David Lisman and Irene E. Harvey, volume editors

Edward Zlotkowski, series editor

A PUBLICATION OF THE

AMERICAN ASSOCIATION
FOR HIGHER EDUCATION

Goodwin Liu's chapter previously appeared in volume 2 of the *Michigan Journal of Community Service Learning*. It is reprinted here by permission of that journal.

**Beyond the Tower: Concepts and Models for Service-Learning in Philosophy**
**(AAHE's Series on Service-Learning in the Disciplines)**
C. David Lisman and Irene E. Harvey, *volume editors*
Edward Zlotkowski, *series editor*

**About This Publication**
This volume is one of eighteen in AAHE's Series on Service-Learning in the Disciplines. Additional copies of this publication or others in the series from other disciplines can be ordered using the form provided on the last page or by contacting:

AMERICAN ASSOCIATION FOR HIGHER EDUCATION
One Dupont Circle, Suite 360
Washington, DC 20036-1110
ph 202/293-6440 x780, fax 202/293-0073
www.aahe.org

ISBN 1-56377-016-4

# Contents

*Part 1:*
*Service-Learning as a Mode of Philosophical Inquiry*

*Part 2:*
*Course Narratives*

*Afterword*

*Appendix*

# About This Series

by Edward Zlotkowski

The following volume, *Beyond the Tower: Concepts and Models for Service-Learning in Philosophy*, represents the 12th in a series of monographs on service-learning and the academic disciplines. Ever since the early 1990s, educators interested in reconnecting higher education not only with neighboring communities but also with the American tradition of education for service have recognized the critical importance of winning faculty support for this work. Faculty, however, tend to define themselves and their responsibilities largely in terms of the academic disciplines/interdisciplinary areas in which they have been trained. Hence, the logic of the present series.

The idea for this series first surfaced late in 1994 at a meeting convened by Campus Compact to explore the feasibility of developing a national network of service-learning educators. At that meeting, it quickly became clear that some of those assembled saw the primary value of such a network in its ability to provide concrete resources to faculty working in or wishing to explore service-learning. Out of that meeting there developed, under the auspices of Campus Compact, a new national group of educators called the Invisible College, and it was within the Invisible College that the monograph project was first conceived. Indeed, a review of both the editors and contributors responsible for many of the volumes in this series would reveal significant representation by faculty associated with the Invisible College.

If Campus Compact helped supply the initial financial backing and impulse for the Invisible College and for this series, it was the American Association for Higher Education (AAHE) that made completion of the project feasible. Thanks to its reputation for innovative work, AAHE was not only able to obtain the funding needed to support the project up through actual publication, it was also able to assist in attracting many of the teacher-scholars who participated as writers and editors. AAHE is grateful to the Corporation for National Service – Learn and Serve America for its financial support of the series.

Three individuals in particular deserve to be singled out for their contributions. Sandra Enos, former Campus Compact project director for Integrating Service With Academic Study, was shepherd to the Invisible College project. John Wallace, professor of philosophy at the University of Minnesota, was the driving force behind the creation of the Invisible College. Without his vision and faith in the possibility of such an undertaking, assembling the human resources needed for this series would have been very difficult. Third, AAHE's endorsement — and all that followed in its wake

— was due largely to then AAHE vice president Lou Albert. Lou's enthusiasm for the monograph project and his determination to see it adequately supported have been critical to its success. It is to Sandra, John, and Lou that the monograph series as a whole must be dedicated.

Another individual to whom the series owes a special note of thanks is Teresa E. Antonucci, who, as program manager for AAHE's Service-Learning Project, has helped facilitate much of the communication that has allowed the project to move forward.

## The Rationale Behind the Series

A few words should be said at this point about the makeup of both the general series and the individual volumes. Although philosophy, concerned as it is with abstract conceptual distinctions, may seem like an unlikely discipline with which to link service activities, "natural fit" has not, in fact, been a determinant factor in deciding which disciplines/interdisciplinary areas the series should include. Far more important have been considerations related to the overall range of disciplines represented. Since experience has shown that there is probably no disciplinary area — from architecture to zoology — where service-learning cannot be fruitfully employed to strengthen students' abilities to become active learners as well as responsible citizens, a primary goal in putting the series together has been to demonstrate this fact. Thus, some rather natural choices for inclusion — disciplines such as anthropology and geography — have been passed over in favor of other, sometimes less obvious selections such as philosophy. Should the present series of volumes prove useful and well received, we can then consider filling in the many gaps we have left this first time around.

If a concern for variety has helped shape the series as a whole, a concern for legitimacy has been central to the design of the individual volumes. To this end, each volume has been both written by and aimed primarily at academics working in a particular disciplinary/interdisciplinary area. Many individual volumes have, in fact, been produced with the encouragement and active support of relevant discipline-specific national societies.

Furthermore, each volume has been designed to include its own appropriate theoretical, pedagogical, and bibliographical material. Especially with regard to theoretical and bibliographical material, this design has resulted in considerable variation both in quantity and in level of discourse. Thus, for example, a volume such as Accounting contains more introductory and less bibliographical material than does Composition — simply because there is less written on and less familiarity with service-learning in accounting. However, no volume is meant to provide an extended introduction to service-learning *as a generic concept*. For material of this nature, the reader is referred to such texts as Kendall's *Combining Service and Learning: A Resource Book for Community and Public Service* (NSEE, 1990) and Jacoby's *Service-Learning in Higher Education* (Jossey-Bass, 1996).

I would like to conclude with a note of special thanks to David Lisman and Irene Harvey, coeditors of the philosophy monograph. Their work has not only demanded patience and resourcefulness, it has also called for considerable personal commitment and a truly pioneering spirit. I would also like to acknowledge the generous assistance of William Clohesy, associate professor of philosophy at the University of Northern Iowa, who provided valuable feedback on the manuscript.

November 1999

# Foreword

## by David A. Hoekema

Anyone who has chosen philosophy as a field of study, whether on the undergraduate or the graduate level, has had to face an insistent question from skeptical family members: "What does philosophy have to do with the real world?" History does not record the first time this challenge was put to a philosopher, but no doubt it was already a familiar question by the time Thrasymachus launched it with particularly biting sarcasm at Socrates in Book I of the *Republic*. Certainly no contemporary American student has escaped it entirely.

But this collection puts forward the suggestion that a new answer is being formed from the experience of philosophy instructors and students across the country.

There has been a quiet revolution in undergraduate education during the past decade or two, a revolution whose standard-bearers were the pioneers of service-learning as an element of liberal arts education. A generation ago, every college and university had a catalog full of academic programs, and many of them also maintained an active policy of encouraging students to volunteer for service to local organizations and agencies. But few campuses — and few students — saw any identifiable relationship between these two parts of the picture.

Today that situation has changed dramatically: Voluntary service to meet community needs has become an integral part of the academic experience of many students. Careful and critical reflection of how academic study informs one's role in community service, and on how community experiences illuminate and flesh out academic studies, has come to be highly valued by students, faculty, and institutions across the nation. The service-learning revolution has brought modest but important changes to nearly every college and university.

The service-learning movement has posed the same challenge for philosophy as the skeptical relative, in slightly revised form: What does the study of philosophy have to do with the real world of community service? It is not hard, after all, to understand how students of 20th-century history can benefit from spending some time working with neighborhood associations, or to identify some significant links between the topics studied in a sociology or an economics class and the challenges of helping a welfare client apply for a job

---

David A. Hoekema, former president of the American Philosophical Association, is professor of philosophy and interim vice president for student life at Calvin College.

or a senior citizen arrange for home health care. In English composition and studio art classes, an assigned essay or a portfolio of drawings can be linked to a student's experiences as a playground helper or a tutor in an urban school. But what about philosophy? How can a class devoted to musing about whether there is any real world, or about whether numbers and emotions and moral rules exist, possibly lend itself to effective service-learning? How can philosophers, whose heads are notoriously enveloped in high banks of clouds, come down to earth in ways that make effective use of community service?

The essays gathered in this book provide an answer to this question — or rather a wide variety of different but overlapping answers. Thanks to the work of those whose reflections are collected here and of hundreds of others in the profession as well, service-learning has come to be one of the means by which students learn philosophy and confront foundational questions of meaning, value, and responsibility. The connections between volunteer experience and philosophical exploration are most readily apparent in courses on social ethics and political philosophy, and the essays collected here provide examples. But there have also been successes, some of them documented here, in using service-learning to shed light on other areas of philosophy, from philosophy of art to epistemology. The pedagogical creativity of these examples may inspire readers to carry the study of other philosophical areas — metaphysics, philosophy of science, philosophy of religion, existential philosophy, and more — into the real world, to intersect with the experiences that voluntary service can provide.

Having spent most of my two decades in academia in administrative positions, I have not yet had the opportunity to incorporate a service-learning component into my courses. (I plan to do this when I return to teaching in the near future.) I have, however, had frequent occasion to observe the profound changes that occur in a colleague's courses — and sometimes in the colleague himself or herself, as a teacher and as a philosopher — as a result of such ventures.

I recall talking many years ago with a highly regarded colleague who had become deeply disillusioned with students' apathy and passivity, despairing of his ability to awaken and motivate them in his introductory philosophy classes. Over the course of a few years, as he began to participate in a number of ventures on his campus and elsewhere that involved some form of service-learning, his outlook changed completely. He told me on one occasion, exaggerating only slightly, that he had found the key to overcoming student apathy by incorporating community service and reflection on it into his philosophy courses. Going out into the community and seeing how institutions meet or fail to meet the needs of real people, he observed, compels students to come out of their cocoons and take both themselves and others more seriously.

Another colleague has spoken about how difficult it was to get students to acknowledge the difficulties and ambiguities of moral choices that they regarded as purely black and white until they spent a few hours in community service agencies. Watching real people who struggled to know what was right — whether to have an abortion or carry an unwanted pregnancy to term, whether to tolerate a teenager's alcohol abuse or to evict him from the household until he goes straight — they began to understand the messiness and difficulty of genuine moral choices in situations where every option seems to untangle good and evil.

Conversely, the uncritical relativism that many students bring to their study of philosophy, the attitude "My morality is true for me and yours is true for you," is one of the first illusions to disappear when students apply philosophical categories to situations they may encounter in their communities. Few people are insensitive enough to fall back on such evasions when they confront the horrors of parental abuse and neglect, on the one hand, or the inspiring example of a high school principal who won't let his staff or his students give up their ideals, on the other. Whether their starting point is an excessively dichotomized moral world or a vague complacency that sees only gray, students learn from community service that good and evil, justice and injustice, compassion and cruelty, are very real — and very different.

These experiences do not provide easy answers, but they do provide a basis for exceptionally fruitful and realistic philosophical discussions. And there is surely more to be gained in the study of philosophy from a serious discussion of the choices that face a pregnant teenager lacking any family support, particularly when several students know this individual as a person and not just a textbook example, than from a science fiction debate about whether it is immoral to unplug a famous violinist who has surreptitiously tapped into your kidney.

What lies ahead? The uses of service-learning in core areas of philosophy beyond moral and social philosophy have only begun to be explored. In some areas of philosophical study, its usefulness may be very limited. It is hard to imagine how an upper-level course devoted to close textual study of Aristotle or Kant, for example, could be enriched, and not merely diluted and discombobulated, by adding a service-learning component. An introductory course in the philosophy of knowledge, on the other hand, might appear an unlikely prospect for service-learning. Yet several of the writers in this collection suggest ways in which classic philosophical issues concerning the mind and the world can be placed in sharper relief through carefully planned community experiences and reflections on them. The same is surely true for other introductory and intermediate courses, ranging from history of philosophy to formal or informal logic.

And what will this achieve, in the end, for teachers and scholars in philosophy? It will bring a renewed sense of engagement and energy in our students and many new challenges for instructors as we search for ways of exploring familiar concepts in unfamiliar contexts.

Service-learning will not turn a struggling teacher into a star. Nor will it solve our most perplexing philosophical problems about the nature of the person or the reality of evil. Rather, it is a tool that, in the hands of a skilled and dedicated teacher of philosophy, can help our students understand that ideas matter, that critical reasoning solves some problems, and that the real world is actually a very good place to do philosophy. I hope this volume will help many of my colleagues in philosophy make creative and effective use of that tool.

# Introduction

by C. David Lisman

This monograph deals with the use of service-learning as an approach to teaching and learning in philosophy. Before providing a summary and analysis of the essays and course narratives included here, I would like briefly to explain this approach and some of the general ways in which it can relate to philosophy as an academic discipline.

Service-learning is a form of experiential education that involves students in community service as part of an academic course and that helps them relate their service experience to course content. Some kinds of service activities students engage in include serving as mentors or tutors in public schools, working at homeless shelters, and working on environmental projects such as park trail improvements and neighborhood cleanups. Integrating service experiences like these into a philosophy course could take several forms. Students in an ethics course could relate their public school tutoring experiences to topics such as racism, gender equity, and distributive justice. They could examine aspects of these topics in the context of their service experience and in a reflective paper explore the relationship among those experiences, course readings, and in-class discussions. Many specific examples of how philosophers have integrated service-learning into academic courses are presented in the pages that follow.

One could, in fact, argue that philosophers have a special role to play in the development and utilization of service-learning as a pedagogical strategy. Philosophers in ethics and in social philosophy classes examine many of the very same fundamental issues that have served to define service-learning as an educational approach. This approach has emerged out of a desire not only to help make learning more practical but also to help promote moral growth, a sense of community involvement, and even a renewal of American education's civic mission. In many cases, philosophers are already discussing in their courses the very issues students are being led to confront in and through their service experiences. Hence, philosophers may rightly be expected to contribute to a deepening of our understanding of this pedagogy as well as to specific techniques for promoting rigorous as well as vigorous student learning.

A major theme of the essays in the first part of this volume is the need for an epistemology that is both implied *by* service-learning and needed *for* service-learning if it is to continue to grow as an effective educational strategy. Several of the essays included here suggest that "postmodernist" philosophical investigations already under way may point in a useful direction.

Indeed, they suggest that service-learning can be seen as another catalyst energizing the broader movement to a postmodernist agenda. "Doing philosophy" in the framework of a postmodernist epistemology may look a little different from doing philosophy in contexts reflecting British and American analytic philosophy or European Continental philosophy.

Another theme articulated here is the need to rethink our moral framework, again in a way relevant to service-learning. While perhaps somewhat less developed, this theme suggests again that philosophy has a critical role to play in articulating a moral theory that can assist us in investigating the many moral and social issues we confront in service-learning. A postmodernist debate on moral theory parallels the debate on epistemology. In the pages that follow, I briefly summarize some of the major ideas of the essays in Part 1, at the same time offering a few tentative suggestions about where we are with regard to postmodernist epistemological and ethical investigations.

## Epistemology

In his article "Knowledge, Foundations, and Discourse: Philosophical Support for Service-Learning," Goodwin Liu describes what he takes to be the theory of knowledge that undergirds conventional pedagogy, criticizes that theory, and proposes an alternative epistemology that affirms the pedagogical value of service-learning. Drawing upon the philosophy of Richard Rorty, Liu maintains that the traditional view of knowledge is foundationalism and dualism.

Foundationalism is the view that there is a bedrock of epistemological certainty. The most influential foundationalist theories are empiricism and rationalism. Empiricism affirms that sense experience provides an adequate basis for knowledge. Rationalism affirms that mind is the source of knowledge. Associated with rationalism is the dualism of Descartes. According to Descartes, mind is distinct from body and that knowledge of the existence of mind as a thinking thing constitutes the foundation for knowledge. Whether one is a rationalist or an empiricist, once a distinction is made between the perceiving subject and the world perceived, epistemological skepticism emerges. How can we be certain that our subjective experiences provide us with a basis for knowledge? Rorty uses the metaphor "mind as Mirror of Nature" to characterize this self-referential view of knowledge. According to Rorty, we understand the mind as a Mirror of Nature in the sense that moving from belief to knowledge is a matter of polishing the Mirror so that its representations can accurately reflect external reality.

Liu criticizes this traditional view. He states, "If we view knowledge as a relation of correspondence between persons and objects, between internal representations and external realities, then we need the ability to offer theory-neutral observation statements as objective evidence for or against particular knowledge claims." However, no theory-neutral procedure is available. We have no notion of what counts as an objective observation, and we therefore have no context-independent language for adjudicating competing claims to knowledge. This criticism applies to both foundationalism and dualism.

Drawing upon the work of Barber (1984), Liu advocates that a community-informed pragmatism provides a more usable epistemological framework. Liu states:

> On this view, knowledge is not discovered by penetrating into the objective essence of reality and representing it accurately on our Mirrors of Nature. Instead, it is created through conversation in which persons with interests and needs attempt to justify knowledge claims stated in languages with particular norms and meanings. What counts as knowledge is understood as a function of conversation and its standards of justification.

Liu suggests that this contextual theory of knowledge may serve as an adequate epistemology for service-learning as a pedagogy. He suggests that rather than trying to develop a view of service-learning that accords with traditional academic practice, we need to protect service-learning's marginal status by recognizing that this pedagogy may be pointing the way to a new epistemology that actually will serve as a critique of the traditional epistemological framework of higher education. Whether service-learning will accomplish this remains to be seen.

In "Feminism, Postmodernism, and Service-Learning," Irene E. Harvey defends postmodernism against feminist and service-learning charges that postmodernism undermines the very possibility of these perspectives. The fundamental complaint of feminist theory is that postmodernism denies or deconstructs concepts such as "subject," "subjectivity," "truth," "gender," and "women in general" that are essential to taking women's particular experience as a basis for theorizing. Service-learning advocates may similarly complain that postmodernism preempts community involvement and observations from experience. Harvey argues that a proper interpretation of postmodernism actually strengthens feminist theory. Similarly, she contends that postmodern theory is at least coherent with service-learning practice.

Developing service-learning projects that enable students to explore the meaning and application of concepts such as "freedom," "determinism," "self," and "knowledge" from a feminist, postmodernist perspective can be a powerful way for those students not only to come to understand the power of postmodernist analysis but also to develop an appreciation of feminist theory. Harvey provides concrete examples of how she has used service-learning in her philosophy courses. In doing service, her students "discover for themselves how philosophical ideas are enacted in practice, institutionalized in regulations, and reinforced in accepted procedures and rule-bound activities."

In "Listening to the Evidence: Service Activity and Understanding Social Phenomena," Hugh Lacey argues that service-learning accompanied by "carefully structured reflections to which a variety of theoretical frameworks are brought to bear" can play an essential role in helping us understand certain social phenomena such as urban poverty. Lacey briefly comments on the widespread view of poverty that has led to welfare reform. This view holds that our previous welfare policies contributed to dependency and a "culture of poverty," thus essentially blaming the poor for their poverty. Lacey observes that these critics of welfare usually have had very little contact with people in poverty, ignore the perspective of the poor themselves, and typically describe the poor in harsh and punitive language.

He suggests instead that we adopt an investigative approach that attempts to "listen to the evidence," to examine the phenomenon of poverty in a more inclusive way. What, he asks, would count as evidence in addressing this issue? He believes service-learning can play a role here because "understanding the phenomenon of poverty requires experiential contact with it," and service-learning projects can provide this kind of understanding.

## The Task of Philosophy

In "The Use of a Philosopher: Socrates and Myles Horton," John Wallace presents an essay whose very style represents a break with more traditional philosophical discourse. Wallace is concerned with how we might teach in a more radically democratic manner, i.e., teaching students not so much *about* philosophy as about *how to be genuinely philosophical* in attempting to promote social change. Wallace draws upon insights of Socrates and Myles Horton, who founded the Highlander Folk School, to develop an approach to teaching philosophy that is useful for students involved in academically based community service. He rejects the traditional view of teaching students to appreciate knowledge for its own sake but acknowledges that this may be the only way to teach philosophy to masses of students who are in college mainly to get the credentials they need to pursue a career. He also rejects as ridiculous and repugnant Nusbaum's view that philosophers are experts on the good life and that the value of philosophy is that it enables students who will gain positions of power to internalize philosophical models.

Wallace develops a more praxis-oriented approach based on comparing similarities and differences between Socrates and Horton. He sees several similarities between the two. They both used conflict and contradiction to move people and to make them think. They placed a high value on the past experiences that people bring to a learning situation. In this regard, Horton believed that people brought with them the seeds of the solutions to their own problems. Both taught through a questioning approach instead of telling or lecturing. Both focused primarily on developing people instead of getting distracted by "practical work." Like Socrates, Horton emphasized education over organizing. Both philosophers also adopted the perspective that the philosopher's "expertise" lies in inquiry and learning and not in having answers, content, or results known in advance. Finally, both philosophers taught by example and were willing to take personal risks.

In my essay "Praxis-Informed Philosophy," I also advocate a more praxis-grounded approach to doing philosophy — one that recognizes that philosophy is a method for clarifying, understanding, and contributing to the achievement of human purposes. I note that many of our purposes are very ideological. To say that a purpose is ideological is to say that the purpose is realized in the context of a set of interrelated beliefs and values essential to our self-esteem. I suggest we need to think about ways by means of which we can effect change in our ideologies. One way that this can come about is through the recognition that having an ideologically laden goal is, in effect, to be "emotionally invested" in a goal.

Because goals or purposes, especially ideological ones, are not merely normative interests but normative interests in which we have strong emotional investment, a change in that emotional investment may result in a change of goal or purpose, or at the very least, greater clarity about that goal or purpose. How might such a change in emotional investment come about?

The cognitive theory of emotions can be very useful as a tool for illuminating emotional investments. According to this theory, emotions are highly self-involved appraisals. While in many cases there is a close alignment between emotionally relevant beliefs and intellectual beliefs, in the case of prejudice, there well may be an inconsistency between the emotionally relevant belief and the intellectual belief. Emotionally relevant beliefs are best characterized as examples of "experience as" rather than "experience that." In other words, they are forms of experiencing in which we experience the significance of something as being of a particular sort. In a situation where there is no tension between an emotionally relevant belief and an intellectual belief, there is no disjunction. However, in the case of a person who is intellectually opposed to racism but harbors racist feelings, such a disjunction does exist. The racist individual intellectually believes that prejudice is wrong but experiences ethnically different individuals in a negative way.

The solution to such a disjunction is for the racist individual to work at bringing the intellectually held belief and emotionally relevant belief in line. Perhaps such an individual should become personally involved with people for whom he or she has racist feelings. By becoming more involved with people who are potential objects of the individual's racist feelings, he or she may begin to experience them in ways that are more convergent with the individual's intellectual belief that all ethnic members are socially equal.

# Civic and Procedural Republicanism

Communitarianism has emerged as a fairly recent postliberal moral and social philosophy in response to perceived difficulties with philosophical liberalism as epitomized by the contractarian theory of Rawls (1971). Barber (1984), Pratte (1988), Sandel (1982, 1996), and Sullivan (1982) have been the most vocal critics of Rawls's theory. Philosophical liberalism (or procedural republicanism, as it is called by some) assumes as its foundation the atomistic individual. But are we, in fact, ontologically sufficient, or are we socially encumbered? Liberal or progressive communitarianism maintains that we need to recognize that we are essential social beings. We need, moreover, to bear in mind that, as Taylor (1991) argues, we come to the recognition of a moral framework through language acquisition in a dialogical process. Thus, we come to acknowledge that the first principle of ethics is to adopt those policies and principles that serve the common good. This approach is called "progressive" or "liberal," because it acknowledges that the common good includes attention to principles of autonomy and justice. That is to say, a society that would define the common good to exclude maximizing fairness and autonomy has a faulty concept of "common good."

It is in this context that Liu's community-based pragmatism figures as a "communitarian" possibility. However, many similar communitarian theories (Barber 1984; MacIntyre 1981; Sandel 1982, 1996; Sullivan 1982; Taylor 1989, 1991, 1992) have been criticized for developing a community-based ethical framework that can be reduced to cultural relativism. What is needed is a moral theory that will enable us to better understand that the good society is a society that promotes the good of all in ways that protect liberty and fairness. But we need to secure such a perspective on something other than the traditional moral foundationalism of either Kantian thinking or utilitarianism.

I would suggest that the linguistic direction of Rorty and others points the way to such a perspective. As with epistemology, ethics may be secured in the recognition that we logico-linguistically must make certain assumptions about moral discourse as a condition of acquiring this discourse through mastering natural language. Fundamental to our narrative acquisition of language is the recognition of others as persons, which in turn entails that to acknowledge ourselves as persons means respecting the dignity of others whom we acknowledge as persons. This, in turn, provides the narrative framework for developing the conception that we necessarily must affirm that ethical decisions should meet the test of the common good tempered by liberty and fairness.

In "Fluid Boundaries: Service-Learning and the Experience of Community," Cathy Ludlum Foos argues for the sufficiency of philosophical liberalism, maintaining that "civic virtue can and should be promoted in the public schools through the teaching of a liberal conception of a limited, political morality." She maintains that we have a responsibility to help promote individuals capable of participating in collectively shaping their society, and that this involves teaching young people "to acknowledge and listen to points of view other than those with which they were raised."

She explicitly acknowledges the communitarian tradition's criticism of this liberal emphasis on the individual. Liberal values do not, however, lead unavoidably to self-centeredness. Rather, this is something that may happen if we are not careful about how we teach the value of individualism. She also defends liberalism against the charge that it fails to take seriously enough the value of community. Communitarians, she maintains, confuse a political emphasis on individualism with a social emphasis on individualism. Liberalism advocates a *political* emphasis on the grounds that the rights of individuals against the tyranny of the majority must be protected. Moreover, in such a society, individuals will be empowered to form strong communal and social relations. The fact that we are fragmented as a society is a result not of social theory but of the failure for us to connect individuals, especially our students, to community.

She concludes by suggesting ways that service-learning can accomplish this purpose. Community service draws students out of themselves as they see the consequences of self-centered behavior. Students also can grasp the power of community as they see what the multiplication of individual effort in a cooperative venture can accomplish.

In his essay "Service-Learning, Citizenship, and the Philosophy of Law," Stephen L. Esquith maintains that if service-learning is to serve as a tool of political education, it must place educating about power at the center of democratic citizenship. Esquith discusses how service-learning can take on this kind of role in the context of the philosophy of law. He notes that prelaw students take philosophy of law mainly for the purpose of gaining a better grasp of the kind of logical reasoning they will need in law school and as attorneys. However, he wants them to develop a more critical or questioning frame of mind about the role of law in our society. Our society tends to seek legal remedies at the expense of other democratic methods and to provide legal remedies at the expense of serving the common good.

Esquith cites Dewey's view of experience as a working conception of the way in which he believes service-learning can enable students to "problematize" their learning in order to understand the ways in which the law is deployed contextually. He finds great value in Emerson's view that we should personally aim at attaining a degree of personal poise in dealing with real-world complexities, in this case, the application of the law. In developing a more contextualized understanding of legal theory through service-learning, Esquith hopes, his law students will come to a deeper understanding of the place of the law, and of their future need as attorneys to trust the "deliberative capacities of common citizens and their potential to grow and keep up with . . . shifting forms of corporatist power."

Finally, to conclude the first part of the volume, Judith Green, in her essay "Deepening Democratic Participation Through Deweyan Pragmatism," discusses an international current of support for what she calls "deep democracy." This is a concept of democracy emphasizing citizen activism that is socially transformative, empirically based, and productive of "human flourishing" in empirically describable terms. Green believes that there are several reasons for believing that we can develop this kind of democracy internationally. Such an approach recognizes, first, that citizens can be knowledge producers rather than merely passive consumers of expert knowledge; second, that their involvement is critical to developing and gaining acceptance of appropriate public policies; and, finally, that active citizen participation in policy deliberation and implementation promotes moral growth. Indeed, an expert-driven model morally diminishes our citizens.

Green considers various obstacles to the development of deep democracy. Citizen activism not only runs up against concentrations of political and economic power but also is a messy affair and can be unpredictable. Other challenges concern how to effectively develop the most appropriate goals and methods for achieving our democratic purposes. Green maintains that the personal and socially transformative process of citizen involvement can serve as a counter to these problems and that Deweyan pragmatism offers us invaluable guidance in developing appropriate social and political goals and methods for solving our problems and strengthening democracy. It guides citizens "to cooperatively create rolling 'experimental' processes of analyzing a problem, formulating an operating hypothesis, agreeing upon a shared objective, acting together, evaluating the consequences, and formulating new hypotheses for the next stage of their ongoing collaborative transformation effort."

## Course Narratives

Eugene J. Valentine's essay, "Service-Learning as a Vehicle for Teaching Philosophy," provides a fairly wide-ranging discussion of how he uses service-learning as a tool for enabling students to examine philosophical concepts they are studying. This essay provides a good introduction to the second part of the volume, entitled "Course Narratives." Here we find essays whose primary purpose is to provide a rationale for why service-learning is being used in a particular philosophy course and what its utilization accomplishes.

In his civics education course, Valentine adopts the view that the goal of such a course "should be to develop the disposition to reflect well on the relationship between a well-lived life and a good community. Its goal should be to educate citizens to participate in civic dialogue concerning how we should connect our lives to the lives of others." In this course, students study Plato, Aristotle, Hobbes, and Kant. Valentine illustrates how students have used their service-learning experiences to deepen their understanding of concepts and concerns central to these philosophers. For example, one student who mentored teen parents in a high school observed that Plato was right in saying that the community plays an important part in shaping our children. However, she also pointed out that today media figures often exercise more influence on young people than do their parents.

In discussing her rationale for integrating service-learning into her Perspectives on Poverty course, Carolyn Magid sees this approach as helping her students deepen their understanding of the plight of people in poverty as well as the implications of current policy. In this way, they also become better able to envision alternatives. Many of her students have worked at the Hamilton School, an urban public school. Their service-learning experiences have provided them with a contextualized base for reflecting on issues of poverty.

Sally J. Scholz discusses the value of service-learning in ethics as a way to help her students develop their moral imaginations, gain a sense of self-awareness, and challenge the intellectualism and insularity of theoretical ethics and traditional practical ethics courses.

Mary Esther Schnaubelt discusses service-learning as the means for providing "content" in her critical-thinking course. In working on local community problems, students learn to both develop and apply critical-thinking skills.

Finally, in his essay "Sojourning in the Art World: Service-Learning in Philosophy of Art," Dan Lloyd discusses how service projects at various art centers, including a small theater, a senior citizens craft center, a cultural center, and an avant-garde gallery, enable students to better understand the cultural and economic forces at play in the development of art. Lloyd points out that students come into his course with a view of art as a socially isolated matter. But through this course and the service experiences it provides, students come to see that there is a strong interplay between the production of art and socially defined opportunities and norms.

William M. Sullivan's afterword places the kind of academic work represented in this volume as a whole in the context of how service-learning "can give new urgency to important questions about the discipline of philosophy and the enterprise of higher education." By practicing self-reflective inquiry such as is modeled here, contemporary academic philosophers can reassert philosophy's claim to being a core liberal arts discipline as well as a powerful vehicle of democratic renewal.

The volume concludes with a brief annotated bibliography of texts especially relevant to philosophers interested in the connection of service-learning and philosophy.

## References

Barber, B.R. (1984). *Strong Democracy*. Berkeley, CA: University of California Press.

MacIntyre, A. (1981). *After Virtue*. Notre Dame, IN: University of Notre Dame Press.

Pratte, R. (1988). *The Civic Imperative: Examining the Need for Civic Education*. New York, NY: Teachers College Press.

Rawls, J. (1971). *The Theory of Justice*. Cambridge, MA: Harvard University Press.

Sandel, M.J. (1982). *Liberalism and the Limits of Justice*. New York, NY: Cambridge University Press.

———. (1996). *Democracy's Discontent: America in Search of a Public Philosophy*. Cambridge, MA: Harvard University Press.

Sullivan, W.M. (1982). *Reconstructing Public Philosophy*. Berkeley, CA: University of California Press.

Taylor, C. (1989). *Sources of the Self: The Making of the Modern Identity*. Cambridge, MA: Harvard University Press.

———. (1991). *The Ethics of Authenticity*. Cambridge, MA: Harvard University Press.

———. (1992). *Multiculturalism and the Politics of Recognition*. Princeton, NJ: Princeton University Press.

# Knowledge, Foundations, and Discourse:
## Philosophical Support for Service-Learning

by Goodwin Liu*

In an earlier article, I used the Kuhnian metaphor of "scientific revolution" to describe service-learning in relation to the pedagogies and concepts of knowledge most typical of American higher education (Liu 1995; see also Kuhn 1962). I hinted at some of the ways in which service-learning signals a departure from traditional academics, and I suggested that service-learning may constitute a shift in educational paradigm. I learned from many colleagues that this latter notion resonates with what they understand service-learning to be and why they use it.

It is tempting to believe that service-learning is reshaping our understanding of education in important and dramatic ways. Yet practice still varies considerably at the program level, and we continue to struggle for a definition of service-learning that is capable of eliciting broad consensus and usage in the field. As a consequence, service-learning has appeared to lack rigor, and it failed to penetrate mainstream educational practice on most campuses.

I believe service-learning will continue to be viewed suspiciously in academia as long as we speak of it as an alternative pedagogy without clarifying the nature of its underlying epistemology. For the most part, we have been making arguments for a change in pedagogy without the support of arguments for a change in epistemology. The premise of this article is that education takes place within an epistemological frame: If we wish to rethink the way we teach and learn, then we need to rethink the way we know.

This article is primarily philosophical. It is an attempt to describe the theory of knowledge that undergirds conventional pedagogy, to criticize that theory, and to propose an alternative epistemology that affirms the pedagogical value of service-learning. Specifically, I discuss foundationalism and dualism as the key pillars of our mainstream intellectual heritage. I challenge these concepts and offer a positive alternative, drawing from Richard Rorty's *Philosophy and the Mirror of Nature* (1979). Rorty, who identifies himself as an heir to the work of Dewey, Heidegger, and Wittgenstein, expands the implications of Kuhn's history of science into a comprehensive theory of knowledge. The epistemology he proposes is an extension of the philosophical tradition called "pragmatism." Pragmatism's preoccupation with discourse, I argue, illuminates the contextual nature of knowledge and implicates community, diversity, and engagement as pedagogical virtues.

# Mainstream Epistemology

I begin by describing the theory of knowledge that we have inherited from Western post-Enlightenment philosophy. This tradition actually consists of not one but several theories of knowledge. For our purposes, what is important is not the relative merits of different theories, but the way they frame the central epistemological problems they try to solve. Indeed, what places these theories within a single tradition are the premises they share about ourselves and the nature of the world.

The traditional view may be understood as having two conceptual pillars. One is foundationalism. Traditional theories of knowledge understand the problem of knowledge to be a problem of locating the epistemological bedrock from which we can make a claim to knowledge with absolute certitude. From a secure foundation, we can build a system of knowledge by establishing rules of inference that allow us to use what we already know to justify claims to new knowledge. Thus, the legitimacy of a knowledge claim derives from the legitimacy of the claims before it, as long as the entire chain of claims can be traced back to a foundation of certainty and reflects the correct application of the rules of inference. For example, the foundational claim "If I have a clear and distinct idea of a chair, then the chair is really there," followed by an observation that "I have a clear and distinct idea of a chair," warrants the claim "There is a chair." Foundational theories differ with respect to the degree of certainty they require of foundations and the degree of certainty they accord to knowledge claims further and further away from the foundation (Code 1987: 4). But in any case, the foundationalist approach has led us to understand the problem of knowledge as a "quest for certainty" (Dewey 1929).

The second pillar of the traditional view is dualism. Among the many foundational theorists in the Western tradition, perhaps none was as influential as Descartes. Through his method of radical doubt, Descartes gave substance to foundationalism by locating the epistemological bedrock in his clear and distinct idea of "I" or "a thinking thing" (what we call "mind"). In carving out inner space and distinguishing it from the notion of "body" or the external world, Descartes privileged the former over the latter in terms of its susceptibility to certain knowledge. Descartes could never doubt his existence as "a thinking thing," and the invention of the mind provided a field of nonempirical inquiry in which certainty was possible (Rorty 1979: 136-137). Without this foundation and the rule of inference he drew from it (the method of "clear and distinct ideas"), he claimed to have no way of distinguishing genuine knowledge of the external world from perceptions generated by illusions, dreams, or a demonic deceiver.

The concepts of foundationalism and dualism go far in illuminating our traditional knowledge paradigm. Foundationalism offers a linear, static, and hierarchical view of knowledge. Dualism gives substance to the hierarchy by drawing a bright line between mind and body. Together these notions privilege the mind over the external world as an object of knowledge, with the first susceptible to nonempirical self-inspection and certain understanding, and the second comprehensible only through contingent, empirical inquiry.

This premise centers the dominant theories of knowledge in the Western tradition on one paradigmatic epistemological problem — namely, the problem of the external world. How is knowledge of the outer, external world possible when our only certain knowledge is of our inner ideas and sensations? How is it possible to lift the "veil of ideas" that separates the world as it appears to us from the world as it really is? It is this line of questioning that introduces the notion of skepticism, and the task of circumventing skepticism in order to ground claims to knowledge has been the central project of epistemology for the past 200 years.

Many solutions have been proposed. Descartes suggested that we could know genuine reality by sorting out confused inner representations from the clear and distinct ones. Locke offered a mechanistic account of how objects of knowledge make impressions on the mind. Berkeley (and Hume to some extent) argued that there is no way to transcend the veil of ideas, that we have no reason to believe in an external reality, and that our knowledge is limited to ideas, perceptions, and our interpretations of them. None of these theories has gained universal acceptance, but they have made important contributions to the way we think about the problem of knowledge.

Within the dominant paradigm, knowledge is understood as accurate representation. The problem of knowledge is the problem of knowing whether our inner representations correspond accurately to an outer reality. On this correspondence theory of truth, the statement "There is a table" is a true claim to knowledge if my sensory idea of a table corresponds to the empirical reality of the table's existence. Thus, knowledge is understood as a relation between the knower and the object of knowledge.

Furthermore, this paradigm models knowledge on sense perception, especially on metaphors of sight. Throughout the literature, philosophers have understood the question of how we can know as a question of how we can see clearly, and the proposed solutions are causal explanations of how objects generate mental representations that correspond with the genuine articles. These explanations spill over into physics, physiology, and psychology, but in metaphorical terms, they conceive of the mind as "something like a wax tablet upon which objects make impressions," and they equate "knowing" with "having an accurate impression" (Rorty 1979: 142).

Rorty uses a different metaphor to characterize the paradigm of knowledge as accurate representation. He suggests that, on the conventional paradigm, "to understand how to know better is to understand how to improve the activity of a quasi-visual faculty, the Mirror of Nature" (1979: 163). If we can find within the Mirror a privileged class of representations whose accuracy cannot be doubted, if we can "polish" the Mirror so that its representations really reflect the external reality, then we will have found the foundations of knowledge that entitle us to judge the accuracy of other representations.

This mirroring metaphor is consistent with the analogy of visual perception used to describe knowledge as a relation between persons and objects. On this view of knowledge, it is clear why the notion of "objectivity" is central. For the mirroring function to work accurately, we must orient both the mirror and the object in a way that prevents contingencies or irrelevant considerations to deflect or distort the lines of reflection.

Rorty's metaphor is useful in illuminating how this epistemological frame guides the search for knowledge, particularly in the paradigmatic enterprise of that search: science. Polishing the mirror to see clearly is analogous to developing a set of methods and rules of inference for objectively characterizing the world. The certainty that attaches to any characterization, to any theory or observation, depends on the precision of the mirroring function, which is to say, the rigor of the method of inquiry. For example, in the biological sciences, basic scientists generally give greater weight to evidence from in vivo experiments than to in vitro evidence. Biochemical explanations that allow us to deduce physiological phenomena are valued over physiological characterizations of the phenomena themselves. Genetic studies are assigned more probative value than cellular research. Depending on the experimental system, the evidence is labeled direct or indirect, explicit or circumstantial. To qualify knowledge claims in finer degrees, scientists employ various tools of statistics. Moreover, the use of probabilities and the demand for replicability may be understood as responses to the problem of induction.

In these ways, we begin to see how the traditional theory of knowledge grounds knowledge claims in the empirical sciences. Knowledge claims are justified in terms of the accuracy of the mirroring function mediated by experimental methods, and degrees of accuracy are understood as varying levels of experimental rigor that yield hierarchies of inquiry and evidence. In science as in philosophy, the problem of knowledge is the problem of bridging the gap between ourselves and the external world, and our answers push against a stingy skepticism that limits the certainty with which we may make any claim to knowledge.

It is not difficult to draw out the implications of this paradigm of knowledge for the way we approach education, research, and teaching. Since dualism dictates that we may have absolute certainty only about our ideas and not about the real world, we elevate the realm of thought above the realm of action.[1] Since the search for knowledge is a quest for the immutable essence of things, we privilege basic research that strives for unconditioned objectivity over applied fields that permit practical needs and human interests to condition inquiry. Since analytic, nonempirical claims are susceptible to greater certainty than synthetic, empirical claims, we value "hard" quantitative inquiry that invokes the necessity of mathematical truth over "soft" qualitative inquiry that relies upon contingent observations. And since foundationalism characterizes knowledge as static and hierarchical, we transmit knowledge using pedagogies that are more didactic than dialectic.

## A Critique of the Mainstream View

There are many ways to criticize this dominant paradigm of knowledge, and many philosophers have offered thoughtful arguments toward that end (see Dewey 1929; Freire 1970; Habermas 1968; Kuhn 1962; Rorty 1979; West 1989). Here I shall give a brief critique with two main thrusts, one aimed at foundationalism and the other aimed at dualism.

### Against Foundationalism

An essential premise of foundationalism is that there is a common ground or neutral framework that constrains the process of inquiry. We cannot understand the structure of knowledge as rational concatenation — the linking of new knowledge claims to the ones preceding it — unless the links are forged from a common substance according to common rules. If inquiry and discourse are to be rational, then the contributions to the discourse must be commensurable, that is, "able to be brought under a set of rules [that] will tell us how rational agreement can be reached on what would settle the issue on every point where statements seem to conflict" (Rorty 1979: 316).

In a dualistic system, the set of rules for adjudicating empirical knowledge claims commonly relies on a distinction between theory and observation. We understand observations to be evidence for or against theoretical claims, in virtue of the way we privilege observational terms with a special degree of certainty. The assumption is that if we look at things in the right way (objectively), then we are compelled (causally) to believe what we see. Thus, observation is the common ground where no rational person can dispute the meaning of terms or the truth value of propositions. It constrains debate over competing theories to a neutral language on which the disputants can agree and through which a rational choice between theories may be made. If we view knowledge as a relation of correspondence between persons and objects, between internal representations and external realities, then we need the ability to offer theory-neutral observation statements as objective evidence for or against particular knowledge claims.

It is inviting to think that we can develop a neutral observation language, since we have at our disposal a wide range of statements whose meanings are rarely disputed — for example, "The bricks are red," "Willy is a whale," "The gas is odorless," or "This pencil is seven inches long." But if we try to specify the parameters of what counts as an observation, we will find this to be a difficult task. If we restrict the range to what we can detect through our sense perceptions alone, we would exclude observational predicates such as " . . . is a bacterium" or " . . . is magnetic." If we allow observations to include what we can detect with the aid of instruments, then we include predicates such as " . . . is a quark" or " . . . is due to hydrogen bonding," which are commonly understood as theoretical postulates.

We will fail in our attempt to construct a language of objectivity because our observational language is pervasively theory-laden. Cellular substructure is observable in light of theories of electromagnetism governing electron microscopy. The topography of Jupiter is observable in light of theoretical principles governing radio-wave transmission (from *Voyager*). Even low-level observational inquiries depend upon some theory-laden frame of reference:

> [A] British mathematician some years ago presented a paper with the intriguing title "How long is the coast of Britain?" The answer is — it depends. Depends on how you're measuring it, and for what purpose. Its length will vary for an observer from a satellite, a person walking around with a yardstick, or a snail crawling around and over every bump and pebble. (Berry 1991: 11)

We have no fixed notion of what counts as an objective observation, and thus we have no context-independent language for debating competing claims to knowledge.

Kuhn's history of science (1962) further supports the idea that there is no neutral arbiter of competition between scientific theories that occur within competing paradigms. During periods of extraordinary (as opposed to normal) science, there is incommensurability not only between the meaning of terms used as evidence for or against competing theories but also between the rules of evidence governing the debate. In deciding between, say, the Copernican theory of celestial motion and the description of the heavens provided by Scripture, we have no agreement between the two sides on what constitutes objective evidence for the movement of the planets. From Galileo's perspective, what the Scripture says bears no evidentiary relationship to planetary motion, yet from the Church's perspective, the observable accuracy of the Copernican theory has little to do with the ultimate configuration of the heavens. And without a neutral language of arbitration, we cannot reduce competing statements of evidence into meaningful terms on which both Galileo and the Church could agree. In sum, debates between paradigms cannot be settled by statements whose meaning and evidentiary significance are determined within paradigms.

Without a common language for grounding knowledge claims, we have no algorithm for rational choice between competing claims. Without an algorithm for rational choice, we have no basis for believing that knowledge accumulates through linear concatenation. And without a view of knowledge as rational concatenation, we have no reason to uphold foundationalism.

## Against Dualism

Rorty's criticism of dualism begins with the idea that the problem of knowledge, in its dualistic construction, is based on a set of unnecessary metaphors: mind as a wax tablet, seeing as a model of knowing, mind as a Mirror of Nature. Rorty's starting point is the suggestion that knowledge is justified belief. To have knowledge is to have reasons for believing a set of propositions, and "what I know" may be understood simply as the collection of propositions completing true statements that begin "I know that . . . " — for example, "the sky is blue," "$F = ma$," "I am holding a pen" (1979: 142). On this view, knowledge is understood as a relation between persons and propositions ("knowledge that"), not as a relation between persons and the objects those propositions are about ("knowledge of").

Where Descartes, Locke, and others went wrong was to understand the primary form of knowledge to be "knowledge of," instead of "knowledge that." Their theories provide causal explanations of how one comes to have a belief (again, the metaphor of imprinting or mirroring), when what we really need is an account of how one goes about justifying that belief.[2] Rorty's point is that "a quasi-mechanical account of the way in which our immaterial tablets are dented by the material world will [not] help us know what we are entitled to believe" (1979: 143). In other words, "knowledge of" does not ground "knowledge that."

This seems right, since knowing does not consist merely in having representations but also in judging that the representations are accurate or reliable or consistent with other representations. To understand how you came to have in mind a present, true-to-life representation of the President will not help you claim "There's Bill," unless you can also justify your judgment that the representation corresponds to the real man and not a life-size cardboard cutout. Knowledge, then, is a relation within the logical space of reasons, not the logical space of causal relations to objects. To propose a causal theory of knowledge is to commit something akin to the naturalistic fallacy in ethics: Just as we cannot derive "ought" statements from "is" statements, we cannot analyze epistemic facts into nonepistemic facts without remainder (Sellars 1967, as quoted in Rorty 1979).

If we understand knowledge as "knowledge that," then the problem of knowledge is no longer the problem of circumventing skepticism, and dualism and its metaphors become optional or irrelevant. On this view, we are concerned with the mind not as a faculty that aims to mirror nature, but as a faculty that attempts to justify our claims to knowledge. The problem of knowledge becomes the problem of defining what it means to justify belief in terms that do not appeal to the support of permanently established knowledge (foundationalism) or to an argument for correspondence between representations of objects and the objects themselves (dualism).

## Pragmatism and the Nature of Discourse

This formulation of the problem of knowledge gives rise to an alternative view that falls under the philosophical banner of pragmatism (see West 1989). On this view, knowledge is not discovered by penetrating into the objective essence of reality and representing it accurately on our Mirrors of Nature. Instead, it is created through conversation in which persons with interests and needs attempt to justify knowledge claims stated in languages with particular norms and meanings. What counts as knowledge is understood as a function of conversation and its standards of justification.

In rejecting the need to ground knowledge in an ultimate foundation, this conception sets knowledge claims and their chains of justification afloat within logical space. But when put in the context of conversation, sound claims and their justifications find a "ground" in the agreement they elicit among interlocutors in light of their agreed-upon norms, conventions, and standards of evidence. So, for a given knowledge claim, although theoretically we may see no end to "the potentially infinite regress of propositions-brought-forward-in-defense-of-other-propositions," practically we may stop the epistemic chain of justification at the point where there is no longer any disagreement in the conversation (Rorty 1979: 159). The agreement envisioned here is neither mindless yea-saying nor thin conformity. Instead, it is a product of dialogue, contention, and justification. It is substantive, hard won, and always open to reconsideration.

Rational certainty, then, is simply a reflection of such firm yet ultimately provisional agreement, not a relation of necessity between ourselves and the objects of our knowledge. In other words, pragmatism interprets our certainty about the Pythagorean theorem or the color of the sky or the existence of this paper not as the ineluctable grip of triangularity or blue-ness or paper-hood upon our rational faculties, but as a reflection of our confidence that nobody will object either to the premises from which we infer these claims or to the patterns of inference we employ. It is in this way that knowledge exists as a relation between persons and propositions, not as a relation between persons and the objects those propositions are about. (See the table on page 33.)

Importantly, pragmatism does not suggest that there are *no* epistemic criteria, but that there are no ultimate criteria and that the only criteria we can have are ones that are internal to discourse.[3] Rorty (1979) makes clear what this implies for our understanding of knowledge:

> *If we see knowing not as having an essence, to be described by scientists or philosophers, but rather as a right, by current standards, to believe, then we are well on the way to seeing conversation as the ultimate context within which knowledge is to be understood. Our focus shifts from the relation between human beings and the objects of their inquiry to the relation between alternative standards of justification, and from there to the actual changes in those standards which make up intellectual history. (389-390)*

In sum, knowledge turns on justification, and justification occurs in the context of conversation. In turn, our inquiry into the nature of knowledge becomes an inquiry into the nature of discourse and justification.

If we reorient our inquiry in this way, we can collapse a set of related distinctions that emanate from the traditional epistemological frame. In particular, we can understand the landscape of academia in terms that do not reify distinctions between "hard" and "soft" disciplines, or between objective and subjective modes of inquiry. Typically, these lines are used to distinguish discourses in which commensuration is possible from those in which it is not. That is, we view science as "hard" or objective in its methodology and epistemic criteria because there exists some common ground — empirical observation, for example — for adjudicating knowledge claims. On the other hand, we conceive of politics, art, and literature as fields that lack an independent ground for resolving disagreement, fields in which points of view cannot achieve the status of genuine cognition but remain simply matters of taste or opinion. The distinction, we believe, is one that separates inquiry into what is "out there" from inquiry into what we "make up" (Rorty 1979: 342), and it is in virtue of the indeterminate ontological status of the subject matter that we cast a suspicious eye toward the latter.

Pragmatism argues that the line between commensurable and incommensurable discourses does not reveal deep distinctions between where certain knowledge is possible and where it is not. The key premise of the pragmatic view is that the line between different discourses is contingent but not necessary, and that it has not been and will not be drawn in the same place throughout the course of intellectual history. Rorty (1979) recasts the substance of this distinction between discourses by generalizing Kuhn's distinction between normal and revolutionary science into a distinction between normal and abnormal discourse:

> *Normal discourse is that which is conducted within an agreed-upon set of*

*conventions about what counts as a relevant contribution, what counts as answering a question, what counts as having a good argument for that answer or a good criticism of it. Abnormal discourse is what happens when someone joins in the discourse who is ignorant of these conventions or who sets them aside. The product of normal discourse [is] the sort of statement [that] can be agreed to be true by all participants whom the other participants count as "rational." The product of abnormal discourse can be anything from nonsense to intellectual revolution. (320)*

On this conception, commensuration in a given discourse does not precede the discourse itself. Instead, it is a by-product of agreed-upon practices of inquiry that have continued long enough for shared conventions, rules, and standards of evidence to develop and come into plain view. It is an indication that the discourse and its norms are useful, productive, or effective in the context in which it occurs. It is not a revelation of something deep about the underlying structure of knowledge, for neither commensuration nor incommensuration is a permanent or necessary feature of any discourse. In certain periods, it may be as easy to determine the aesthetic merit of a painting as it is to determine the scientific validity of a measurement, while in other periods, "it may be as difficult to know which scientists are actually offering reasonable explanations as it is to know which painters are destined for immortality" (Rorty 1979: 322).

Thus, the line between commensurability and incommensurability is nothing more than the line between normal and abnormal discourses. And this latter distinction does not parallel the distinctions between "hard" and "soft," objective and subjective, finding and making, nature and spirit, or facts and values.[4] Natural science and other fields of inquiry do not necessarily line up, respectively, as normal and abnormal discourses, although they may at particular slices in time. Both modes of discourse occur within science as well as nonscience, and on a long view of intellectual history, we will find that the patterns of argumentation and justification in the natural sciences do not differ qualitatively from the types of discourse in the humanities and social sciences.

The point of distinguishing between normal and abnormal discourses is not to prioritize one or the other as a better way of knowing. It would be ineffective if not impossible to teach, to learn, or to conduct a program of research without rules, conventions, shared vocabularies, and other means of systematizing inquiry. Normal discourse allows us to apply foundational reasoning when it is useful to do so. In a sense, it is the starting point for intellectual activity, for abnormal discourse is possible and meaningful only when it occurs with a consciousness of how it departs from a well-understood norm. Abnormal discourse always presents itself as an alternative (e.g., to tradition, to a dominant view). As a consequence, it "is always parasitic upon normal discourse" (Rorty 1979: 365-366).

Nevertheless, because normal discourses are the products of substantial intellectual and material investments, perhaps we need a more forceful reminder that "normal participation in normal discourse is merely one project, one way of being in the world" (Rorty 1979: 365). Instead of "reducing all possible views to one" through some means of universal commensuration (377), abnormal discourses illuminate the ways in which epistemic norms occur within, not outside of, various historical contexts and human communities. By making room for alternative paradigms, they can clear the way (as they have in the past) for new sciences, new research programs, and new normal discourses to emerge. Thus, we must "prevent abnormal inquiry from being viewed as suspicious solely because of its abnormality" if we wish to stay open to the fullest range of intellectual possibilities (363).

In sum, pragmatism shifts our epistemological aspiration from finding objective truth to sustaining a meaningful conversation. In doing so, it identifies important roles for both normal and abnormal discourses in the elucidation of knowledge.

## The Contextual Nature of Knowledge

The need to examine the nature of discourse in order to determine how and what we know illuminates the contextual character of knowledge:

> Evolving descriptions and ever-changing versions of objects, things, and the world issue forth from various communities as responses to certain problems, as attempts to overcome specific situations, and as means to satisfy particular needs and interests. . . . To put it crudely, ideas, words, and language are not mirrors [that] copy the "real" or "objective" world but rather tools with which we cope with "our" world. (West 1989: 201)

In contrast to conventional dualism, pragmatism centers our epistemic concerns not on how well knowledge claims can circumvent skepticism but on how well they "work" in particular contexts for particular people with particular purposes. What counts as a justification may depend not only upon its logical relation to a given claim but also upon the circumstances in which and the persons for which it is being offered.

In this section, I discuss the examples of politics and moral development in order to illustrate the contextual nature of knowledge. However, I want to be clear that this context-dependence is not peculiar to knowledge in the social sciences. Instead, it is characteristic of knowledge in all disciplines, including the natural sciences. A pertinent example is my earlier discussion of the incommensurability of evidence for the theories of planetary motion offered by Galileo and the Church. Indeed, Kuhn's book *The Structure of Scientific Revolutions* (1962) is devoted almost entirely to making this point.

## Political Knowledge

In *Strong Democracy* (1984), Benjamin Barber argues that within the sphere of modern liberal democracy, contextual knowledge is the only knowledge we can have and exactly the kind of knowledge we need. Barber traces the malaises of liberal politics (e.g., voter apathy, distrust of government, gridlock) back to the epistemological stance that reifies the quest for certainty. This quest, as it relates to politics, is a search for an immutable, prepolitical foundation from which all concepts, values, standards, and ends of political life may be derived, an independent ground for conflict resolution, "a basis for social knowledge secure beyond all challenge, one that will endow political practice with the absolute certainty of generic truth" (Barber 1984: 47). The futility of this effort, he argues, has made us into hesitant political skeptics, rightly critical of those who claim to know ultimate solutions, yet too unsure of right action to be citizens who participate vigorously in public life. Thus, while our skepticism has helped us to resist orthodoxy, it has limited our confidence in politics as a means of securing justice, freedom, and other contested ideals whose objective existence in nature we are unable to find. The operating premise of modern liberal democracy appears to be "If we can never know anything for certain, we should never do anything for certain" (61).

In proposing a conception of politics as epistemology, Barber relates the problem of political knowledge directly to the problem of action. The defining question of politics becomes "What shall we do when something has to be done that affects us all, we wish to be reasonable, yet we disagree on means and ends and are without independent grounds for making the choice?" (120-121). In the context of action, what is primary is the recognition that "[we] must act even while [we] know how little [we] know. [We] know that action can afford neither the agnosticism of skeptical philosophy nor the dogmatism of the quest for reflective certainty" (Barber 1984: 66).[5] The object of inquiry, then, is not "to uncover the antecedently real" but "to gain the kind of understanding [that] is necessary to deal with problems as they arise" (Dewey 1929: 17). Thus, we derive knowledge that is meaningful to politics not by applying prepolitical truths to human interactions made generic but by dealing with real demands for action in the context of actual situations, interests, and contingencies.[6]

We arrive at the provisional knowledge we need for political choice and application through concrete, intentional discourse, which Barber calls "political talk."[7] It is through talk that we achieve working agreement on concepts of law, right, freedom, and justice as they relate to practical political problems. And it is through talk that these concepts "are constantly being adjudicated, challenged, modified, transposed, reinterpreted, emended, unpacked and repacked, depreciated and revalued, and edited and transformed in accordance with the historical circumstances and evolving needs of concrete political communities" (Barber 1984: 156). If we understand political discourse — both normal and abnormal — as the autonomous epistemology of politics, then the contextual character of political knowledge is simply a reflection of the contextual character of political discourse.

## Moral Knowledge

Using similar arguments, Carol Gilligan provides an account of moral knowledge that affirms its provisional and contextual nature, and that rejects conceptions of moral judgment as grounded in some ultimate and necessary foundation. In her book *In a Different Voice* (1982), Gilligan criticizes the dominant psychological theories of moral development for their failure to include women as subjects in empirical studies, and for their linear, normative, and putatively scientific ordering of development in terms that deny or subordinate the ways in which women come to moral judgment.[8] The conventional ordering, based on psychological studies of men, equates development with individuation and separation. Developmental advances are associated with an increasing ability to conceive of oneself as an autonomous moral being, to recognize the formal equality of all persons, to articulate universal principles of justice and abstract moral rules, and to apply them to moral dilemmas consistently, logically, and systematically. With an idealized notion of individual freedom at its core, this conception of moral development is based on a "morality of rights." And with its demand for certainty in the logic of moral justification, this conception is "geared to arriving at an objectively fair or just resolution to moral dilemmas upon which all rational persons could agree" (21-22).

Drawing on empirical studies of women's experiences, Gilligan points out the limitations of this dominant conception, and she describes a different path of moral development that suggests an alternative moral theory. In rough terms, while development in men is associated with increasing independence, women develop their sense of identity through ongoing relationship. Consequently, women tend to interpret moral dilemmas not as a problem of conflicting rights (i.e., how to minimize interference with each other's freedom) but as a problem of conflicting responsibilities (i.e., how to minimize "the possibility of omission, of your not helping others when you could help them" [21]). On this view, morality encompasses what we should do not only to limit abridgements of abstract rights but also to respond to the particular needs of others. In drawing the contrast, Gilligan argues that a moral problem arising from conflicting responsibilities rather than from competing rights "requires for its resolution a mode of thinking that is contextual and narrative rather than formal and abstract" (19), one whose framework for moral choice aims to consider rather than disregard circumstantial human needs and interests. Indeed, Gilligan observes that in response to moral dilemmas, women tend to focus on the contextual details and particularities of a case in order to determine a solution, instead of interpreting facts as an abstract pattern to which a general rule may be applied. She detects this difference in approach early in the path of human development,[9] and the developmental trajectories that arise from differing approaches play out the contrasts between impersonal objectivity and interpersonal relation, between abstract reasoning and situational choice.

Thus, the differences between the male and female voices in Gilligan's work "point to the contextual nature of developmental truths" (174). Her point is not that we should construct a developmental theory solely from the experiences of either women or men but that we must include both voices in the discourse of moral and psychological theory if we hope to have a truly encompassing theory of human development. On the one hand, to understand moral choice as a purely contingent act is to lack a coherent framework for making moral judgments. But on the other hand, to construe moral judgment as the logical and dispassionate application of universal principles is to miss the ways in which relational and contextual reasoning can lead to defensible moral choices.

In Rorty's terms, we might understand developmental theory as an abnormal discourse, in which male and female voices "typically speak of the importance of different truths, the former of the role of separation as it defines and empowers the self, the latter of the ongoing process of attachment that creates and sustains the human community" (Gilligan 1982: 156). We should not regard the abnormality as an impetus to decide which view should subsume the other; there is no independent ground that can help us decide that question. Instead, we should understand it as a challenge to sustain the conversation, to exploit its creative tensions, and to hold out the possibility of agreement on a broader conception of moral development.

## Implications for Pedagogy

Up to this point, I have suggested that knowledge may be understood as a product of discourse and that the contextual nature of knowledge — moral, political, or scientific — is a function of the contextual nature of discourse. While this alternative epistemology has its own difficulties,[10] I believe it offers a more persuasive account of intellectual history than does the foundational paradigm. It also liberates us from a set of insoluble philosophical problems (e.g., skepticism, universal commensuration) that give rise to false distinctions, unnecessary hierarchies, and limiting frameworks of analysis.

Let us now turn the corner from arguing for a different epistemology to examining briefly what our epistemology entails for educational practice. I shall discuss community, diversity, and engagement as three pedagogical virtues implicated in the transformation of a way of knowing into a way of teaching and learning.

## Community

In abandoning foundational theories of knowledge, we are likely to feel uncomfortable with the prospect of granting the status of "knowledge" to claims of less-than-absolute certainty. This is understandable: If we cannot have an ultimate ground for justification, then we need at least a way of distinguishing knowledge from opinion or taste. Otherwise, we slip down a dangerous slope toward relativism. However, the slippery slope is problematic only if it is understood as a hill with absolutism at the top and relativism at the bottom. Alternatively, we might imagine the slope as one side of a valley, "a concave world where the bottom is the middle [and where] once we're in the middle we tend to stay there rather than slip to the extremes that are on high peaks on either side" (B.R. Barber, Feb. 1, 1995: personal correspondence). Philosophically, we locate this middle by understanding knowledge in the context of conversation; pedagogically, we find it by putting teaching and learning in the context of community.

Rejecting foundationalism does not doom us to relativism if we conceive of knowing and learning not as individual acts of discovery but as communal acts of creation. Individuals in isolation are not entitled to legitimize knowledge; that function is reserved for communities in which truth claims are continually tested and contested in the context of discourse. Thus, while "mak[ing] no claim to be universal or to proceed from an independent order of things," political judgment "is not subjective, because it arises out of social interaction and out of the imaginative effort by individuals to see in common" (Barber 1984: 171). Similarly, moral judgment without an ultimate Moral Law need not be a simple matter of opinion if we see "a world comprised of relationships rather than of people standing alone, a world that coheres through human connection rather than through systems of rules" (Gilligan 1982: 29).

From this epistemology, community emerges as a critical pedagogical virtue. It is a precondition of learning in two senses: First, community is the place where discourse occurs (e.g., a community of scholars), and second, community is the ethic that enables discourse to occur (e.g., a spirit of community). If discourse is what makes knowing possible in a world without foundations, then community is what makes learning possible in educational institutions where thinking alone is still the norm. Community (in the second sense) is not "an affective or emotional supplement to cognitive education" but one of its integral elements:

*Without the soft virtues of community, the hard virtues of cognitive teach-*

*ing and learning will be absent as well. Our ability to confront each other
critically and honestly over alleged facts, imputed meanings, or personal
biases and prejudices — that is the ability impaired by the absence of community. (Palmer 1987: 25)*

In sum, knowing and learning are not possible without discourse, and discourse is not possible without community.

## Diversity

If community is a bulwark against relativism, then diversity is a bulwark
against dogmatism. The process of knowing and learning in community may
lead to little more than group orthodoxy when it does not include a spectrum of voices whose differing criticisms and interpretations are brought to
bear on knowledge claims. While the relation between knowledge and discourse "is precisely what makes it possible to legitimize (or delegitimize)
truth claims," a truth claim carries legitimacy only if it reflects a "consensus
arising out of an undominated discourse to which all have equal access"
(Barber 1993: 213-214). Moreover, just as diversity in discourse gives knowledge claims greater or lesser warrant, it also engenders the creative conflict
that leads to new discourses and new knowledge. Thus, from the standpoint
of pedagogy, diversity is another precondition of learning in virtue of its epistemic functions.

This precondition consists not only of the need to achieve diversity in
educational settings but also of the need to manage diversity in ways that
deepen our knowledge. Quite importantly, if diversity is not to degenerate
into fruitless intellectual politics, we must understand discourse as a combination of both speaking and listening. To make sense of divergent views
within normal discourse, we must say to ourselves, "I will put myself in his
place, I will try to understand, I will strain to hear what makes us alike, I will
listen for a common rhetoric evocative of a common purpose or a common
good" (Barber 1984: 175). To argue within an abnormal discourse, we cannot
appeal to "objective" standards of justification. Instead, we must engage our
opponents' claims on their own terms and "show how the odd or paradoxi-
cal or offensive things they say hang together with the rest of what they
want to say" (Rorty 1979: 365). Thus, the pedagogical challenge is not only to
bring diverse views into a given discourse but also to keep the conversation
going, to prevent divergent voices from talking past one another, and to
ensure that opposing sides do not opt out in frustration.

## Engagement

Finally, just as community is the counterweight to relativism and diversity is the counterweight to dogmatism, engagement is the counterweight to
dualism. Since Descartes wrote, we have aspired to achieve the position of

ultimate objectivity by maximizing the distance between the knowing subject and the object known. We adopt this epistemological stance in an effort to grapple with the problem of the external world, to keep our knowledge from being contaminated by subjective interests, circumstances, or contingencies. As a consequence, we "create a world 'out there' of which we are only spectators and in which we do not live" (Palmer 1987: 22). From this separation of perception and reality, it is a short stretch to the separation of student and subject, campus and community, education and the real world. Pragmatism, with its metaphor of "coping," is indifferent to the distinction between perception and reality. It locates us simply and literally within the world in which we live (however real or unreal), where knowledge is understood as concrete, purposive, and contextual — "issu[ing] forth from various communities as responses to certain problems, as attempts to overcome specific situations, and as means to satisfy particular needs and interests" (West 1989: 201). In essence, the contaminants of knowledge in dualism are the precursors of knowledge in pragmatism.

By associating knowledge with human context in an integral way, this alternative epistemology shifts our "ideal of knowledge as a correspondence between mind and form" to a "conception of knowing as a process of human relationship" (Gilligan 1982: 173). In turn, it suggests a pedagogy that is distinctively relational — a way of teaching and learning that narrows the gap between abstraction and circumstance, between theory and practice, between knowing and doing, between the knower and the known. In addition, it transforms the "banking" concept of education[11] into a pedagogy that envisions teachers and students as related participants in a process of discourse. Thus, engagement — understood as developing and exploring the relations between the very concepts, activities, persons, and institutions that dualism split asunder — is a third precondition of learning.

It is important to note that these three pedagogical virtues — community, diversity, and engagement — are genuine virtues only when they occur together. Community without diversity is a prelude to groupthink. Diversity without community is a recipe for academic warfare. And engagement without either community or diversity amounts to humdrum relationships that exist in a void. Clearly, none of these is an enabling condition for teaching, learning, or knowing. The pedagogical challenge presented by pragmatism, then, is to balance these virtues without appealing to a predetermined formula. Because pragmatism's epistemic criteria are internal to discourse and because discourse is fundamentally narrative, we can understand the "proper" balance only as the "most productive" balance in the evolving context of purposes, norms, and circumstances that characterize a given discourse.

# Implications for Service-Learning

The connection between an alternative epistemology and service-learning is now clear: The pedagogical virtues implicated by pragmatism are among the defining features of service-learning. In its effort to promote learning through communal processes of reflection, service-learning requires community. In its effort to bring unconventional voices into the discourse of academia, service-learning embraces diversity. In its effort to close the divide between knowledge and action, service-learning insists on engagement.

I suspect that "thin" conceptions or practices of service-learning may find their support in what I have labeled "mainstream" epistemology. Here I am thinking of clinical programs in law or medicine, in which the activity resembles "practice" or "demonstration" and maintains a division between persons capable of knowing and objects (e.g., clients, patients) capable of being known (i.e., "knowledge of"). This stands in contrast to "thicker" understandings of service-learning, in which the activity resembles "creation" or "interaction" and engages persons in communal processes of knowing (i.e., "knowledge that"). Those who share this "thick" conception may find in pragmatism the much-needed philosophical support for their current practice.

In any case, whatever more can be said about the relation between epistemology and service-learning should be said, I believe, not by an armchair philosopher but by reflective practitioners who witness the actual ways in which teaching, learning, and knowing occur. As a philosophical inquiry, this article does not emanate from a base of practical experience with service-learning programs. If the goal is to articulate an epistemology that authentically supports service-learning pedagogy, then I have gone only halfway starting from one end. I hope one or more readers will supply the other half by assessing — from the standpoint of practice — the relevance of this alternative epistemology.

I want to conclude with two thoughts about philosophical inquiry as it relates to service-learning as a movement, not as a pedagogy.[12] First, this article and its pedagogical consequences are "overbroad" relative to what is needed in order to give service-learning adequate philosophical support. A review of Dewey's theories on knowledge and action might have been sufficient (see Giles and Eyler 1994; Dewey 1929). Nevertheless, I believe the importance of Dewey is amplified when his work is put into larger philosophical contexts by Rorty, West, Barber, and others. Similarly, I believe the field of service-learning stands to gain from aligning itself with other intellectual agendas — for example, multiculturalism and critical thinking — that are struggling for legitimacy from the same or a related epistemological base. Seeking out and forging natural alliances in the academy may enhance strategies for institutionalization and improve practice.

Second, my effort to articulate an alternative epistemology that supports service-learning runs counter to an oft-articulated view in the field — that we should move service-learning from the margins to the mainstream of higher education by showing how it is consistent with the educational mission of the traditional academy. As a practical matter, virtually all practitioners strive to institutionalize their programs in this way. Yet many of these practitioners also maintain that service-learning is what it is in virtue of its departure from the foundations and goals of the traditional academy. On this latter view, the marginal status of service-learning is what certifies its authenticity, and moving from the margins to the mainstream would undermine the conception of service-learning as a critique of traditional ways of knowing. This glaring inconsistency — between the practical issue of program sustainability and the philosophical issue of program integrity — is the central tension inherent in any attempt to institutionalize service-learning. Resolving this tension is fundamental to determining the future of service-learning in higher education.

## Acknowledgment

*Reprinted with permission from volume 2 of the *Michigan Journal of Community Service Learning*.

## Notes

1. John Dewey elaborates on this point in Chapter 1 of *The Quest for Certainty* (1929).

2. Rorty borrows Wilfrid Sellars's observation that "in characterizing an episode or a state as that of *knowing*, we are not giving an empirical description of that episode or state; we are placing it in the logical space of reasons, of justifying and being able to justify what one says" (Sellars 1963: 169 in Rorty 1979: 141, 389).

3. Rorty distinguishes pragmatism from relativism by defining the difference between pragmatists and their critics as the difference "not between people who think one view as good as another (relativists) and people who do not, [but] between those who think our culture, or purpose, or intuitions cannot be supported except conversationally (pragmatists) and people who still hope for other sorts of support" (1982: 167).

4. Against the fact-value distinction, Rorty writes: "To use one set of true sentences to describe ourselves is already to choose an attitude toward ourselves, whereas to use another set of true sentences is to adopt a contrary attitude. Only if we assume that there is a value-free vocabulary [that] renders these sets of 'factual' statements commensurable can the positivist distinction between facts and values, beliefs and attitudes, look plausible" (1979: 363).

5. Barber explains: "Antecedent reality, whether sensed, intuited, or dreamed, is always beyond politics, is always utopian in the sense of being nowhere with respect to its realities. For politics is defined by its *somewhereness*, its concrete historicity in the real world of human beings. Knowledge grounded in nowhere, even where it has a philosophical warranty of truth and certainty, cannot serve politics" (1984: 64).

6. What we require in the real political world are "not reflexive truths garnered in reflective equilibrium but enabling norms developed amidst concrete common problems; not absolute certainty but relative conviction; not philosophical incorrigibility but practical agreement; not ultimate knowledge but shared ends, common values, community standards, and public goods in a world where ultimate knowledge may be unattainable. . . . Truth in politics seems, as William James said of truth in general, to be something [that] is 'made in the course of experience' rather than something discovered or disclosed and then acted upon" (Barber 1984: 65).

7. See Chapter 8 of *Strong Democracy* (1984). Barber offers a conception of "talk" that entails listening as well as speaking, that is affective as well as cognitive, and that relates to the realm of action as well as the realm of reflection.

8. Gilligan (1982) notes at the outset that the association she describes between gender and contrasting paths of moral development is only an empirical observation: "This association is not absolute, and the contrasts between male and female voices are presented here to highlight a distinction between two modes of thought and to focus a problem of interpretation rather than to represent a generalization about either sex" (2). The problem of interpretation she refers to is the following: "When women do not conform to the standards of psychological expectation, the conclusion has generally been that something is wrong with the women," not with the psychological theory (14).

9. In one study, two 11-year-old children were asked the question "When responsibility to oneself and responsibility to others conflict, how should one choose?" The boy answered, "You go about one-fourth to the others and three-fourths to yourself." The girl offered a more discursive response that began, "Well, it really depends on the situation. . . ." One invokes the certainty of mathematics to deduce solutions abstracted from human circumstance, while the other responds contextually instead of categorically, explaining how choice might be conditioned by the facts at hand (Gilligan 1982: 35-38).

10. Among the philosophical problems that pragmatism leaves unresolved, two seem particularly poignant. First, if pragmatism does not permit any theory to claim objective truth, then pragmatism itself — as a theory of knowledge — cannot make a claim to truth. Pragmatism's argument against the existence of essences appears to undermine its own claim regarding the essence of knowledge. (This paradox is the analogue to foundationalism's problem of "first foundations" — that is, any claim to have found the foundations of knowledge itself must have a foundation, which itself must have a foundation, and so on. For an elaboration of this point, see Habermas 1968, ch. 1.)

Second, in denying the existence of an independent ground for theory choice, pragmatism faces the difficulty of explaining the progress of science. If Kuhn's history of science constitutes evidence for the nonrationality of knowledge development, then don't our ever-improving powers of prediction, observation, and explanation constitute evidence for an ultimate, directional scientific method? Kuhn (1977) himself acknowledges this problem: "Even those who have followed me this far will want to know how a value-based enterprise of the sort I have described can develop as a science does, repeatedly producing powerful new techniques for prediction and control. To that question, unfortunately, I have no answer at all. . . . The lacuna is one I feel acutely" (332-333 in Rorty 1979: 340).

11. See Paulo Freire, *Pedagogy of the Oppressed* (1970), ch. 2. Freire describes conventional pedagogy (e.g., lectures, narration) as "an act of depositing, in which the students are the depositories and the teacher is the depositor. . . . In the banking concept of education, knowledge is a gift bestowed by those who consider themselves knowledgeable upon those whom they consider to know nothing" (58). Freire traces this pedagogy back to its Cartesian roots: "Implicit in the banking concept is the assumption of a dichotomy between man and the world" (62).

12. I raise these points in recognition of the need to complement my philosophical discussion with a sociological inquiry into how people come to adopt and defend certain knowledge paradigms, how these paradigms cohere with particular social, political, and economic norms, and how in actuality people are persuaded to relinquish one paradigm in favor of another. These questions are beyond the scope of this article. But if our concern is to institutionalize an alternative pedagogy, then they are at least as important as the epistemological questions I have discussed.

## References

Barber, B.R. (1984). *Strong Democracy: Participatory Politics for a New Age*. Berkeley, CA: University of California Press.

———— . (1993). *An Aristocracy of Everyone*. New York, NY: Ballantine Books.

Berry, H. (February 1991). "Education, Chaos, and the Participatory Universe." Presentation at the Partnership for Service-Learning Conference, Raleigh, NC.

Code, L. (1987). *Epistemic Responsibility*. Hanover, CT: University Press of New England.

Dewey, J. (1929). *The Quest for Certainty: A Study of the Relation of Knowledge and Action*. New York, NY: Capricorn Books (1960 edition).

Freire, P. (1970). *Pedagogy of the Oppressed*. New York, NY: Continuum Publishing Corporation (1981 edition).

Giles, D., and J. Eyler. (1994). "The Theoretical Roots of Service-Learning in John Dewey: Toward a Theory of Service-Learning." *Michigan Journal of Community Service Learning* 1(1): 77-85.

Gilligan, C. (1982). *In a Different Voice: Psychological Theory and Women's Development*. Cambridge, MA: Harvard University Press.

Habermas, J. (1968). *Knowledge and Human Interests*. Boston, MA: Beacon Press (1971 translation).

Kuhn, T.S. (1962). *The Structure of Scientific Revolutions*. Chicago, IL: University of Chicago Press (1970 edition).

——— . (1977). *The Essential Tension.* Chicago, IL: University of Chicago Press.

Liu, G. (1995). "Service-Learning: A Paradigm Shift in Higher Education?" *NSEE Quarterly* 21(1): 8f.

Palmer, P.J. (September/October 1987). "Community, Conflict, and Ways of Knowing: Ways to Deepen Our Educational Agenda." *Change* 19(5): 20-25.

Rorty, R.M. (1979). *Philosophy and the Mirror of Nature.* Princeton, NJ: Princeton University Press.

——— . (1982). *Consequences of Pragmatism.* Minneapolis, MN: University of Minnesota Press.

Sellars, W. (1963). *Science, Perception, and Reality.* New York, NY: Humanities Press.

——— . (1967). *Philosophical Perspectives.* Springfield, IL: C.C. Thomas.

West, C. (1989). *The American Evasion of Philosophy: A Genealogy of Pragmatism.* Madison, WI: University of Wisconsin Press.

## Pragmatism: An Alternative Epistemology

| | Foundational dualism | Antifoundational pragmatism |
|---|---|---|
| **Ideas, words, and language are ...** | mirrors that "copy" the real world | tools for "coping" with our world |
| **Propositions are objective and true insofar as they ...** | correspond with objective reality | elicit agreement among interlocutors |
| **Rational certainty is ...** | a necessary relation between persons and objects of knowledge | a hard-won, provisional consensus |
| | established through interaction/confrontation with nonhuman reality | established through conversation between persons |
| **Justifying knowledge claims involves ...** | finding an unshakable foundation | making an airtight case |
| | by appealing to how objects "grip" us and compel us to belief | by bringing propositions forward in defense of other propositions |
| **Knowledge claims are adjudicated by ...** | rational commensuration on an independent common ground (e.g., observation language) | contextual standards of evidence and justification (no independent or common ground) |

# Feminism, Postmodernism, and Service-Learning

by Irene E. Harvey

It is a truism that the history of feminism[1] is a history of activism. The energy and direction of feminism have always been drawn from social action, resistance to the oppression of women, and the demands and desires for gender justice. Thus, the idea of service-learning, as an active community involvement program for higher education, introduces nothing new to feminism and indeed even to women's studies programs in the most general sense. However, these forms of direct involvement are most often seen as capstones in a long program of academic work in the classroom, even in women's studies. Nonetheless, the integration of theory and practice, community involvement, and testing and forging ideas in experience have always been the hallmarks of feminist work. In this sense, service-learning projects fit neatly within the basic principles and history of feminism.

Postmodernism, however, may seem to represent the opposite end of the spectrum in terms of its relation to application, the community, experience, and even subjective documentation. Where much of feminism relies on what is now called "standpoint theory"[2] — taking women's particular experiences not only into account but also as a basis for theorizing — postmodernism seems to have deconstructed the very ideas of the subject, subjectivity, truth, gender, and women in general. The resistance to postmodernism can be understood as twofold here. First, many feminists resist all that falls under the rubric of postmodernism as represented by such thinkers as Lyotard, Derrida, Foucault, and, on occasion, Rorty. I shall explore these objections systematically in my next section. In addition, the association of postmodernism with service-learning is also suspect. The very postulates of postmodernism may seem to preempt any active community involvement, testimonial, empirical data, and observations from experience as relevant epistemologically or ontologically. I shall attempt in what follows not only to correct this perception of an uncrossable abyss between postmodernism and service-learning but in fact to demonstrate, if not the necessity, at least the coherence in principle and in fact of the trajectories of postmodern theory and service-learning practica. My own courses will be used as examples in this regard, since they represent experiments in situating postmodern theory in practice.

This paper will thus involve a theoretical portion exploring the feminist objections to postmodernism and a practical, experimental portion describing ways in which postmodernism has been used as the basis for service-learning courses. Finally, to sum up, I will show how these courses demonstrate the answers to current feminist objections to postmodernism as apolitical, amoral, and hopelessly relativist, to name only a few.

## Feminist Objections to Postmodernism

It must be said that some feminists embrace the insights of postmodernism — in whole or in part — and find this work useful if not essential to the continuing development of feminist work — in theory and in practice.[3] But there is a substantial group that resists this direction and even claims that it may lead to the demise of feminism as we know it. The stakes are thus high and the issues are central to the current state of feminist theory. I shall focus on seven of these objections and several major theorists[4] who all find postmodernism to be problematic if not disastrous for feminism today. It is also true that these debates have already taken place and are continuing, and thus the issues here are far from resolved one way or the other. Further, feminism is clearly not a single, unitary project, though it has some unifying threads that identify feminists as feminists. Thus, resolution of these tensions is not necessary or even essential for feminism as a whole. The tensions are themselves a sign of the multiplicity of voices, directions, and tactics within the field of feminist theory today. They are, I would argue, a sign of health and strength, not weaknesses. It is therefore not my aim to resolve tensions or reduce opposition for the sake of some supposedly underlying or overarching sameness, unity, or totality. Rather, I aim here to show that some feminist objections to postmodernism involve a caricature of the enemy rather than an accurate representation. Fears and traditional prejudices tend to creep into the most academic of enterprises, and this debate is no exception.

The key issues feminists who object to postmodernism tend to focus on are the following: (1) the loss of the "subject" — the agent or agency is deconstructed just at the moment when women begin to take the reins of power and become agents or subjects of history rather than its objects; (2) the loss of a collective subject — categories such as women in general, oppression in general of women, patriarchal cultures, societies, systems are notions that have been deconstructed or shown to be fictional; (3) the loss of the idea of a continuity of history — just at the moment when women are writing their own histories, the very idea of a history of a concept of something is lost; (4) the loss of the idea of progress — the ideals of justice, freedom, equality, truth are all being deconstructed; (5) the loss of referents — all is now reduced to texts, language, signs, signification, and we lose the "real" world; (6) the loss of the body as gendered — embodiment, the empirical, the sensuous are lost in postmodern theory; and (7) the loss of the capacity to make ethical, political, moral judgments — all decisions and choices have been marked as undecidable, relativist, partial, and thus without grounds.

These are no doubt serious objections to postmodernism, and they are not restricted to feminists. These issues crosscut most criticism of deconstruction and postmodernism today, and they have not yet been adequately or sufficiently answered. Each side ends up shaking its head and muttering, "You just don't understand what is really at stake here." Traditionalists and feminists seem ironically to end up on the same "side" against the so-called threat of postmodernism's unraveling the world as we know it. This irony has been mirrored in Andrea Dworkin's resistance to pornography as the source of violence against women and her "alliance" with the Christian Right (which she resists at every other turn), whose argument is against the "sins" of pornography. Analogously, in the debate over "free speech," differing reasons have led to the same stand and the same positioning for both feminists and those representing the most patriarchal of traditions. "We don't want feminism deconstructed" is walking hand in hand with "We don't want our tradition deconstructed."

In all these instances, the seemingly corrosive and destructive power of postmodernism is the main target — though that target may turn out to be something of a mirage. In the end, we shall see that postmodernism and feminism are actually very closely aligned despite their apparent differences.

## Losing the Subject

Deconstruction, as developed by the work of Derrida, has indeed long focused on the issue of the subject and its philosophical counterpart, subjectivity.[5] It is true that the "subject" can be said to have been "deconstructed." The question is, which concept of subject and subjectivity are we referring to here, and which are feminists concerned to save and protect?

Feminists' concerns, one should recall, are always focused on the empowerment of women as subjects. Relatedly, a service-learning course partnered, for example, with a women's resource center devoted to counseling battered and abused women can also be seen as empowering women in disempowered situations. The role of the "subject" here — as counselor and counseled — is as central in practice as in theory and not expendable. But the question remains, in what sense is the "subject" to be understood?

Derrida, following Heidegger, was concerned to unmask the notion of subjectivity developed primarily by Descartes and Cartesianism following him. This "subject" would be for Descartes, and later for Husserl, present to itself by a critical backward glance of reflection insofar as "reflection" was thought to provide immediate access to the subject by itself. Thus, Descartes uttered the famous "I think therefore I [know that with certainty I] am," and further, whatever I perceive with clarity and distinctness I can with certainty claim as a valid perception. That is, I can know, according to Descartes, that I am not deceived by either thought or sense data if the quality of the experience entails both clarity and distinctness. For Derrida, this Cartesian subjective foundationalism, which of course is writ large with Kant and the so-called Copernican turn in the history of philosophy, is itself suspect. There is, first of all, language that mediates the relation of the subject to itself — in thought and in perception. On this level alone, what we think we think and perceive we perceive is itself multiplied and open to multiple readings. Language is the element of plurivocity. It is, in its essence, Babelian, rather than clear and/or distinct.

Derrida's arguments for the mediation that orients and hence disorients the subject's relation to itself also rely on the insights of both Freud and Lacan in their work on the unconscious and its central role in psychoanalysis. The "subject" becomes a fiction we produce for ourselves via our relation to others and the world at large. The "subject" is a fiction in the sense of a foundational cornerstone found inside the individual — as an instinctive or inborn character, or framework. In this sense, the idea of the subject as a fixed entity guaranteeing itself can no longer be used as a warranty for truth in science, mathematics, epistemology, or ontology. Rather, we must analyze the constitution of subjectivity as a multifarious process that happens, in a real sense, behind our backs and out of the corner of our conscious eyes. This constituting process can be traced back by the effects it produces in consciousness as our "images" of ourselves. Here we enter the simulacra of what may appear from a traditional viewpoint as a hall of mirrors. What really enters here are precisely the dimensions of experience that feminists insist upon not forgetting — the social, political, historical, intersubjective dimensions involved in the constitution of all subjects. This is not the end of "agency," but it does effectively decenter the idea of a "free will" that "starts" from a subject with an idea. That we have the illusions of free will, subjectivity, and idealism is not denied and that we act as such is also undeniable. But the issue becomes, what is behind this directedness of a subject toward a focused idea or project? What is pushing or pulling the subject in this or that way? What meanings are produced or assumed along the way that empower this acting agent? In short, the deconstruction of the Cartesian subject is a form of complication or enrichment and thickening, a socializing, languaging, intersubjectivizing of the notions of freedom, the will, the subject, subjectivity, and, ultimately, agency.

## Loss of the Collective Subject: Woman in General

How can feminism continue if there is no such thing as "woman in general" for whom all feminist action, analysis, and resistance is done? How can a concept of a people, or a nation, or an oppressed group unified precisely by their history of oppression be erased, deconstructed, unraveled, or eroded? And must not feminism itself build the dam that will keep this destructive storm at bay till it passes of its own accord and wears itself out? Many feminists believe this and argue that deconstruction (and postmodernism in general) is at its most pernicious on this issue.

Yet, in my service-learning courses, students have found time and again that institutions in practice rarely act on the basis of the collective subject as such. Rather, a specificity and particularity and indeed an Aristotelian *phronesis,* or practical wisdom, most often took precedence over a general rule for all clients or all participants. For example, students who worked in seniors' facilities or halfway houses often found that general rules for all clients were rarely applied as such to particular persons. Rather, the general rules were held in abeyance, and the specific, detailed needs of a particular client held sway. Hence, the collectivity or essence of "the subject in general" was revealed as mythic.

But I want to return to concept formation. It was Nietzsche who insisted, "There is no such thing as truth," or "The truth is there is no truth" — ironic statements that, not unlike Zeno's paradox, are false if true, and true if false. But Nietzsche also discussed the nature of language itself as involving, of necessity, collapsing differences into identities. Names and naming necessarily make the differences the same. If we did not inflict such violence on things, we would need a new word or name for each instance of each thing. This, in turn, would destroy and nullify the very functioning of language, since it functions precisely *because* it is primarily not a system of proper names but a system of conceptual formulations. We speak of "cups" in general, but in speaking of this cup here we are also speaking of cups in general, or indeed the cup as such. We need not have Plato's Form or Idea of the cup in mind, or even assume it to be a reality in order to use language in this way. Indeed, we can use it in no other way. Schizophrenics' use of language, by inversion, consists precisely in taking words themselves for things and defying this concept-formation assumption behind them. "This cup here" itself becomes a thing, not interchangeable or synonymous with "this cup here" written later in a different place. These are not even different instances of the same thing but different things, each uniquely situated in its own time and place.

"Normal" or "proper," let us say nonschizophrenic and indeed nonpoetic, language use, however, requires that again we make the difference the same. We use the same term "cup" for this cup, and that cup, the one I broke yesterday, the one I will buy tomorrow. In short, we inevitably use language as concept-forming and thus producing and reproducing the effects of the idea of the cup — or woman — in general, for example.

Deconstruction and postmodernism in general simply point out this Nietzschean insight into the violence inherent in naming and in all language use, not just verbal abuse, or name-calling. All uses of language — but for the notable exception above — require that concepts be invoked. At the same time, we know that these concepts are also fictions once we try to articulate the supposed essences behind this functional usage. Thus, their functioning itself is belied and no longer possible. A certain paralysis takes place, and we, as St. Augustine put it, no longer know what this is once we ask the question. We no longer know (and never did) what cups are, apart from the performative use of language that names this thing here as a cup. In short, the violence of language is unavoidable — of totalizing and synthesizing and erasing the differences — and at the same time, language is in its very structure fictional. We make things "the same" by calling them by the same names or in some cases by not naming them at all.

As to the "woman" question, feminists argue this issue both ways. On the one hand, there is no such concept as woman in general: We are black, white, Hispanic; first, second, third world; working, middle, upper class; and so forth. There is no single collection of traits — even biological — that makes all women cohere as a group. Using the concept of "woman" as such thus does violence to all the other "others" who are by definition erased by this term that — also by definition — takes some women as the example or model (the prototype) for all women, or all feminists. Black-American and third-world feminists have been effectively raising the consciousness of middle-class white feminists on this issue.

But other feminists argue, in First- and Second-Wave feminism especially, that we need such a concept — whether fictional or not — to galvanize the movement of women in general (and we know who we are) in order to create and propel social change and resist collective oppression. Though "women in general" or "woman as such" is a fiction, it is also a historical reality that patriarchal societies have used to oppress half of their populations. The issue of the content of the concept becomes irrelevant as one realizes its very form has had and continues to have life-and-death consequences for women in particular. Naming, feminists have long realized, has a political effect. "Chauvinism," "sexism," "racism," for example, have become political weapons in wars of words, flesh, and bone. Thus, once again, deconstruction's and postmodernism's refusal to essentialize such concepts and their movements in order to unearth the violence inherent in naming goes hand in hand with the feminist demand for a kind of action that speaks "louder than words." Rejecting "essentialism," now a common feminist buzzword, is a parallel project consistent with the motivations and analyses of postmodernism. Few feminists today would argue for a concept of woman in general in the way Susan B. Anthony — or even Simone de Beauvoir — did. But they would argue that such a concept is useful politically both to describe the cage "women in general" have lived inside for centuries and to unite this population both self-identified as women and identified by the other as women. Whether seeing themselves as selves or others, women in general both are and are not a concept of woman as such.

## Loss of Continuity and Coherence of History

Much feminist work has been and continues to be devoted to the creation of women's history in the largest cultural and global forms as well as in the form of individual life-stories.[6] This work is thought to constitute the new sub-jectivity — as distinct from objectivity — of women generally. As we women begin to speak for ourselves, we are no longer foreclosed from history either as a network of great men taking great action or as the social, cultural, politi-cal, and economic work of the multitudes. This other side of history continues to develop and expand as various groups — all designated as "other" — begin to voice their own stories, legends, and legacies of the past. Thus, history as testimony, biography, and autobiography is valorized within current feminism as part of the liberating process of women speaking for themselves and recon-stituting their own identities as actors and subjects of history.

In service-learning courses, we have also seen evidence for this trans-formed notion of historicity as subject- or client-centered rather than spec-tator-centered or allegedly objective. The story of the client holds sway as the veracity of the testimony of that person's experience of his or her experience rather than giving way to a search for some objective standard of a truth independent of the first person singular perspective. In their work with the women's resource center, students have repeatedly found that a client's expe-rience was what counted as the historicity of a situation that had to be dealt with — and no other judgments could overrule this. The same lesson was learned through AIDS counseling and work with the gay-lesbian hot line.

Thus, it is not surprising that much feminism rejects what it sees as a postmodern unraveling of the very possibility of such histories. Notions of coherence, narrativity, continuity through time, and progress are all under fire due to the postmodern rethinking of such traditionally "metaphysical" and, by some accounts, essentially "modernist" terms. As a result, feminists are led to reject the value, virtue, and consequences of such a disqualifica-tion — postmodernism's epistemological prohibition of the use of such terms and the production of such texts.

Paul Ricoeur,[7] among others, has argued that narrative is the very form of intelligibility. Not only is it language that situates, names, and contextu-alizes a thing or an event (such as a riot, an uprising, a skirmish, etc.); the "emplotment" of events and things is what truly makes them what they are for us. Thus, meaning arises not simply from naming but from the story telling that emplotment and narrativity give rise to. In this way, for Ricoeur, narrative forms the foundation for both fiction and history, prior to all dis-tinctions and judgments made concerning truth and falsity. An event has no meaning "by itself" — without context, story, or narrative of what came before and what may or does come after. The temporality of things and events is thus the key to their meaning. In terms of women's lives for the past, present, and future, this is no less true, and thus feminists reaffirm this narrative foundation as a necessary opening to the (re)writing of women's history as their own, as what women's lives mean to and for women, not as the product of dominant structures and the loudest voices of societies past and present.

## Loss of the Notion of Progress

Many postmodern thinkers (for example, Foucault) reject an essentially progressive view of history. Since the guarantee for such a view — either God or rationality — is no longer credible or believable, on what grounds can one insist that history moves, of its own accord, forward? Dialectics, as the structure of History instantiated by Hegel and motivated by Marx,[8] is also in question here as a form that all historical change would necessarily fall into. Seen as an imposition on events that falsifies them, dialectics is again no guarantee of a forward movement to events or progress in history.

An example of this loss in service-learning courses was seen by the students who worked for the local SPCA and tried to grapple with the difficult and unnerving issue of euthanasia for unwanted animals. This "solution" can no more be considered progress or a forward movement than it can a regression. Its moral components can be argued both ways and ultimately leave one in a state of, if not undecidability, at least paralysis regarding the dialectics of redemption. The killing of innocent animals by a humane society was a wrenching experience for the students who worked there and saw it firsthand. Such an experience was no more dialectical than it was pure evil, and as such represented a good illustration of how dialectics as progressive history fails us.

Feminism is far from blind to this problem, though those influenced by Habermas[9] tend to adopt a dialectical strategy that gives hope to all oppositional movements. As a stage of resistance, overcoming is ultimately guaranteed: The only question is how much time it will take, how many lives or lifetimes. Hence, without such an ideal of justice and of the value of resistance to oppression, feminism loses both its direction and its passion — its eros. Indeed, the vision of a better future for women is surely one of the key factors that animates all feminism, driving both theoretical and practical agenda. How, then, could it not refuse to give up either the idea of dialectics or the notion of progress in history?

If, however, progress is viewed not as a given but as an end, an aim toward which one works, the differences between postmodernism and feminism's objections to it in some respects evaporate. Granted, there is no common ground with regard to dialectics: Its foundational function is either granted or challenged. However, on the issue of history as History and as something in itself necessarily progressive, most feminists and postmodernists are on the same shifting ground. Both camps would seem to agree the guarantees here are illusions. The liberation of any oppressed group does not happen by itself, since by the very nature of institutions and institutional power, the forces of current institutions are focused on their own self-maintenance. Thus, transformation of the loci of power in society today and the world at large will not come of its own accord. Resistance — both in theory and in practice — is the means to this end, and, as with all political action, we cannot know in advance if we will obtain the desired results. The risk of undecidability or inconclusiveness haunts both postmodern and feminist action.

## Loss of Referents: Nothing Outside the Text

Derrida has been cited as having said, "There is nothing outside the text." He is also credited with the assertion that the "proper name is [for him] nothing but the index of a problem."[10] When decontextualized, both these phrases invert and suggest the reverse of what they claim in context. First, the proper names. This claim was made in defense of his choice of Rousseau to illustrate the play of the supplement, or the process of supplementarity. Here he argued that "the proper name is nothing but the index of a problem" in that the proper names of philosophers in the history of philosophy function largely as an "index" of problems or issues.

Similarly, the claim that "there is nothing outside the text" has been misconstrued to represent the solipsistic view that only the reader Jacques and the text exist, or, more sparsely perhaps, only the text really is. The world and others, the subject, history, flesh and blood are thus discarded. This caricature, for that is what it is, has been used to charge Derrida with irresponsibility concerning "the real world," its sociopolitical and ethical problems, and his withdrawal from any connection with them.

There are many responses to this charge. To begin with, it is obvious that Derrida's sense of the term "text," far from merely indexing an actual book or piece of writing, refers to a writing behind writing; a textuality of the world; events, self, and others that constitute the fabric of meaning and nonmeaning, sense and nonsense, visibility and invisibility. His claim here is that these pairs are interwoven rather than opposed, with each feeding and making possible the other — sense and nonsense, visibility and invisibility, etc. It is through this fabric or tapestry that we perceive what we perceive, think what we think, and do what we do. Hence, such an assertion represents not a turning away from the world but, as Heidegger earlier called it, a turning toward the "worldhood" of the world. What makes the world a world, what makes things accessible, visible, invisible, perceptible, imperceptible, obvious, or obscure? What gives us access to the world? What prevents such access?

For students involved in service-learning projects, the truth of this position was vividly demonstrated through their work. The performative nature of language as designating a person to be poor, not mentally competent, delinquent, juvenile, or aged emerged in their very efforts to dispel the meanings linked to such appellations. That institutions need to name and categorize their clients in certain ways in order to treat or respond to them in accordance with those names became all too clear. Furthermore, they also came to see that the name has a referent only after such naming rather than, as is most often assumed, the reverse. A person might or might not receive food at the food bank, counseling at a shelter for the abused, etc. depending on the designation assigned to her or him.

These are certainly also feminism's issues — particularly concerning women as gendered subjects in a gendered world. Far from turning away from sociopolitical reality, Derrida's work provides new access to what makes "reality" reality, how institutions function, how language functions, how intersubjectivity is created and destroyed. Thus, the feminist charge against postmodernism as being amoral, apolitical, and ahistorical is quite unfounded. Only if one takes terms such as "text," "writing," and even "proper names" literally can one (mis)read Derrida in this way.

## Loss of the Body, Embodiment, and Gender

It has been argued that postmodernism occludes and precludes access to the body in general and the female gendered body in particular.[11] If all is text, then all are signifiers, and both the body and gender are just signifiers in their own and in larger systems. They are part of the play of signs that produces and at times destroys meaning. Even biology, that apparent basis of positivistic facticity, can be seen merely as a system of signifiers that organizes the world in particular ways. Thus, semiotics holds sway as a more primordial locus of inquiry than either the notion of the body or that of gender.

Second, historicity, at least as re-created by Foucault, is thought to unravel any fixed notions of either the body or gender. These are, after all, "discursive objects" that are produced in particular historical contexts and are systematically oppressed, constructed, distorted, and sculpted through the practices of various institutional and institutionalizing structures. This is reflected, for example, both in clothing style and in the fashion of a particular type of erotic body. Thus, far from forgotten, for Foucault, the body is understood as a site to be archaeologically and genealogically rearticulated. In this way, it can be seen as an effect, a product of various forces articulated in its appearance. Women's bodies are frequently rewritten and rearticulated in this way.

The service-learning courses that encountered this phenomenon most often were those associated with the gay-lesbian hot line and the local AIDS project. Gender issues surfaced constantly, for example, in the situations of callers whose sense of their true gender did not necessarily coincide with societal or parental expectations, let alone sociobiological assumptions. The social constitution of the body and, hence, gender became an experienced reality for students who took such calls.

Also troubling to feminists when it comes to body issues is the perspectivalism seemingly inherent in postmodernism, i.e., the denial that meta-narrativity has greater validity than other smaller, more local narratives. In asserting that women's bodies have been the site of patriarchal oppression across the globe for many centuries, we move to such a level of meta-narrativity to transport analysis beyond any particular time and place. The transcultural and indeed transhistorical framework that crosscuts women's studies in theory and practice would here be eliminated if one were to accept a blanket prohibition on meta-narrativity. To be sure, patriarchy has always used, and indeed is characterized by, universalizing gestures of this sort that sweep up the particular in the general and thereby impose one particular reality on the whole. However, many feminists argue that such oppressive meta-narrativity must not be confused with *all* meta-narrativity. Transcultural and transhistorical perspectives can be both cultural and historical — i.e., situated — and still remain valid at their widest, most extensive levels. Such an extension is not hyperbolic but instead remains based on the truth of each particular. In short, patriarchal narrativity entails an invalid induction from some particulars to all, whereas feminist meta-narratives entail a reality that parallels the statement. It is not an induction at all.

Furthermore, some feminists argue that gender itself is lost in postmodern analyses and descriptions. When Derrida, for example, speaks of "woman" in Nietzsche, he speaks of the figure, as figure of speech, trope, the word as thing, in Nietzsche's text. He is not referring to the gender of woman, or to women as embodied beings on the planet. The charge here includes the notion that women as subjects, as opposed to objects of discourse, are nowhere to be found in postmodern work. The body, when and where it is discussed, is inextricably the male body, or from the vantage point of male sexuality, male eros. An apparent gender neutrality, parallel to an apparent concept neutrality (i.e., man, one, chairman), actually betrays a hidden allegiance to one gender over the other, as both representing the missing other and also as foreclosing their difference.

Women as embodied subjects are thus not to be found in the texts of postmodern male theorists. To be sure, such a conclusion must overlook the works of Irigaray and Butler, who represent postmodern feminist amalgams that do indeed focus on women's embodiment. Nonetheless, more empirically positivist feminists would still argue that individuals such as these, as thinkers heavily influenced by postmodernism, still leave the basic problem unresolved: namely, the tendency to regard women, gender, and women's bodies only as textual, discursive objects, not as real, flesh and blood things. The assumption, of course, is that one can simply step out of and away from discourse and reach "the real thing." I shall explore both of these directives in my examples of postmodern feminist service-learning.

## Postmodern Feminist Service-Learning

Although seemingly oxymoronic several times over, such a phrase accurately describes the actual experiments in service-learning I have used in my classroom. In the following pages, I shall discuss two of these and show how each responds to various feminist objections concerning the supposed limits and drawbacks of postmodern thinking. Nonetheless, it must be admitted that postmodernists, for the most part, have not experimented with service-learning and have done little or no work on the transformation of pedagogical practice.[12]

The two examples I will discuss here involve a wide range of student activities. The particular projects the students chose to participate in represent already existing projects ongoing in our local community of State College, Pennsylvania. Students' choices included such work as ambulance assistance, women's resource center counseling and support, food distribution at the local food bank, Big Brother/Big Sister participation, Senior Full Care Facility work, coaching a soccer team, caring for injured raptors in a nearby shelter, and so forth. The community work assignment for both courses included a minimum of two hours per week or 32 hours per semester. This could be distributed in sessions once a month, every week, or in a single block, as some worked in another city for Habitat for Humanity during their spring break. Students were instructed to keep journals on their work experiences, their own reactions and reflections on those experiences, as well as a preliminary analysis of the same as preparation for their written assignments. Beyond these common features, the projects were quite distinct for each course, so I shall discuss further details individually. In both cases, however, it was evident that the service-learning course served many positive purposes for the students involved, the university in its relations with the community, and the community itself. I will discuss the particular strengths of these projects in light of the theoretical issues relating to feminism and postmodernism as discussed above.

### Philosophy 1. Introduction to Philosophy: Justice

Readings for this course were drawn from Plato's *Republic,* Thomas

Paine's *Rights of Man,* and Simone de Beauvoir's *The Second Sex.* These texts discuss very distinct notions of justice, which variously relate to natural and innate differences, socially constructed differences and inequities, and gender-based differences as played out in literary, philosophical, social, and cultural articulations of women's oppression and secondariness.

The task for students was to situate themselves in a regular program of community work throughout the semester (with a few, rare exceptions) and begin to unearth the implicit yet assumed concepts of justice at work in the practices and institutional structures of their particular service-learning situation. For instance, one student worked at the local food bank and was concerned to explore the regulations concerning food distribution and availability. Who was included, who was excluded from obtaining free food at the food bank? What were the reasons or rationale for this difference? What were the assumptions being made behind the official rationale or policy? Likewise, another student worked at a halfway house for juvenile offenders and focused on the regulations that limit and restrict the freedom and rights of the young people in its care. What assumptions are latent yet active within these proscriptions, and what is their foundation? Were there different rules for different genders? ages? races? sexual orientations? Again, another student worked at the women's resource center and was concerned to explore the access structures in place that allow women to obtain various services free of charge from the center versus restrictions placed on men's participation or access. This was analyzed in terms of both staff and clients.

These are just a few concrete instances of ways in which students were instructed to attempt to deconstruct the institutions at which they were performing services and with which they were working. From the inside, they could see that very often the rules were what the institution, and perhaps its board members and funding agencies, would tell itself it was doing, whereas in practice these same rules were often inappropriate or did not apply to a particular situation at hand. The reality of specific circumstances and actual experience showed again and again the rupture between the principles of an organization and its practice, between what it says it is doing and what in practice it is doing. Such a discrepancy lies at the heart of the deconstructive project and highlights the rupture between principles and experience, ideals and reality, language or naming as inherently general and life or experience as inherently singular. Though certainly at times the rules were strictly applied, inevitably a specific situation would arise that would transcend the categories the rules were meant to apply to and for which the rules were written. The violence of naming, the meta-narrativity of the institutional regulating strictures, and the inherent exceptional, out-of-bounds, illegal (unlawful) nature of the idiomatic and unnameable became concretely manifest for students in their actual service-learning practice. No classroom theory could substitute for or more clearly illustrate these notions.

## Philosophy 218. Contemporary Philosophy

For this course, I again used postmodernism as the subtext and orientation point in juxtaposing community practice with actual texts and classroom theory. It goes without saying that I intended the students in both these courses to use their experiences as a supplement to all the regular readings, lectures, and classroom discussions and participation. Community-based work was in no way a substitute for these traditional pedagogical methods. In this second course, the feminist component was more explicit, since we discussed four texts, all of which were written by women (an incidental fact though still unusual in most college courses today), and more important, we explored women's reawakening spirituality, black women's reinscription in a new discourse as subjects, and women's ways of knowing that detail very specific gender differences in epistemological practice.

The service-learning assignment in this case, as in the former course, included 32 hours of work for the entire semester at an agency of the student's choice. Students were instructed to search beneath the surface of their experiences and encounters with others to find the embedded and implicit philosophical allegiances buried within. For example, in some cases, students were to seek to make explicit the spiritual bases of practices and encounters, the epistemic bases, the political theory animating various power structures in place, the metaphysics behind and within the institution and its discursive practices, and even the ontological framework within which the experiences took place as they did. In short, they were instructed to perform an archeological analysis of the situation and practices they worked within and were exposed to by their project.

Some examples of specific projects may help to clarify more precisely the kinds of work students undertook. One student worked at a nursing home for seniors — a full-care facility — and explored the way residents' days were structured, limited, organized, and restricted for them. What assumptions lay behind these institutional practices, what ethics, politics, metaphysics, and even ontology?

Another student became a Big Sister to a young adolescent without a present father and whose mother worked full-time to make ends meet. This student explored her Little Sister's self-image and self-concept as a person, as a female subject, as an agent in the world, but also her sense of powerlessness, victimization, experience as an object of racial attacks, and so forth.

Yet another student worked with raptors — birds of prey — and found interesting issues to tackle concerning animal rights. Another worked for the

SPCA, and she, after much prodding, decided to explore the difficult issue of euthanasia with respect to the unwanted animals kept and eventually killed at the shelter. She investigated the institutionalization of the killing: which would be killed, when, where, and why, and which would not and why. The values of life and death, of animals as such, and ethical issues concerning animal rights in general were all addressed in her outstanding project.

It is safe to say that for many students involved in these projects their assignments, participation, and eventual analysis became life-changing events. Their intimate comprehension of the connectedness of theory and practice, of philosophy with life, were results that seldom come from exclusively classroom-based learning. Not only was their understanding of philosophy extended and deepened, I believe, as a result of these experiences but also their sense of its role in everyday life as the institutions around us became clear to many for the first time. In addition, many students' personal commitments to the community work at hand extended beyond the semester and course assignment proper.

## Conclusions

Service-learning, in my experience, can form a bridge between feminist concerns for agency, meta-narratives, subjectivity, historicity, ideals, and nonlinguistic materiality, on the one hand, and abstract postmodern theory, on the other. There is no gap and no opposition between these realms if one uses service-learning as the map that helps identify the pathways between them. In my experience, students have felt that taking the classroom outside into the community agency arena has been an invaluable expansion of their education. Learning not only about the agency and its mission but also about its successes and failures, students discover for themselves how philosophical ideas are enacted in practice, institutionalized in regulations, and reinforced in accepted procedures and rule-bound activities.

The process of seeking what is not explicit or manifest as such reveals to them not only the hidden biases of agencies that can never measure up to their own standards or principles but also a way of learning that reveals the inherently philosophical basis — the ethico-political bedrock — of all activity, all speech, all agency, all historicity, all processes of inclusion and exclusion. Questioning this implicit foundation is the only effective way to reveal its presence and to open up the possibility of real social change for the better. Such goals are, of course, shared both by feminism as a whole and by postmodernism at its best.

## Notes

1. For a thorough but brief history of feminism by the major feminist writers, see Schneir (1972).

2. For a good overview of "feminist standpoint theory" and a review of the positions of its leading protagonists, see Di Stefano (1990).

3. Such feminists in this camp include Judith Butler, Luce Irigaray, and, to a lesser extent, Nancy Fraser. For a good selection of articles contending the uses and abuses of postmodernism for feminism, see Nicholson (1995).

4. These theorists include the following, who henceforth will be named by positions that overlap rather than by proper names as such: Nancy Hartsock, Seyla Benhabib, Sandra Harding (notably ambivalent), and Susan Bordo, to name just a few.

5. For more on my reading of Derrida's work as a whole from a philosophical standpoint as it relates to the history of philosophy, see Harvey (1986).

6. For a good example of this direction in feminism, see Belenky et al. (1986).

7. See, in particular, Ricoeur (1985).

8. For his most recent remarks on Marx and the dialectics of history, see Jacques Derrida (1994).

9. Most notable in this regard is the work of Nancy Fraser, who admits her debts to Habermas in her feminist theory.

10. For the context here, see Derrida (1974).

11. One of the leading theorists on gender issues today is Susan Bordo. She squarely lays out her objections to postmodernism in Bordo (1990).

12. Derrida, for his part, has worked extensively on the transformation of pedagogical institutions in France, particularly when it comes to philosophy. He has established a major new institution for interdisciplinary research in Paris, and continues to be actively involved in teaching and recruiting there.

## References

Belenky, M.F., et al. (1986). *Women's Ways of Knowing: The Development of Self, Voice, and Mind.* New York, NY: Basic Books.

Bordo, S. (1990). "Feminism, Postmodernism, and Gender-Skepticism." In *Feminism/Postmodernism,* edited by L. Nicholson, pp. 133-156. New York, NY, and London, Eng.: Routledge.

Derrida, J. (1974). *Of Grammatology,* translated by G. Spivak. Baltimore, MD: Johns Hopkins University Press.

———— . (1994). *Specters of Marx,* translated by P. Kamuf. New York, NY, and London, Eng.: Routledge.

Di Stefano, C. (1990). "Dilemmas of Difference." In *Feminism/Postmodernism,* edited by L. Nicholson, pp. 63-92. New York, NY, and London, Eng.: Routledge.

Harvey, I.E. (1986). *Derrida and the Economy of Difference.* Bloomington, IN: Indiana University Press.

Nicholson, L., ed. (1995). *Feminist Contentions: A Philosophical Exchange.* New York, NY, and London, Eng.: Routledge.

Ricoeur, P. (1985). *Time and Narrative, Vol. 2,* translated by K. McLaughlin and D. Pellauer. Chicago, IL, and London, Eng.: University of Chicago Press.

Schneir, M. (1972). *Feminism: The Essential Writings.* New York, NY: Vintage Books.

# Listening to the Evidence: Service Activity and Understanding Social Phenomena

by Hugh Lacey

The university, as an institution, plays many roles in contemporary society. In recent years, it has also become increasingly fragmented to the extent that now there is difficulty in discerning any common purpose and shared core values, or even common language for critical discussion of them, among members of the university. With the fragmentation — accompanied by the widespread adoption of epistemic and moral relativism or skepticism, and the language of "valid educational experience" coming to ascendancy over the traditional language of "truth" — it is difficult to find a ground to argue rationally about the place (if any) of service-learning in the curriculum. Consequently, argument on this matter has tended to become replaced by pragmatic compromises that have provided little insight into important educational values. The difficulty is exacerbated by the fact that "service-learning" has become a general label for a diverse range of activities with various degrees of educational value whose only common element is that they involve some sort of integration of service into academic credit-gaining activities. I do not think that it is fruitful to attempt to discuss the value of service-learning in general terms.

I have a very limited objective in this paper: to argue that certain practices of service, accompanied by carefully structured reflections to which a variety of theoretical frameworks are brought to bear, may be able to play an important (and, under current historical conditions, perhaps an essential) role in coming to *understand* some social phenomena currently of great significance. My focus will be on the phenomenon of urban poverty in the United States, including the repercussions of the recently enacted welfare reforms. The role that I have in mind is played out neither by treating the practices of service simply as a means to gaining understanding, nor by subordinating the gaining of understanding to service, or to those moral virtues that may be cultivated within the practices of service. Instead, the role is played out in the course of a complex dialectic of service and understanding, that keeps in awareness that the service activities themselves become part of the phenomena that are to be understood and that, in principle, they make a difference to assessments of what possibilities the phenomena allow. Despite the fragmentation referred to above, I assume — though my assumption will be contested — that *one* of the core tasks of the university remains to gain understanding of the significant social phenomena of the times, those phenomena from which no lives are isolated and response to which largely defines the moral character of an age.[1]

At the present moment, following the enactment of welfare reform legislation, the conditions of the lives of the poor in the United States are undergoing rapid change. Interestingly, much of the debate surrounding the legislation has rested upon a mode of understanding of urban poverty, with respect to which there appears to be broad agreement: (in impressionistic summary) that the current condition of the poor represents a state of dependency on government, which has reinforced numerous vices (laziness; avoidance of work; violence, criminality, and other forms of social destructiveness; irresponsible sexual, child-bearing, and child-raising habits; drug use; absence of personal initiative and lack of preparedness to make use of opportunities; manipulativeness in blaming their condition on racism and playing on feelings of guilt among the well off) that entrap the poor in a "culture of poverty"; that, on balance, recent government programs on behalf of the poor represent a net harm (perhaps, in some versions, because they could not be efficacious, since the causes of poverty are not social or structural but rather located in individual attributes such as low "intelligence" and alleged genetic proneness to violence); that government spending for programs targeted to alleviate poverty represents a burden on, or even an injustice toward, the middle-class taxpayer; and hence that possibilities for empowerment of the poor require putting in place conditions that will impel them toward "self-sufficiency" and "taking responsibility for their lives."

Several features of the debate on welfare reform have struck me as worth noting. In the first place, the participants in it tend to display remarkable certitude about their diagnoses and their prescriptions, though few have had close contact with any poor people or ongoing dialogical relations with them, and though the "evidence" offered to support their diagnoses is hotly contested and, at best, partial and riddled with ambiguities. In a work originally published almost a century ago (1903), Du Bois wrote, "We must not forget that most Americans answer all queries regarding the Negro a priori, and that the least that human courtesy can do is to listen to the evidence" (Du Bois 1982: 130). It seems that his remark still holds, and applies as well more generally to the poor.

Second, the voices of the poor themselves are largely absent. Little effort has been expended to find out how poor people characterize themselves, how they diagnose the causes of their condition, how they express their hopes, and how they identify and articulate the possibilities that they consider worthy of their aspiration. They — "the evidence" — are not being much listened to. They tend not to be seen as parties to developing the "solution" to the "problem" that they, their behavior, their traits, and their communities are perceived to constitute.

Third, the language of the debate is often harsh, punitive, scornful, humiliating, coercive, "tough," and disengaged, dominated by appeal to "realism" — a realism (framed at the moment by such certitudes as the value of the free market, private control of capital, down-scaled government, and extended realms for private initiatives, and the "naturalness" of prioritizing self-interest) that does not recognize any viable possibilities outside the framework of its core certainties. It is a realism, I might add, more responsive to the realities of power than to the fruits of careful, systematic, empirical inquiry. Absent from this language is any sense of mercy, love (except "tough love"), compassion, solidarity, brother- and sisterhood, sacrifice for the sake of the common good, and any sense that our lives are intertwined. No doubt they are absent because they do not figure in the equations and calculations of "realism." Could it be that there is a connection between the certitude of diagnosis and the harshness of language, so that the "a priori" is grounded in the preparedness to use power (and the institutions of violence, e.g., prisons) to ensure compliance with the tenets of "realism"? Or perhaps it is grounded in the widespread tendency to replace the full exploration of the causal nexus of poverty with the premature (and morally righteous) assignment of responsibilities for the failure to eliminate its pathologies.

These are, of course, just impressions and polemical comments on the debate about welfare reform. I state them here to provide a context for raising the question about what it is to gain understanding of a social phenomenon such as urban poverty in the United States. What would we find out if we "listened to the evidence"? How must we be placed and what must we do in order to listen to it? With what language must we transcribe the evidence, and how do we learn that language? What possibilities (if any) for the future, and what varieties of them, are there in the communities of poor people to be identified that are not recognized in mainstream discourse? These questions generally are not considered at length in the mainstream because, I think, it is widely taken for granted (another "a priori"?): (1) that there are no significant possibilities for the foreseeable future outside the structures framed predominantly by the free market, private control of capital, and private enterprise, and, consequently, that individualist values will continue to be celebrated, manifested, and embodied in societal institutions ever more completely so that any attempt (for example) to cultivate values such as solidarity or to work toward creating significant cooperative institutions is flying in the face of reality; and (2) within these structures and their supporting institutions, there are continually expanding opportunities — eventually, in principle, open to everyone — for individuals to achieve their wants and to satisfy their needs, provided that they take the appropriate individual initiatives (for detailed discussion of these assertions, see Lacey 1997).

# Understanding

Now I will turn directly to the questions: What is it to gain understanding of a social phenomenon such as urban poverty in the United States today? How is that understanding gained and how ought it be gained? What criteria of evaluation should it meet?

I suggest that gaining understanding of such a phenomenon involves three interacting components that describe, explain, and encapsulate the possibilities allowed by the phenomenon (see Lacey 1991, 1993, 1995a). Gaining understanding involves, first, a comprehensive descriptive charting of the phenomenon and of the agents whose lives are part of it, which includes accounts of its variations, differences, and conflicts, and is sensitive to all of its dimensions, concreteness, historicity, and particularity as well as to statistical generalizations, and to the sources for (i.e., realized anticipations of and proposals for furthering) hope and transformation present within it as well as to the sufferings and pathologies that have brought it to mainstream attention as a "problem."

It involves, second, a historical-sociological analysis of how the phenomenon has been shaped and maintained, together with an analysis of the social and material conditions as well as the mechanisms and regularities of the various modes of life that the structures that frame the phenomenon allow (and require), and of the interactions and structural relations among these modes of life. This provides the background for assessing and appraising the relative importance of the various factors (natural, individual, behavioral, interpersonal, cultural, institutional, structural — and their interactions with one another) that might have made causal contributions to the phenomenon, recognizing that explanatory adequacy requires that attention be given to all the detail charted descriptively.

Third, gaining understanding involves attempts to diagnose what the range of future possibilities may be, including those for fundamental transformation, given the conditions and constraints provided by the present phenomena and their structural framing; and to identify what practices, what alliances with other people and institutions, and what restructuring of institutions and structures would be necessary to bring some of these possibilities to realization. Crucial here is the recognition that on the one hand the currently predominant structures, their regularities, and their tendencies significantly constrain the range of future possibilities, but that on the other hand there are genuine possibilities, realized in anticipatory forms in the marginal spaces of these structures, that may be able to gain the conditions to develop.

I think that certain kinds of service activities (which I will specify below) can play useful roles in gaining understanding of phenomena such as those of urban poverty. In order to make the argument for this in its minimal form, I will focus on the third component, the question of future possibilities (though clearly it presupposes the descriptive charting component). I emphasize that understanding cannot be reduced to description and explanation; it also involves encapsulation of future possibilities and, in turn, cannot be reduced to prediction that, in the social sciences, is achievable only under stable structural conditions. I will address how the question of future possibilities can be pursued in a disciplined and empirical way that avoids simultaneously the pitfalls of ideology (accepting the inevitability of the tendencies of the status quo as defined by actual relations of power) and illusion (fueled by a value-driven voluntarism, deriving possibilities from what one deems desirable). While sound understanding is opposed to both ideology and illusion, it is not uninformed by values. From values one cannot derive what is possible, but values can attune us to realms of possibilities that are worthy of investigation. Moreover, in human affairs, certain possibilities can be realized only if there are people who hold certain values, who desire that those possibilities be realized, and who are motivated to act to bring them to realization.

Any human phenomenon can issue in myriad possibilities, since it involves (among other things) the behavior of intentional agents and relations among them, and it is open to transformation in the light of reshaping its relations and interactions with any number and variety of individuals and social institutions. (Remember: Service activities of members of the university become part of the phenomenon of urban poverty.) Not all genuine possibilities can be realized, for the conditions required for the realization of some may preclude what is required for others. Furthermore, since the investigation of social possibilities itself requires material and social conditions, not all genuine social possibilities and the means toward their possible realization can be investigated. We cannot expect to be able to develop theories in which all genuine possibilities will be encapsulated. In order to investigate future possibilities, a selection of the kinds of possibilities of interest must be made, a selection that will reflect a value commitment, even if the selection made is just to investigate the trajectory of actual structures and their predominant tendencies. When we turn to a phenomenon such as contemporary urban poverty, however, understanding is seriously incomplete if it does not identify possibilities (if there are any) for the lessening of the suffering (in all of its dimensions) experienced by the poor and for the transformation of their condition so that possibilities for human flourishing become more available to them, and if it does not identify the social processes and the institutions that might serve to bring these possibilities to realization, or if it does not explain (with explanations that have been well tested empirically) why no possibilities for transformation are available.[2]

Thus, if we want to understand poverty, we need to address: (3) Do the tendencies and regularities of current structures open up (or prevent) possibilities of expanding the well-being of the poor and the suffering (without diminishing that of others)? (4) Do alternative social arrangements — aspired to in movements for social change in poor communities and present in anticipatory forms among them — offer greater possibilities? Could modifications of current structures, and transformations of its institutions, provide space that would permit such possibilities to expand and come to realization?

## Evidence

How can such questions be investigated in a way that is systematic and empirically grounded — without being constrained by the "a priori" reflected in questions (1) and (2), or by presumptions tailored to fit our hopes and desires, but recognizing both that future possibilities are constrained (not determined) by prevailing structures, powers, and conceptions of well-being (as well as by natural and ecological factors), and that what the future will be depends largely on the agency and choices of human beings, interacting together?[3] Answering this question in a comprehensive way is beyond the scope of this article. I focus on an important detail. What should count as *evidence* when addressing issues such as (3) and (4)?

Relevant evidence includes detailed accounts of the phenomenon as it is experienced by members of poor communities themselves, accounts therefore that are attentive not only to the sufferings and the pathologies of the community, to the usual demographic and statistical analyses, and to the micromechanisms underlying them. It must also include (since we wish to investigate alternative possibilities that may be germinating in the communities) the concrete daily experience of members of the community, their histories, struggles and achievements, values, knowledge, visions and images of hope, motivations, practical ideas, leaders, alliances and affiliations, budding initiatives, frustrated previous efforts, programs for transformation, and interpretations of their condition, of ongoing events, of whom (persons and institutions) they trust and distrust, and why. Such evidence cannot be gained without contact — extended, multifaceted, and involving considerable listening and dialogue — with those who experience the phenomenon of poverty.

## Service

How can the appropriate contact be obtained? One way is through carefully designed projects of service, and often it is the only way practically open to university personnel. Other ways would include living or working in a poor community or participating in its religious life. Obviously the poor themselves have the contact simply by virtue of being poor. That is why reflective testimony of the experience of the poor made by poor people themselves has an authority that is not readily discounted; nor, of course, is it the last word on an issue. Service, as such, is not sufficient, for it may be performed while making very little contact with the experience and context of the lives of the poor, and with little understanding of the conditions that must be in place for service to be effective. Under certain conditions, it may even hinder gaining understanding of the possibilities of transformation. (That is one of the reasons why a general defense of service-learning cannot be given.)

To be able to provide the appropriate contact, service activities normally should be part of a well-planned set of programs, where the activities and programs display the following four interacting levels (Lacey 1995b; Lacey, Bradley, and Eldridge 1994):

1. Each of the programs and activities has value by itself by virtue of its attempting to address a need identified by community members in an urban poor neighborhood — bringing resources, skills, training, and *above all* knowledge and the capability to generate knowledge into the community (see Note 9).

2. These programs and activities are integrated in a process of comprehensive community-wide (and, where possible, broader social) change — building institutions that all participants will share — directed toward goals established in collaboration with the community members.

3. They are carried out at a site (or sites) where students and others can perform community service (whether motivated by voluntarism or activism, charity or justice) that has been approved by the community and that is subject to ongoing supervision and evaluation, and where efforts are made to foster discussion and interaction between community members and those engaged in the service activities, to nurture respect and friendships, and to explore together further forms of collaboration.

4. They are conducted with a spirit of reciprocity, with all involved conceiving what they are doing as part of a common task whose goals are important for all of them. University personnel, community residents, and representatives of other public, private, and community organizations conceive themselves as working together for the same goals while playing different roles. The university personnel are not helpers or providers, but accompany and participate in the process of social change for the long haul, aiming, among other things, to create a new kind of institution of learning in which poor people can participate at all levels and from which they can gain knowledge and research to inform their projects for social change.

The four levels interact. All are equally essential. Some are not for the sake of others; rather, each is for the sake of all the others. All are essential if the service activity is to provide the kind of contact that locates one adequately for gaining evidence of the kind referred to above, while not treating service to the poor simply as a means to ends held by various university personnel. Service alters the phenomenon. Ideally, it becomes part of the means to bringing about social change of the kind desired by the community members and — at the same time — to bringing about transformations in the structures of learning and research in the university. Where all the levels are in place, programs of service become (in part) tests of certain types of possibilities of social transformation, e.g., the possibility of shaping social institutions (of which the university is an important instance) so as to exhibit the widest possible inclusiveness, diversity of perspectives, visions, and people, where there is special attention to including those currently excluded or neglected. Then, assessment of their success and progress (or failure) is itself a partial provider of relevant evidence about what future possibilities may be.

My point is a very simple one and, if one holds that one's claims to understand should be submitted to the tribunal of broadly empirical criteria, a quite obvious one: Understanding the phenomenon of poverty requires experiential contact with it, and projects of service — structured in the way outlined — can provide the opportunity for having that contact. The contact, of course, does not provide the understanding but the occasion for gaining the evidence to bring to bear in gaining understanding. Thus, projects of service of these kinds, provided that they are accompanied by careful and systematic reflection, and the further study, analysis, and research necessary for the formation and testing of an emerging understanding of poverty, play useful roles in connection with one of the fundamental tasks of the university.

## Service and a Course in the Philosophy of the Social Sciences

While my point is simple, the conditions that I have proposed are not easy to put in place. So it is reasonable to ask whether my general, abstract argument can be turned into concrete implementations. What difference to what is understood is made by engaging in these service practices? I cannot answer this in a general or in a conclusive way. By way of a partial (even oblique) and far from conclusive answer, let me offer some reflections on how an obligatory service component affected discussions in a class, Methodologies of the Study of Poverty, I recently taught in the philosophy of the social sciences (for details of the course, see Lacey 1995b). Most of the students were involved in weekly tutorial activities in the community center of a public housing development in an impoverished city (Chester, Pennsylvania, which is very close to Swarthmore), accompanying which were opportunities to talk with adults from the community, and occasionally for some of the students to attend community meetings.[4] The following is a list of some of the ways in which directed reflection and discussion of the service activity enhanced the philosophical discussion of the class. I do not claim that these matters cannot be discussed fruitfully without the context provided by the experiential contact, only that the contact lends a measure of concreteness and urgency and thus generates motivation to delve deeper into them.

1. It provided a rich context for the discussion of observation, particularly of how observation may or may not be a function of such factors as what one is looking for, one's personal history, one's location, what one is doing, how one is interacting with people, one's expectations, and one's cultural background. When students compared their own observations of the community center and events happening in it with those of their fellow students, those of the community members, and those of the public housing officials, they were struck by differences (on occasion, even contradictions), and so the issue of the objectivity (or not) of observation in the social sciences became an immediate and concrete issue.

2. What is the phenomenon of poverty that social science aims to understand and the public policymakers want to redress? Is poverty (and its attendant phenomena, e.g., racism and abuse of women) just a problem? Is it also a site for hope, struggle, and novel possibilities? How does one's characterization of poverty interact with one's social values and commitments about programs to transform the condition of the poor? How is poverty experienced by the poor, how is their experience relevant to how one characterizes poverty, and what sort of language do they use to describe it? Engaged contact with the phenomenon seemed to attune the students to the ways in which social science studies (and the public discussion about welfare reform) tend to presuppose answers to such questions, and so raised sharply the questions about evidence that are central to this article.

3. What is, and what ought to be, the relevance of local knowledge (including of local history) to understanding the phenomenon of poverty, to public policy formation, and to the decision-making processes of public authorities? The students quickly became aware that the residents know a great deal that they do not know, and would not come to know except through organized contact with the residents, e.g., about (in our case) Chester and its history, about the public housing development, about the hopes, visions, and motivations of the residents as well as about their sufferings and frustrations, and about their struggle (and sometimes organized efforts) to create a better life, especially for their children. This experience, in turn, raises critical questions about the "privilege" that tends to be granted to knowledge gained in the social sciences. What (if anything) grounds the privilege of "scientifically generated" knowledge? Does it properly dis-

place local knowledge when we seek comprehensive understanding and the grounding of the social values that shape public policy? How, for instance, might local knowledge provide relevant evidence for testing assumptions about "dependency" often appealed to in the current welfare reform debate?[5]

4. Questions about certain social science methodologies were sharpened. Concerning ethnographic studies, for instance, what are we to say of the reliability of a study if its subjects disagree with it? This question is sharpened when one can discuss with the subjects the reasons for their disagreement. The general adequacy of quantitative methods was raised, too, especially when students heard articulate residents characterize the community's condition with emphasis on concepts such as "brokenness" rather than measures such as low income or unemployment rate. "Brokenness" is used by Ella Thompson[6] to characterize the core sufferings experienced by and within a community — brokenness of personal lives, brokenness of relations among residents, brokenness from the life of the city and public affairs — that must be "healed" if the cycle of despair and violence is to be overcome. And the students tended, for example, to move beyond the statistics about how many children finish their schooling and began to ask about the motivations and motivation-formation processes of those who do and those who do not.

5. The students experienced the residents as agents, people with an interest in developing themselves and transforming their community, whose leaders have their own ideas about how to go about doing so (and a history of attempts, with some successes and some failures, to implement their ideas). They also observed the public housing authorities making a decision to relocate residents without discussion with them and without taking into consideration their forcefully articulated objections and alternative proposals. In short, the authorities ignored the residents' agency (knowledge, understanding, values, and aspirations), thus acting on the basis of an understanding of who the residents are that is not faithful to reality.[7] The students also became aware that in the ongoing debate about welfare reform, welfare recipients have in general not been invited to participate, thus coming to perceive it as a debate that presupposes that it is appropriate to make far-reaching decisions about the lives of poor people without engaging them in the process. This provided a context for asking how to investigate a group while simultaneously recognizing the agency, proper to human beings, of its members. Also, how could public policy be developed in ways that respect the agency of poor people, rather than treating them as objects for whose lives decisions are made in accordance with what "experts" and "authorities" think is good for them? What sort of social science do we pursue when we take these questions seriously? This raised the potential salience of "participant action" research and the centrality of

interpretive methods that attempt to understand actions, habits, motives, and predispositions as springing from agents' self-understandings.

6. What is the range of possibilities afforded by current realities? Are these possibilities fully framed by what can be done within prevailing socio-economic structures in accordance with current dominant tendencies? The students met residents who aspire to different, novel possibilities in which the community would exercise control over itself and be an active agent in public affairs (see Note 7). The aspirations are often expressed in a language that involves interesting twists in the use of commonplace terms. Where "empowerment," typically implying strong individualist connotations, is often used to express the objective of welfare reform, community residents speak instead of aspiring to "community empowerment." I have attempted to sum up what is intended by community empowerment as follows:

> It aims for the sharing of responsibilities and for community transformation, rather than encouraging individuals to "get out," just to cope, to live with lowered expectancies, or to accept the dependency that can accompany welfare; it aims to motivate community members to participate actively and authoritatively in the process of community transformation so that they have a genuine choice: to construct a fulfilling life in their own community, or to follow some other path. Community empowerment is thus part of a process of social transformation that is grounded in democratic means, and that at the same time enhances the expression of democracy. It puts democracy ahead of efficiency, the considered judgment of community leaders ahead of the generalizations and assessments of possibility of social analysts, and community involvement ahead of programs designed and implemented by outside experts. It builds the conditions for genuine democratic decision making at the community level so that the community members become active agents and decision makers in the process of change, and do not become reduced to recipients of aid, the goals and programs of which are determined by outside agencies. It holds that the authority for determining what is good for the community lies — in the final analysis after appropriate dialogue with agencies that wish to offer services and with due consideration given to the experiences of other communities — with the community members themselves. (Lacey, Bradley, and Eldridge 1994: 45)

How (repeating the question posed above) does one deploy empirical evidence to answer this question? There is virtually no philosophical literature that addresses this matter of evidence concerning claims about future possibilities (Lacey 1995a), yet I believe that it is the most urgent epistemological matter facing us today. One of the major achievements of the course was that the abstract question "Are there genuine alternative possibilities afforded by current realities?" became converted into the concrete one, "Do the residents' alternative proposals represent genuine possibilities?" That question is open to a measure of empirical investigation: by ongoing observation of

- the unfolding of the proposals,
- their being turned into a series of concrete projects for addressing needs,
- their gradually bringing about recognizable changes in the community that the residents recognize as positive, and
- their becoming linked institutionally with the projects and structures of other groups and institutions (including universities)

so that they begin to obtain the structural conditions for permanent maintenance and growth. The last consideration here also turns attention to the link between transformation of the condition of the poor and transformation of major societal institutions, including universities. One component of service activities is that friendships may be established among community and university personnel; such friendships can be the source of motivation for institutional change. (For a more detailed discussion of the issue of evidence/future possibilities, see Lacey 1997.)

7. Contact with the phenomenon of poverty engenders a strong sense both of complexity of problems and of tenuousness of opportunity, as well as a realization of the presence of resistance and struggle. To understand the phenomenon, one must grasp the full causal nexus — the macro and micro causal factors; the structural, interpersonal, and behavioral; matters of public policy and personal responsibility and initiative — and gaining such understanding cannot properly ignore the input derived from the perspective of poor people themselves.[8] Transformation of the condition of the poor requires both structural and personal transformation in dialectical interaction. There are no quick fixes; there is no one (principal) or one type of causal factor that has only to be changed and transformation will be ensured. Awareness of such complexity tends to move one away from using explanatory analysis as a means for assigning blame or moral responsibility. Frequently, the public debate is more about who is to blame for the pathologies of poverty, and who is responsible for initiating and funding solutions, than it is about understanding the phenomenon as it is and what could be done to transform it. While I do not think that the social sciences can be value free (Lacey 1997), I think it is a profound error to confuse explanatory analysis with the assignment of blame, and to remove from the causal account factors that one thinks ought not be changed (e.g., private control of capital) because of considerations of rights.[9] Responsibility can be exercised in a variety of ways (depending on who one is and where one is located); when we look to the full causal nexus, it becomes possible to discern

where one can make constructive interventions in order to exercise one's own responsibility — and different people and institutions may be better suited to make interventions in different places and ways.

## Concluding Remarks

My conclusions are modest. In order to understand certain phenomena (e.g., urban poverty), I have maintained, one must draw upon appropriate contact with the phenomena, and service activities may provide the vehicle for this contact. The difficult part is to design the service activities and their place within a curricular structure so that they do, in fact, contribute to the gaining of understanding. I offered a summary of the outcome of my effort to create such a design. I think that the outcome is promising, as are those of other courses developed within the Chester-Swarthmore College Community Coalition (Lacey, Bradley, and Eldridge 1994), and they will be replicated and further developed. These outcomes become part of the empirical record testing whether service-learning (and which forms of it) really does enhance the gaining of understanding. No general epistemological argument about service as a possible vehicle for entering into the appropriate contact with the phenomenon can justify failure to scrutinize the empirical record of how service has functioned in learning projects. Sound epistemology does not guarantee sound pedagogy. Attention must also be paid to the limitations of any effort to implement service-learning. In connection with my own course, it became clear that a one-semester contact is not enough to gain a good grasp of things. Short-term contact, even supplemented by a few interviews with residents, is not enough. A longer-term interaction, with multiple phases and multiple dimensions, involving participation in several courses or research projects clearly would be conducive to nurturing greater interpretive abilities and also be more consistent with the fourth level of collaboration listed above.[10] Meanwhile, the approach that I have presented remains exploratory and its conclusions provisional.

Despite these qualifications, it seems to me clear that if we can learn how to "listen to the evidence" and to incorporate it into our efforts to understand the morally significant social phenomena of our day, we will be indeed constructing a path that avoids the twin pitfalls of ideology and illusion.[11]

### Notes

1. Clearly, my argument is not limited in application to the case (urban poverty) I discuss, but I will leave the limits of its generalization as an open question. I emphasize, however, that my argument does not provide support for the value of much of what

has been included under the label of "service-learning." It remains open that other arguments may support other forms of service-learning, e.g., internships that contribute to professional formation, although severe criticism of many forms of service-learning is implicit in my argument (see also Note 10). Furthermore, that the service activities are of value in themselves or that in the course of them certain moral virtues (e.g., compassion, charity, justice) may be cultivated has little to do with the merits of their inclusion in the university curriculum (but see Note 8) — as distinct from their inclusion in a university's social outreach programs. My argument supports a place for certain forms of service-learning in the curriculum on the basis of their (potential) contribution to gaining understanding. It is not meant to be an argument that any form of service-learning become required of all students.

2. This sentence expresses simultaneously both a value judgment and a judgment about the requirements of adequate understanding. Denial of it also involves both kinds of judgments. Some may say that gaining understanding of urban poverty involves only predicting or anticipating its likely trajectories, perhaps under the conditions of welfare reform. But this involves the value judgment that identifying "lost possibilities" is not part of gaining understanding, and that there is no obligation to attempt to gain understanding that might usefully inform projects whose likelihood of reaching a successful outcome is (under current conditions) low.

3. Any judgment about future possibilities inevitably involves subtle mixtures of prediction and promise, anticipation and intention, awareness of current realities and desire for novelty. Keeping the proper balances is necessary for gaining sound understanding. Such judgments always remain conjectural. But the degree of confidence one accords to them can change with changed motivations of human agents.

4. The activities were part of a set of programs, developed by the Chester–Swarthmore College Community Coalition (CSCCC), attempting to implement the four conditions stated in the text. These conditions have not yet been put in place as fully as I, and my collaborators both from the community and from Swarthmore College, consider desirable. For some details about CSCCC, its history, philosophy, and programs, see Lacey, Bradley, and Eldridge (1994). The CSCCC idea came from the model developed at the Central American University in El Salvador, and articulated in the writings of I. Ellacuría and I. Martín-Baró, the most important of which are published in Hassett and Lacey (1991b). I have discussed it further in Hassett and Lacey (1991a) and Lacey (1993, 1995a). Ellacuría and Martín-Baró did not discuss service-learning as such. Their concern was to integrate the "social outreach" programs of their university systematically with its teaching and research programs.

5. This also raises the question of the possible teaching role in the university of the bearers of local knowledge, an important question in the light of the fourth level of collaboration indicated above (see Lacey, Bradley, and Eldridge 1994).

6. Ella Thompson is president of the Resident Council, William Penn Homes, in Chester, and cochair of the board of CSCCC. She is a long-term resident of public housing and community organizer. "Brokenness" is just one term where students found descriptive language (with rich "theoretical" content) used by articulate members of the community that is not a commonplace in social science and public policy discussions. The adequacy of "translations" of community analytic and explanatory idiom becomes an important question in these contexts, e.g., in connection with my attempt to summarize the content of "community empowerment."

7. Shortly after the completion of the course, as a consequence of concerted pressure from the residents, the authorities dropped their plans and agreed to reconstruct the housing development with a design that the residents worked out in collaboration with an architect appointed by the authorities. Efficacy of action and practicality of (some of) their ideas are further "data" that the contact, acquired through service, would bring to the students' attention, and they also would furnish partial concrete content to what projects that further community empowerment could be like.

8. In Note 1, I maintained that the justification of a pedagogical form depends principally upon epistemic considerations, and that that is not sufficient to appeal to moral virtues that may be cultivated by it. This is consistent with certain practices for gaining understanding being dialectically intertwined with the cultivation of certain moral virtues (Lacey 1993). Indeed, it is difficult to imagine participation in the kind of service-learning that I have advocated if one does not aspire to manifest particular moral values in one's life, or if one is not prepared to have one's imagination stirred with a view to entertaining critical confrontations with the predominant social structures and perhaps lifetime commitments to social transformation, working with community leaders toward building new institutions. This kind of service-learning, thus, seems to require and imply *conscientização* (Freire 1970), or the development of "morally critical awareness" (Martín-Baró 1991). I asked, What kind of contact with the phenomenon must we have — what must we do — in order to gain the relevant evidence? It may well be that, in order to do what must be done, one must be of a certain type of character or hold certain values. If so, service-learning will be involved with the cultivation of moral virtues, but its place in the curriculum derives from its contribution to gaining understanding.

9. It is also an error to predict disastrous consequences simply from what one judges to be (morally) ill-motivated policies. The possibilities afforded by the moment are always more encompassing than what can be grasped by a priori or moralistic analysis. It may well be that the new realities created by the implementation of ill-motivated policies will become the occasion for a new level of motivation and energy among community members to develop their own programs of community empowerment. The matter is an empirical one, and one about which we can draw little insight from past regularities. Since there is so much new to be understood following the passage of welfare reform, this is a fitting time to be engaging in the kind of service-learning that I am advocating. It is worth noting that one very important form of service at this moment is bringing to the community knowledge about such things as legislation, regulations, new agencies, rights and legal protections, and opportunities that may have been opened up by the new policies.

10. Numerous objections, not always mutually consistent, have been made to the idea of requiring service in courses for academic credit: that it involves treating poor communities as laboratories; that it politicizes the curriculum; that it lowers standards; that it permits the curriculum to be shaped by subjective preferences and special-interest moral agendas; that it clashes with the "nonpartisan" character of an educational institution and may even threaten its autonomy; that it reinforces those who would put educational experiences rather than disciplinary inquiry at the center of the curriculum; and that it downplays that the distinctive role of the university is to gain knowledge rather than to be a direct agent of social change. I believe that these objections need to be taken seriously and responded to. Some of them may constitute

valid objections to some instances and conceptions of service-learning. I cannot, however, address these matters here.

11. This article includes extracts from "Methodologies of the Study of Poverty" (Lacey 1995b), which are used with permission of Pennsylvania Campus Compact.

## References

Du Bois, W.E.B. (1982). *The Souls of Black Folks*. New York, NY: New American Library.

Freire, P. (1970). *Pedagogy of the Oppressed*. New York, NY: Herder.

Hassett, J., and H. Lacey. (1991a). "Comprehending Reality From the Perspective of the Poor." In *Towards a Society That Serves Its People: The Intellectual Contribution of El Salvador's Murdered Jesuits*, edited by J. Hassett and H. Lacey, pp. 1-15. Washington, DC: Georgetown University Press.

————— , eds. (1991b). *Towards a Society That Serves Its People: The Intellectual Contribution of El Salvador's Murdered Jesuits*. Washington, DC: Georgetown University Press.

Lacey, H. (1991). "Understanding Conflicts Between North and South." In *Cultural Relativism and Philosophy: North and Latin American Perspectives*, edited by M. Dascal, pp. 243-262. Leiden, Netherlands: E.J. Brill.

————— . (1993). "Notes on the Dialectic of Truth and Justice." In *Educating for Social Responsibility in a Multicultural World. The Swarthmore Papers* 1, edited by B. Schwartz, pp. 107-116. Swarthmore, PA: Swarthmore College.

————— . (1995a). "The Legacy of El Salvador's Murdered Jesuits." *Journal for Peace and Justice Studies* 6: 113-126.

————— . (1995b). "Methodologies of the Study of Poverty." In *Service-Learning: Linking Academics and the Community*, edited by J.W. Eby, pp. 139-147. Harrisburg, PA: Pennsylvania Campus Compact.

————— . (1997). "Neutrality in the Social Sciences." *Journal for the Theory of Social Behavior* 27: 213-241.

————— , T. Bradley, and M. Eldridge. (1994). "The Chester-Swarthmore College Community Coalition: Linking Projects for Community Empowerment in a Public Housing Development With a College's Academic and Outreach Programs." *Universities and Community Schools* 4: 41-49.

Martín-Baró, I. (1991). "Developing a Critical Consciousness Through the University Curriculum." In *Towards a Society That Serves Its People: The Intellectual Contribution of El Salvador's Murdered Jesuits*, edited by J. Hassett and H. Lacey, pp. 220-242. Washington, DC: Georgetown University Press.

# The Use of a Philosopher:
## Socrates and Myles Horton

by John Wallace

In this paper I want to explore a conceptual territory — a kind of field of force — between two quotations. One quotation is from Frank Ramsey, the distinguished British economist and philosopher; it makes an apparently strong claim to the effect that philosophy should be useful. The other is from James Bevel, the distinguished American civil rights leader; it compares Socrates with Myles Horton. Reflecting on Ramsey's claim, in the context of my work as a teacher, caught me up in a quandary; reflecting on Bevel's comparison has suggested a way of moving through the quandary to a new place. Ramsey pushes us to ask what philosophy is for. Bevel points a direction in which to look for an answer.

## The Quotations

It will be useful to have the quotations in front of us at once. Ramsey writes:

> *Philosophy must be of some use and we must take it seriously; it must clear our thoughts and so our actions. Or else it is a disposition we have to check, and an inquiry to see that this is so; i.e., the chief proposition of philosophy is that philosophy is nonsense. And again we must then take seriously that it is nonsense, and not pretend, as Wittgenstein does, that it is important nonsense. (1965: 263)*

Before quoting Bevel, I want to set the context of his words by drawing on Taylor Branch's *Parting of the Waters: America in the King Years 1954-63*. According to Branch, in the fall of 1958 a busload of students from Nashville, including John Lewis and James Bevel, went to a workshop at the Highlander Folk School, which Myles Horton had helped start in the 1930s and of which he was currently the executive director. Concerning Bevel's experience at this workshop, Branch writes:

> *Of the Highlander speakers, it was Myles Horton who first cracked Bevel's sense of mastery. Horton questioned the claims of students who said they had separated themselves from segregation's assertion that they were inferior. He made them doubt who they were, what they were saying. Bevel had never heard a white man speak so bluntly and yet so deftly. He seemed like Socrates, always challenging assumptions, boring deeper toward the core. The effect put Bevel on edge. He began to feel an oppressive weight. At a*

*later session, he sizzled when another speaker berated the students for cowardice. "Just look at the Polish students," said the speaker. "They are busy helping to get the government of their country straightened out, and you are all here winding around the may-pole, and going up the side steps to see a movie, and playing bridge. How do you feel?" Bevel's temper snapped. He walked out on the heavy-handed speech and slammed the door. (Branch 1988: 263)*

Branch's source for his account of this workshop is Aldon Morris's book on the origins of the civil rights movement. Morris quotes from an interview with James Bevel as follows:

*That's when I first met Mrs. Septima Clark, Myles Horton, and I guess for the first time in my life, I was introduced to a man who reminded me of Socrates. Myles was a guy who'd ask questions about your assumptions. He would challenge you on your inferior feelings. He sort of decrudded Negroes from being Negroes and making them think of themselves as men and women. His psyche didn't agree with a "nigger" being a "nigger." So that's not a game with him. He has arrived at a self-respect and self-appreciation of mankind. He, in that sense, is not a liberal, he's an enlightened man. When you come upon it, and you assume that you're a Negro, and you assume that white folks are oppressing you, he would tear your assumptions up. He, like, destroyed all the false assumptions of the oppressor and made us deal with the fact that we were cowards, and that we were lying, and were not serious about being who we said we were. (Morris 1984: 147)*

## Starting With Ramsey

Ramsey's words that "philosophy must be of some use" have been ringing in my mind since graduate student days. They came to life in a fresh way about eight years ago when I began to teach a course (Social Justice and Community Service) in which I attempt to help undergraduate students link their experiences in doing service work in the wider community with writings on ethics and politics from the philosophical tradition. Not all at once, but slowly over the time I have repeatedly taught and repeatedly revised this course, my view of philosophy as a subject to be taught to these students has undergone a radical change.

My old view saw philosophy as a cultural inheritance, a cultural treasure, to be learned and appreciated for its own sake. Courses expose students to some of the central monuments of the subject, exposure that includes their learning some of the intellectual strategies and skills used in building the monuments. Students then are free to make what use of the subject they will. In effect, I presented students with the following division of labor: "My job, as teacher, is to present and help make accessible to you important examples of philosophical thinking; your job, as students, is to learn them and to figure out their relevance, if any, to your own life."

Teaching the course, participating with students and sometimes with community leaders in class discussions, reading students' writing, and simply talking almost every day with students who were working in the community to meet human and environmental needs forced me to reexamine this view. Students' motivations for doing this work are complex and varied, and not always uniformly admirable, and I have no wish to simplify or idealize. If someone were to say, "Every racist, classist, sexist attitude that is divisive in the wider society, every blinding partialness of vision, understanding, and sympathy to be found in the society, is present in one or more students in your class," I would not deny it. I could not help but be struck and moved, however, by the evident strong desire of virtually all of the students to act in response to real needs and to begin to act and to live to meet them.

The students want to make a difference. If, in the course of their work, they begin to see that they are making a difference — to a child being tutored, to a senior citizen needing a friend, to a park needing fix-up — one sees a tremendous burst of energy and commitment. The students are not passive learners, but are searching for knowledge and understandings that will help them be more effective in their immediate service work and in their larger and long-range roles as citizens. They want to work, and work smart, in the short run, and in the longer run to build a more just and more humane society. It became uncomfortable for me to say to them, "I admire and support what you are doing. As for the philosophy we are learning here, it may or may not be relevant to your interest in building a better society; that is for you to figure out." I needed to go further, to develop a commitment that matched theirs. If I were going to ask these students to spend time studying philosophy, I would have to be able to say something, to believe something, about how they can use what they learn from the study. I needed to develop my own view of how philosophy can be relevant to, and useful for, someone who wants to dig in and work for social justice. Not that I wanted to impose such a view on the students, but I did want to be able to bring to the class ways of thinking about what the relevance might be and, if I succeeded in finding a view of my own, to share it.

So the question I had to face was a version of Ramsey's question: What relevance do teaching philosophy and doing philosophy have to building a more just and humane society? I should emphasize that this is the force that Ramsey's question has taken on for me, given my experience of the subject and of the world. I do not attempt to give a scholarly account of what it meant for Ramsey, a question that interests me, but not here.[1]

It has been instructive and encouraging to discover Martha Nussbaum also wrestling with this question. In the introduction to her book *The Therapy of Desire: Theory and Practice in Hellenistic Ethics* (1994), she contrasts the "happy and self-expressive" life of a philosophy professor with the "hunger, illiteracy, and disease [that] are the daily lot of a large proportion of human beings." She asks, "What business does anyone have living in the happy and self-expressive world, so long as the other world exists and one is a part of it?" (3). In responding to this question, she holds out an attractive possibility: "It seems possible that philosophy itself, while remaining itself, can perform social and political functions, making a difference in the world by using its own distinctive methods and skills" (3). And she claims that the Hellenistic philosophers she discusses in her book "practiced philosophy not as a detached intellectual technique dedicated to the display of cleverness but as an immersed and worldly art of grappling with human misery" (3).

This sounded splendid, and just what I was looking for: a way of taking and doing philosophy that is not a mere "display of cleverness" but performs social and political functions that make a difference in the world. How does philosophy with these attributes come about, what does it look like, how does it work, and in what way does it engage usefully with the world? Nussbaum turns explicitly to these questions in Chapter 4 of her book. She writes:

> The practical value of good philosophy [lies] in really getting to the most powerful and justifiable pictures of human excellence, human functioning, human social justice. Such philosophical accounts are not at all useless: for once they are worked out, they can offer a great deal of guidance to public life — to judges, legislators, economists, policy-makers of many kinds. Those people will not themselves all be philosophers; but they will be able to use the results of philosophical inquiry to design social institutions better. And in that way they will bring the benefits of philosophy to many people who are never going to study philosophy at all, thus helping in their own way the very people Epicurus claims the Aristotelian cannot help. (Nussbaum 1994: 138)

As I understand it, this view can be summarized as follows: Philosophers are experts of a special kind. They are experts at creating designs for good lives and good social institutions. They are experts at creating pictures of human excellence, both individual and social. Not only are they experts at creating such pictures; they are also experts at "justifying" them, that is, I suppose, at giving good reasons for preferring one picture to another picture that at first sight may seem equally or more appealing. Philosophers are therefore experts who know what good lives and good institutions are, and why. This view of the philosopher fits naturally with the view that the point of teaching philosophy is to bring students to appreciate what these experts have created, with enough understanding of the tools with which they create to support this appreciation. This view of the point of teaching philosophy, in turn, fits naturally with Nussbaum's view of how philosophy is useful "as an immersed and worldly art of grappling with human misery." That is, some of these students in later life will move into positions of power where they can implement the designs that they learned to appreciate in their youth. This might be called the expertise/appreciation/trickle-down model of philosophy as a cultural enterprise to be pursued by professors and taught to students in universities.

The part of this view that sees the teaching of philosophy to undergraduate students as the teaching of philosophical appreciation seems to me an honorable and reasonable view. In the circumstances in which we teach at universities in the United States — with students being forced into college in order to have any chance of a decent economic future, and forced into philosophy courses in order to meet requirements for degrees — it is the best that can be done with some students. The other parts of the view, that philosophers are experts on the good life and good social institutions and that the impact of this expertise comes via persons in positions of power who in their youth internalized the good "pictures" of their philosophy teachers, seem to me both ridiculous and repugnant. Not that something like what it holds out as desirable might not sometimes happen. (See Keynes's remark about madmen in authority.) But I am not going to argue this further. My purpose in this paper is rather to develop an alternative view, and let readers choose for themselves.

The view that teaching philosophy is teaching appreciation of philosophical monuments, honorable and sometimes necessary as it is, simply does not work for the students who come to my Social Justice course. If this were the only view available, I would stop teaching the course. George Eliot's depiction, in Chapter 20 of Middlemarch, of Dorothea Brooke's unhappiness in Rome helps me explain this. Dorothea and Edward Casaubon are on honeymoon in Rome. Dorothea spends a good deal of time visiting the great monuments and museums of that city. But they bore her and leave her cold: "She had been led through the best galleries, had been taken to the chief points of view, had been shown the greatest ruins and the most glorious churches, and she had ended by oftenmost choosing to drive out to the Campagna where she could feel alone with the earth and sky, away from the oppressive masquerade of ages, in which her own life too seemed to become a masque with enigmatical costumes" (Eliot 1994: 183). Students come to my course tired of being led through the best galleries and monuments, of philosophy and other academic subjects, and wanting something that is alive for them and advances their work in the community. If philosophy cannot support this life and work — if it cannot go with my students into the Campagna — then my course has to stop. Of course, there are other students who do not want this and for whom philosophy-appreciation may be appropriate, as George Eliot also acknowledges: "The weight of unintelligible Rome might lie easily on bright nymphs to whom it formed a background for the brilliant picnic of Anglo-foreign society; but Dorothea had no such defense against deep impressions" (Eliot 1994: 184). These are not the students who come to my course.

## Socrates and Myles Horton: Similarities

Back to the question to which my students had led me: What relevance do teaching philosophy and doing philosophy have to building a more just and humane society? Wrestling with the question had led me to the impasse I have sketched: I needed an answer to the question to go on teaching the course; I didn't have an answer, and the kind of answer, perfectly thoughtful and serious in its way, suggested by Martha Nussbaum was definitely wrong for me and my students. Stuck in this impasse, Bevel's comparison of Myles Horton with Socrates came to me as a surprise and a freeing revelation. For it offered a bridge between Socrates's doing of philosophy, social justice, and my classroom. Horton had been a powerfully effective educator for social justice. Rosa Parks, Martin Luther King, Jr., James Bevel, John Lewis, Bernice Johnson Reagon had been his "students," though he would certainly not have used that word to describe them. If in doing this educational work he was being a philosopher, doing philosophy, well then, here was a path for an approach to teaching and doing philosophy, a path at once fresh and as old as Socrates, a path that promises to be quite different from the expertise/appreciation/trickle-down approach.

The hypothesis that we need to explore is that, in his educational work at Highlander, Horton was doing and teaching philosophy. We can explore the hypothesis by playing with the comparison between Socrates and Horton. I say "playing," because I think that play is the right spirit in which to approach a field of evidence that is amazingly complex and varied, and that can take us in the span of a few seconds from being surprised, to being moved, to being amused.

Let's play first with similarities between Socrates and Horton. I find 10 of these that are worth being struck by.

### Using Conflict and Contradiction to Move People and Make Them Think

Socrates and Horton are alert to the power of bringing out conflicts and contradictions within the thinking of an individual person, or among persons in a group, as a way of moving people's thinking, getting them to change, grow, and learn. Socrates used the strategy of *elenchus* (Socrates's strategy of inquiry), of questioning his interlocutor's beliefs about the topic in hand to unearth contradictions and so force revisions of the person's belief system. Horton worked primarily with groups of 25 or so in workshop settings. In *The Long Haul,* Horton talks about how studying with Robert Park at the University of Chicago in 1930 helped shape his ideas about the use of conflict in workshops:

> I took classes with Robert Park and learned about group problem solving and conflict as a tool for learning. At this time I began to realize that learning that came from group effort was superior to learning achieved through individual efforts. I also began to understand how to use conflict and contradictions to promote learning. . . . In a workshop, conflict gets the whole group involved. You don't even try to referee between two people. At this point the group takes over the discussion, since the problem being debated is everyone's problem. And when this happens, everyone discovers that the issue is not as simple as the two people have stated it, and a lot of the complications surface and get aired. (Horton 1990: 47)

Horton involved groups at the workshops in making decisions about what to discuss and how to proceed, so forcing groups to work through differences to common action. In addition to using conflicts that arise between individuals in a group, Horton, like Socrates, looked for and used tensions in the thinking of individuals. He writes:

> If you ever lose track of where people are in the process, then you have no relationship to them and there's nothing you can do. So if you have to make a choice between moving in the direction you want to move people, and working with them where they are, you always choose to work with them where they are. . . . Then I set up a tension between where people are and where they can be, and I make people uncomfortable quite often because I keep pushing them, trying to help them grow. (Horton 1990: 132)

### Placing High Value on the Past Experience That People Bring to a Learning Situation

Socrates and Horton are dedicated to getting people to respect and take seriously their past experience, and to giving them ways of building on that experience and achieving future growth that is fully "from" that experience. Socrates and Horton proceed as though, and sometimes say explicitly that, people already have within them the answers they need.

Socrates proceeds by questioning, a process that says to the interlocutor, "What you have in your mind is important and worth having out on the table; it is what we are going to work with." And in the *Theaetetus* at 150D, we find this admission:

*I'm not at all wise myself, and there hasn't been any discovery of that kind [wisdom] born to me as the offspring of my mind. But not so with those who associate with me. At first some of them seem quite incapable of learning; but, as our association advances, all those to whom God grants it make progress to an extraordinary extent — so it seems not only to them but to everyone else as well. And it's clear that they do so, not because they have ever learnt anything from me, but because they have themselves discovered many admirable things in themselves, and given birth to them. (Plato 1973: 13-14)*

Horton always worked in the light of the premise that participants in a workshop brought with them the seeds of solutions to their own problems. The following is just one of many statements that illustrates this:

*We have always made a number of assumptions about workshops. First, a workshop has to have a goal arising out of a social problem that the students perceive; second, people have within themselves the potential, intelligence, courage, and ability to solve their own problems; third, the Highlander experience can add to and enrich the educational experience that the students normally would have; fourth, in addition to learning from their peers during the workshop experience, the Highlander staff members should have an opportunity to interact in the field with students. The most important parts of a workshop come from what has happened in a community before the workshop itself, and what happens when people go home and act. (Horton 1990: 153)*

## Using Questioning and Avoiding Telling and Lecturing in Teaching

For both Socrates and Horton, this strategy is a way of respecting the experience that people bring to the learning encounter and of taking care that the course of the interaction never breaks connection with the learner's experience. As Horton notes:

*I use questions more than I do anything else. They don't think of a question as intervening because they don't realize that the reason you asked that question is because you know something. What you know is the body of the material that you are trying to get people to consider, but instead of giving a lecture on it you ask a question enlightened by that. Instead of you getting on a pinnacle you put them on a pinnacle. I think there's a lot of confusion in the minds of academicians as to what you mean when you say you have to intervene. (Horton and Freire 1990: 146)*

## Making Sure That Learners Care About the Topic of Discussion and Say About It What They Believe

Socrates and Horton do everything they can — from explicit insistence to the tacit ways in which interlocutors are selected and in which their encounters with learners are staged — to ensure that participants speak from their own experience, that the topics of discussions are alive and real in their lives, and that they say what they believe. Gregory Vlastos (1994) calls attention to the "say what you believe requirement" in Socrates's method in the paper "The Socratic *Elenchus*: Method Is All" in his *Socratic Studies*. For example, in the *Protagoras* at 331C, Socrates insists on just this principle:

> Protagoras: Socrates, I can't really admit that justice is holy and holiness just; I think there is some difference there. However, what does it matter? If you like, let us assume that justice is holy and holiness just.

> Socrates: Excuse me. It isn't this "if you like" and "if that's what you think" that I want us to examine, but you and me ourselves. What I mean is, I think the argument will be most fairly tested, if we take the "if" out of it. (Plato 1956: 63-64)

Vlastos argues that this principle is a necessary part of Socrates's inquiry into "what is the way we ought to live":

> Thus the elenchus has a double objective: to discover how every human being ought to live and to test that single human being who is doing the answering — to find out if he is living as one ought to live. This is a two-in-one operation. Socrates does not provide for two types of elenchus — a philosophical one, searching for truth about the good life, and a therapeutic one, searching out the answer's own in the hope of bringing him to the truth. There is one elenchus and it must do both jobs, though one or the other will be to the fore in different phases of it. From this point of view, too, the "say what you believe" makes sense. How could Socrates hope to get you to give, sooner or later, an account of your life, if he did not require you to state your personal opinion on the question under debate? (Vlastos 1994: 10)

Horton was concerned to understand what prevents people from speaking up for their own interests and expressing their own views. He also was concerned to understand what prevents teachers from perceiving the interests and views of their students. Thus, he writes:

> This is the problem, how we can have a body of knowledge and understanding and resist the temptation to misread the interest of the people

because we're looking for an opportunity to unload this great load of gold that we have stored up. . . . One of the things I've found is that if any one of a group of people with similar problems asks a question then there is a good chance that the question will reflect some of the thinking of the peers. Even if it doesn't, everybody in that circle is going to listen to the answer to that question, because one of their peers asked it. They can identify with the questioner. It's a clue that there's some interest there. Short of questions, I have found that I'm secure in a discussion when people actually say what they perceive the situation to be. (Horton and Freire 1990: 139)

## Focusing Primarily on Developing People

Socrates and Horton are fiercely single-minded in focusing on the ideas, the minds, the growth of their interlocutors, and are not deflected from this concentration by any task or job set from outside the learning situation. Socrates and his interlocutors are never writing a report or getting on with a concrete task. They may have interrupted a task to have their discussion, but the discussion itself is conducted as if there were infinite time. Socrates comments on this in the *Theaetetus* at 172D:

If you compare people who have been knocking about in lawcourts and such places since they were young with people who have been brought up in philosophy and other such pursuits, it's as if you were comparing the upbringing of slaves with that of free men — in that the philosophers always have plenty of time; they carry on their discussions in peace and with time to spare. For instance, look at us now, taking up one argument after another: we're already on our third. That's what they'll do, too, if the next argument to come up attracts them more than the one in front of them, which is what happened to us. It doesn't matter at all whether they talk for a long time or a short one, provided only that they hit on that which is. (Plato 1973: 48)

Horton emphasizes the difference between education and organizing:

One of the examples I used to use got me into trouble and still gets me into trouble when I use it. I'd say if you were working with an organization and there's a choice between the goal of that organization, or the particular program they're working on, and educating people, developing people, helping, helping them grow, helping them become able to analyze — if there's a choice, we'd sacrifice the goal of the organization for helping people grow, because we think in the long run it's a bigger contribution. . . . If you're into having a successful organizing campaign and dealing with a specific project, and that's the goal, then whether you do it yourself or an expert does it or some bountiful person in the community does it, or the government does it without your involvement, it doesn't matter, because that solves the problem — then you don't take the time to let people develop their own solutions. If the purpose is to solve the problem, there are a lot of ways to solve the problem that are so much simpler than going through all this educational process. (Horton and Freire 1990: 116-119)

## Insisting That the Proper Expertise of the Teacher Lies in Being an Expert on Inquiry, Not Answers

Socrates and Horton have no elaborate, previously constructed theories to tell to or impose on learners; they practice and share with interlocutors and workshop participants a capacity for learning and a process of inquiry. Socrates's depiction of himself as a midwife (possibly, scholars think, an invention of Plato, but still presumably true to Socrates's practice) gives powerful expression to this idea. In the *Theaetetus* at 150C, Socrates puts this as follows:

> My art of midwifery has, in general, the same characteristics as theirs [that is, as real midwives], but it's different in that I attend to men, not women, and in that I watch over minds in childbirth, not bodies. And the greatest thing in my art is this: to be able to test, by every means, whether it's an imitation and a falsehood that the young man's intellect is giving birth to, or something genuine and true. Because I have, in common with midwives, the following characteristic: I'm unproductive of wisdom, and there's truth in the criticism [that] many people have made of me before now, to the effect that I question others but don't make any pronouncements about anything myself, because I have no wisdom in me. (Plato 1973: 13)

Horton has this to say about not coming across as an expert:

> You have to work through that business of getting them to be comfortable with trusting themselves a little bit, trusting their peers a little bit. They hear Mary say something and Susie says well, if they listen to Mary, maybe they'll listen to me. It's a slow process, but once the people get comfortable with it, then they begin to see that you aren't going to play the role of an expert, except in the sense that you are the expert in how they're going to learn, not in what they're going to learn. It's a slow and tedious process but it seems to work. (Horton and Freire 1990: 162)

## Teaching by Example, by Who You Are

Socrates and Horton educate not only through the learning situations that they facilitate but by the choices they make and the lives they lead. I don't know if Socrates ever describes himself in this way. Certainly others have done it on his behalf, for example, Robert Nozick in his recent paper

"Socratic Puzzles." Nozick writes:

> Socrates has doctrines but what he teaches is not a doctrine but a method
> of inquiry. . . . Socrates shows something more: the kind of person that such
> sustained inquiry produces. It is not his method alone that teaches us but
> rather that method (and those doctrines it has led him to) as embodied in
> Socrates. We see Socrates within his inquiries and his inquiring interactions
> with others; we see the way his inquiries shape and infuse his life, and his
> death. Socrates teaches with his person. Buddha and Jesus did this as well.
> Socrates is unique among philosophers in doing this. (Nozick 1995: 153)

In a Public Broadcasting System interview with Bill Moyers, Horton says, "We
were talking earlier about education, about how you educate. I was telling
about structural aspects of how we educate at Highlander. Really, the way
you educate is by example. You educate by your own life, by what you are"
(Horton 1981).

## Creating Theories That Are One-Liners,
## Useful as Discussion-Starters, Not Discussion-Enders

It is striking that while Socrates and Horton both have "theories" associated with their names, the theories and the way they are presented differ
radically from the practice of current academic philosophy. The theories of
both have the feature that they can be stated in single short sentences. It is
as if they are intended to be not freestanding discourses but sparks to discussions whose outcomes are indeterminate and will differ from context to
context. Vlastos lists 10 of Socrates's theories on about half a page of text.
Some of them are that we should never return wrong for wrong or evil for
evil, that the just man will not harm his enemies, that to teach men justice
is *ipso facto* to make them just (Vlastos 1994: 11).

Horton's "theories" are similarly short:

- A teacher needs to have two eyes that are not used in the same way
(Horton 1990: 130);
- I have no rights that shouldn't be made universal (Horton and Freire
1990: 51);
- The way to do something is to start doing it and learn from it (Horton
1990: 40).

## Emphasizing the Importance of Unlearning

This is another aspect of valuing and respecting the experience students
bring to a learning situation: Some of the things you bring with you from your
past experience and think you know on the basis of that experience are false
and need to be rejected. Socrates and Horton undermine the idea that important learning is a steady, cumulative, additive progress toward a goal. Both

emphasize the importance of backing up and fresh starts. When Socrates's method of *elenchus* unearths a contradiction in one's thinking, something has to be given up. The theme of unlearning is often an explicit part of Highlander workshops; along with "what are you taking home?" the question "what have you unlearned in this workshop?" will be raised toward the end of the workshop. Horton writes about unlearning in the context of accounts of the beginning of Highlander. For example, in *The Long Haul*, he writes:

> We had accepted a theory we had grown up with in school: that the way we'd been taught was the right way to teach. But we were now in an out-of-schooling situation where the ways of learning were different. The problem was we didn't know that. We tried to impose our school experience on this different situation. We didn't understand that the socialization we went through made us willing to be bored to death for years while we accumulated all kinds of useless knowledge. We had to pass exams because we had to finish high school, go to college, do graduate work. We found that all these things that made us learn didn't connect with the people we were dealing with, the out-of-school people. So we had to unlearn and relearn from them. It was only then that we could begin to build a base for Highlander that gave us roots among the people and in their problems. (Horton 1990: 141)

## Celebrating and Encouraging Risks

> If you aren't afraid to die for your cause, then nobody can get at you. Nobody can push you around: jail won't do it, harassment won't do it, beatings won't do it, death won't do it, so you're home free. There isn't anything anybody can do to you but kill you. That's what liberation is, being willing to die for what you believe in. I practice it myself, and I advocate it for other people. (Horton 1990: 187)

Horton and his colleagues took risks throughout their lives and work. The Highlander Folk School, at its original site in Monteagle, Tennessee, was closed by the state on trumped up charges in 1961 during the initial wave of strong reaction to the civil rights movement. A few weeks later, vigilantes burned one of the buildings.

Socrates, of course, expressed and acted on views that are strikingly similar to Horton's. In the *Apology* at 28B, we find Socrates saying:

> Perhaps someone will say: "Are you not ashamed, Socrates, of leading a life which is very likely now to cause your death?" I should answer him with justice, and say: "My friend, if you think that a man of any worth at all ought to reckon the chances of life and death when he acts, or that he ought to think of anything but whether he is acting justly or unjustly, and as a good or bad man would act, you are mistaken." (Plato 1988: 34)

# Socrates and Miles Horton: Differences

It will be useful also to have a just sense of differences between Socrates and Horton. I have identified three of them: (1) that Socrates's teaching strategy worked with individuals one-on-one, Horton's with groups of 25 or so; (2) that Socrates was a "street philosopher" who would engage in dialogue with anyone he met up with in the *agora,* while Horton carefully selected participants for Highlander workshops; (3) that Horton had as an educational strategy that is integral to Highlander workshops giving people "an experience [that] embodies what you are trying to teach" (Horton 1990: 68).

## Kinds of Individuals/Students Worked With

Socrates worked with individuals in one-on-one conversations; Horton worked with groups of 25 or so in workshops. Dick Couto once remarked to me when we were discussing Highlander, "Myles was an artist, and a genius, in working with groups; that was his medium." Horton writes about his time working with Robert Park at the University of Chicago: "At this time I began to realize that learning [that] came from group effort was superior to learning [that] came through individual efforts" (Horton 1990: 147). Highlander workshops are always experiences in group learning, though they allow plenty of time "off task" for walks, individual reflection, and conversations in pairs. Even with this emphasis on groups, Horton's lifelong strategy for changing society was to do it through education, which means changing individuals. Horton writes: "My position was that I believed in changing society by first changing individuals, so that they could struggle to bring about social changes" (Horton 1990: 184). This perspective on Horton's work makes it look less different from Socrates's than at first appears. Myles Burnyeat writes about Socrates: "[His] aim for the city is moral reform. . . . It is a reform that must take root in the minds of individual citizens" (1988: 14). It is also worth observing that when Socrates carries on extended conversation with one person, there usually are others gathered around listening.

## Nature of Teaching/Learning Situations

Burnyeat, in his review of I.F. Stone's *The Trial of Socrates,* says that Socrates "is the marketplace philosopher" (1988: 14). Gregory Vlastos, in his description of the National Endowment for the Humanities summer seminar he gave on Socrates several years ago, called him a "street philosopher." Socrates would engage, with his characteristic probing and questioning, anyone he met in the *agora* who would put up with it and play by the rules: give short answers; say what you believe; follow the argument. Vlastos emphasizes this aspect of Socrates's practice. In this, Socrates's modern counterpart is more Peter Maurin than Horton, for Horton and his colleagues carefully chose those who were invited to Highlander. Horton writes about his approach to selecting workshop participants:

> Highlander workshops are based on the mining of the experience that the students bring with them, their awareness that they have a problem to deal with, and the relationship of that problem to conflict. They have to be opposed by mine owners or government, prevented from eating in some restaurants or denied their fair share of public resources. They must know that they have problems [that] can't be solved on a personal level, that their problems are social, collective ones [that] take an organized group to work on. For this reason, an individual can't come to a Highlander workshop with a personal problem. People have to be selected by their organizations and report back to the organizations that sent them. (Horton 1990: 148)

Workshop participants are leaders and actors: grass-roots leaders of collective action. Moreover, all the participants in a given workshop will normally be working on actions having to do with the same problem — perhaps different aspects of it, but the same problem.

## Supplementary Learning Experiences

An important part of Horton's overall educational strategy is to "give people an experience [that] embodies what you are trying to teach" (Horton 1990: 68). Now it might be said — truly — that conversation with Socrates is an experience that embodies the qualities of mind and character he is trying to teach. But Horton has in mind providing experiences that go beyond what happens in a Highlander workshop. He writes:

> When you believe in a democratic society, you provide a setting for education that is democratic. You believe in a cooperative society, so you give them opportunities to organize a cooperative. If you believe in people running their own unions, you let them run the school so that they can get the practice of running something. (Horton 1990: 68)

What would correspond to this in Socrates's practice would be experiences, which Socrates would help set up, that go beyond Socratic conversations. I do not see anything like this in the relevant dialogues and other information we have about Socrates. Horton wanted to give people the experience now of ways of living and interacting that model and give a foretaste of the kind of just and democratic society that will result if the work participants are being educated for is successful. The idea is to create environments in the overall residential workshop setting such that the environment itself is a teacher; the norms of the environment are themselves an innovation that herald a changed person and a changed society. Perhaps the most striking example of this strategy is the racially integrated workshops that were

Highlander's signature from its beginnings in the 1930s. Horton writes as follows about the thinking behind those workshops:

> The way that was used by most people working in what was then called race relations was to talk about it and pray over it and wait for magic changes, I suppose. Some dealt with segregation by having segregated programs, and educating Blacks here and whites there, like it was the traditional thing to do. We chose to deal with it directly, knowing that a discussion and analysis wouldn't change their minds. We decided to hold integrated workshops and say nothing about it. We found that if you didn't talk about it, if you didn't force people to admit that they were wrong — that's what you do when you debate and argue with people — you can do it. People didn't quite understand how it was happening. They just suddenly realized they were eating together and sleeping in the same rooms, and since they were used to doing what they were supposed to do in society, the status quo, they didn't know how to react negatively to our status quo. We had another status quo at Highlander, so as long as we didn't talk about it, it was very little problem. Then later on participants started talking about it from another point of view, a point of view of experience. They had experienced something new, so they had something positive to build on. When we started talking about it, it wasn't to say: "Now, look you've changed. We were right and you were wrong." We said: "Now you've had an experience here. When you get back you'll be dealing with people in your unions who haven't had this experience, and they're going to know that you've been to an integrated school. How are you going to explain it to them?" So they started, not ever talking about how they had changed or how they had faced this problem, but with how they could explain it to other people. (Horton and Freire 1990: 134)

## Socrates and Myles Horton: Indeterminate

A final area of comparison that is worth considering concerns the stances that Socrates and Horton take toward democracy. Here the comparison must be uncertain because of scholarly dispute, which the available evidence is as yet unable to settle, over where Socrates stands on democracy. There is no uncertainty about where Horton stands. He names democratization of society, the empowerment of people to take responsibility for and control over their own lives, as the overarching aim of his work. The role of Highlander in the civil rights movement is pledge and confirmation of this commitment. As for Socrates, Vlastos argues persuasively for the following two theses. In his own time and place, Socrates was widely perceived as antipopulist. Vlastos adds, "This public perception of him was a misperception: He had not been the crypto-oligarch many had thought he was" (1994: 87).

However Socrates and Horton may have agreed or differed about the possibility and desirability of a truly democratic society, they were certainly in agreement in being harsh, unrelenting, and vocal critics of the societies in which they lived, both of which proclaimed themselves to be democratic. Like Socrates, Horton was perceived by his surrounding society in the American South as antidemocratic, as a "communist." The State of Tennessee put him through a trial in which he lost his school and all its property. Like Horton's, Socrates's method of teaching was profoundly democratic. Martha Nussbaum makes this point very well in her review of Vlastos's book *Socrates: Ironist and Moral Philosopher:*

> *Vlastos' portrait of the elenchus shows, moreover, how democratic structures are built into the entire Socratic enterprise. Each and every person is to search for truth within himself or herself. Deference to external authority has no place in the search for wisdom. (1991: 36)*

It is difficult, I think, not to sense a profound affinity between Socrates and Horton in the belief they share in the capacities of people to (learn to) think for and to govern themselves. Both dedicate themselves to developing people who can operate institutions characteristic of a democratic society.

## Taking It Home

My problem was how to teach philosophy in a way that is useful to students who are doing service work in the community and who want to make a positive difference in their service work and, in the longer run, in building a more just society. I aligned myself with Ramsey's emphasis that useful for my students would be a philosophy through which they learned to clarify their thoughts and actions. Some currently widespread ways of teaching philosophy, perfectly honorable and reasonable in their own ways, do not do this. James Bevel's comparison of Socrates and Myles Horton held out the hope and possibility of a fresh approach — because Socrates personifies philosophy and Horton personifies educating for social justice. We have now played at some length with Bevel's comparison and explored various facets of it. It is now time to try to bring it home.

It needs to be acknowledged at once that there is much that does not transfer from Socrates's situation and practice, and from Horton's situation and practice, to the American college classroom. Socrates's one-on-one teaching is impossible for us, because it is too expensive. We can in part approximate this Socratic responsiveness to individual students by giving feedback on individual journals and papers and by skilled use of small discussion groups of three or four students. Horton's selection of students who are already leading grass-roots collective action for structural change is also out of our reach. We must take all comers. Students who are involved in community service have taken a first step toward social action, and this is a crucial resource for the teaching we can do with these students, but the vast majority of them have not stepped out for structural change. Horton himself made a conscious decision not to go into college teaching because students have too little power to do anything to change society. He writes:

> Commencement speakers always make the same speech that young people are the future leaders of this country. It's up to young people to make this a decent country and solve these problems. And I discovered what every-body else discovered, that they never had any intention of letting the peo-ple they were talking to do anything about society. It's a kind of pacifica-tion speech. The adults run society. Students don't run society. They have very little to say within the schools let alone the society, the larger society. So I decided I wanted to deal with the people who had the power, if they wanted to use it, to change society, because I was interested in changing society. (Horton and Freire 1990: 183)

It would be a big mistake for teachers of undergraduates to suppose we can simply replicate a Highlander workshop in our classrooms.

So let me personalize all of this and talk about what is transferable to my practice as a philosopher and a teacher of philosophy to undergraduates. As a way of thinking about this, I want to examine the area of overlap between Socrates's practice and Horton's to see whether there are some "things to aim at" and some "things to watch out for" that stand out and can be described at a level of generality that makes them usable in my setting.

On the side of things to watch out for, I see two related things to avoid. I need to avoid taking on the role of an expert on content and avoid making myself, or my students, slaves to some predetermined swatch of content that must be covered in a course. The idea that content has some magic power, that having an expert control a body of content lets one partake of that power, and that telling that content to students can transfer the power to them — these ideas are profoundly mistaken and are to be utterly reject-ed and kept away from my practice as a teacher.

On the side of things to aim at, what jumps out at me in the overlap between Socrates and Horton is an array of interlocking strategies that have to do with respecting the autonomy of the learner and making my teaching serve to enhance that autonomy. Part of this is starting where the students are — in terms of interests, concerns, values, questions, and needs and capacities to act. A commitment to start where the students are, in turn, implies that I must learn where they are and must give time and attention to this learning. Then I must design experiences — possibly engaging students in the design of these experiences — that overlap with the students' interests, concerns, values, questions, and needs and capacities to act in ways that enable them to stretch and grow from within. I need to be responsive to the students in these ways, but I am not passive, and having started where the students are, I need to have an idea of where they can move to. As this movement proceeds, I need to take care never to break the connection with the students' experiences. These are the "democratic structures" in the learning situation that Martha Nussbaum so aptly names.

The phrase "starting where the students are" hides a basic complexity, in that no two students start in exactly the same place. That all the students in my course have taken the step of becoming involved in service work in the community is a crucial resource in that it creates a shared experience through which individual differences can be refracted.

As I look back over what emerges from playing with the comparison between Socrates and Horton, I find one other thing to aim at that is present in Horton's practice but not in Socrates's. This is building up in the students in a class a willingness to listen to and respect one another's views and voices. This seems to me a fundamental capacity for democratizing society that can come from group learning but not necessarily come from one-on-one Socratic teaching.

Another set of ideas that I find useful in thinking through this matter of the usefulness of philosophy comes from the British psychoanalyst D.W. Winnicott. Winnicott develops the idea of a potential space or transitional space that is essential for nurturing interactions among people. Such spaces are found in the relation between the child and the mother in good-enough mothering; they are found in the relationship between patient and therapist in good-enough psychotherapy; they are found in good cultural experiences. I want to suggest that they are found in the relationship between student and teacher in good-enough teaching. What is so valuable in Socrates and Horton is that they show us how to get going on creating potential spaces in education.

A potential space is a setting in which people can play. It is a setting characterized by confidence, trust, spontaneity, back-and-forth responsiveness. People in this setting feel free to be themselves; they feel real and alive. Boundaries between selves partly dissolve; the distinction between my-self and your-self partly breaks down, and selves can overlap in the play-focus at hand. The distinction between creating and finding also partly breaks down; old truths are found in ways that make them fresh and one's own. Though the topic can be serious, there is a shared sense of fun and surprise.

One of Winnicott's key expressions of this idea runs as follows:

> When I come to state my thesis I find, as so often, that it is very simple, and that not many words are needed to cover the subject. Psychotherapy takes place in the overlap of two areas of playing, that of the patient and

*that of the therapist. Psychotherapy has to do with two people playing together. The corollary of this is that where playing is not possible then the work done by the therapist is directed towards bringing the patient from a state of not being able to play into a state of being able to play. (1971: 38)*

Transposing this to philosophy, and adjusting it to the group situation, we can frame a parallel statement as follows: Learning philosophy takes place in the overlap of two or more areas of playing, that of the teacher or teachers and that of the students. Learning philosophy has to do with people playing together.

We need to dig further into this. Not all play is the same play. Philosophy is not psychotherapy. In philosophy we play with questions: "What is a good life?" and "What is a good society?" are old favorites that are very much alive in the students in my class and on which they have the capacity to move. "What is it to help someone else?" and "How can intentions to help go wrong?" are also very much alive for them. I think that in philosophy we also play, as it were, with the way in which we play with questions. Developing qualities of reflectiveness and patience; strategies for probing for hidden assumptions; strategies for giving reasons and arguments, for finding gaps in reasoning, for plugging those gaps; strategies of detecting ambiguities, drawing distinctions and sticking to them; skills of imagining new examples with fresh facets, counterexamples, contrasting cases, intermediate cases; qualities of openness to hearing other views, of listening to and letting oneself be struck by, feel the force of, views different from one's own; ability to change one's mind; qualities of being able to hear the fake, the false, the misleading in uses of language — these are some of the ways in which we play. One of the great things about philosophy as a subject to teach is that virtually everyone has the capacity not only to be engaged by "philosophical" questions but also to play with questions in these ways. However, the circumstance depicted by Winnicott in the second half of his statement occurs in philosophy classes as well — a frozenness or reluctance with regard to play — and then it is the teacher's task to bring students into a state of being able to play.

Socrates and Horton do not give us an algorithm for orchestrating this kind of play. They give us some useful "things to aim at" and "things to watch out for." They give us some example of things they tried that help us begin. We can, if we are lucky, if we have students and colleagues to talk with, be able to follow up on these beginnings, learn as we go along, and "make the road by walking." When I try this with my social justice class, I find that sometimes, not always, the class is alive. I sense an incredible robustness in philosophy, for I see that the subject can grow again, fresh, from its beginnings, in this circle of learners today.

But is it useful? I have tried to bring about a shift in the way the notion of "use" is being applied here. Now we need to say: The students use me. When I treat students with the kind of responsiveness to where they are and with the kind of respect for and concern to build up their autonomy that I have described, drawing on Socrates, Horton, and now Winnicott, the students use me. When I help to create, and enter into, the potential space where my philosophical personality and theirs overlap, and begin to play, the students use me in play. Of course, I use them as well: The play makes the subject fresh for me, it sometimes surprises me and opens up fresh vistas in territory over which I have traveled many times before, and I have the satisfaction of seeing their enjoyment and growth. All of this reciprocal use is what I call "the use of a philosopher."

But is this use of a philosopher *useful,* in the earlier sense of contributing to a movement toward a more just society? The question is out of bounds; of course, we can have no guarantees here. Socrates perhaps thought that being a philosopher and allowing oneself to be used as a philosopher could lead to nothing but good, at least in the long haul. The Athenian jury, for the short haul that they took into account, thought otherwise. All I feel confident of is that if one is an academic philosopher, one has a choice whether to teach in authoritarian ways that preclude one's being used or in the ways of Socrates, Horton, and Winnicott through which one makes oneself available for use by one's students. If one chooses the latter way, I know no group of students with whom it is more rewarding to work than those doing community service. These students have taken a first good step toward social justice; as their teacher, one feels close to some action, perhaps the only real action there is anyway — that of making the road by walking.

## Note

1. The reader who would like to pursue this question may find it helpful to consult John Maynard Keynes's biographical essay on Ramsey. See especially Keynes's comments on Ramsey's movement toward "what he himself described as a sort of pragmatism, not unsympathetic to Russell but repugnant to Wittgenstein" (Keynes 1972: 338).

## References

Branch, Taylor. (1988). *Parting of the Waters: America in the King Years 1954-63.* New York, NY: Simon & Schuster.

Burnyeat, M.F. (March 31, 1988). "Cracking the Socrates Case." *The New York Review* 35: 14-18.

Eliot, George. (1994). *Middlemarch*. New York, NY: Random House.

Horton, Myles, and Paulo Freire. (1990). *We Make the Road by Walking: Conversations on Education and Social Change*. Philadelphia, PA: Temple University Press.

Horton, Myles, with Judith Kohl and Herbert Kohl. (1990). *The Long Haul: An Autobiography*. New York, NY: Doubleday.

Horton, Myles, with Bill Moyers. (1981). "Adventures of a Radical Hillbilly." *Bill Moyers' Journal*. Originally broadcast on WNET, New York, June 5, 1981.

Keynes, John Maynard. (1972). *Essays in Biography*. London, Eng.: Macmillan.

Morris, Aldon D. (1984). *The Origins of the Civil Rights Movement: Black Communities Organizing for Change*. New York, NY: Free Press.

Nozick, Robert. (1995). "Socratic Puzzles." *Phronesis* 40: 143-155.

Nussbaum, Martha. (September 16 and 23, 1991). "The Chill of Virtue: Review of Gregory Vlastos, *Socrates: Ironist and Moral Philosopher*." *The New Republic*: 34-40.

————— . (1994). *The Therapy of Desire: Theory and Practice in Hellenistic Ethics*. Princeton, NJ: Princeton University Press.

Plato. (1956). *Protagoras and Meno*, translated by W.K.C. Guthrie. New York, NY: Penguin Books.

————— . (1973). *Theaetetus*, translated with notes by John McDowell. Oxford, Eng.: Clarendon Press.

————— . (1988). *Euthyphro, Apology, Crito*, translated by F.J. Church. New York, NY: Macmillan.

Ramsey, Frank. (1965). *The Foundations of Mathematics and Other Logical Essays*. Totowa, NJ: Littlefield, Adams, and Company.

Vlastos, Gregory. (1994). *Socratic Studies*. Cambridge, Eng.: Cambridge University Press.

Winnicott, Donald W. (1971). *Playing and Reality*. New York, NY: Routledge.

# Praxis-Informed Philosophy

by C. David Lisman

In this essay, I hope to clarify the way I have increasingly been doing philosophy. I do not see this as so much a new method as a matter of emphasis — although there may be broader implications for how philosophy should be done. Like many of my colleagues, I have been schooled in the analytic tradition but have grown weary with that approach. Why I am less than enthusiastic about the analytic approach will become evident in the following discussion.

## Philosophy as a Method for Clarifying Human Purposes

I have come to see philosophy as a method for clarifying, understanding, and contributing to the achievement of human purposes. On the surface, one may say that is one way to express the commitment to doing analytic philosophy. For this method also presumably involves a concern with fundamental concepts as expressions of purpose. But there is a difference. In the first place, analytic philosophy is ostensibly more inclusive. Analytic philosophy analyzes all basic concepts, whether perceived as candidates for a purpose or whether ostensibly unrelated to purposes. At a very abstract level, the referential theory of truth is an example of a concept assumed to be unrelated to any particular purpose. Analytic philosophers may be interested in the referential theory of truth purely for its own sake or only because the concept seems intellectually interesting. Thus, although the concept of the "Good" is related to human purpose, the analytic philosophical interest is in the concept itself, or so it is believed. In this way, there is at least a surface difference between an approach to philosophy that upholds disinterested analysis of concepts for the sake of philosophical wisdom and one that is primarily interested in conceptual clarity in order to contribute to the enrichment of human purpose. What I wish to accomplish here is to explore and deepen that difference, to show specifically what is different about a praxis-based approach to philosophy.

As Jurgen Habermas points out, *praxis* has long been associated with a socially transformative approach to intellectual work. Although I shall appropriate the concept for a different purpose, that purpose is not unrelated to social transformation. Indeed, I maintain that if philosophy went about doing its business "correctly," it would naturally be socially transformative. The view I shall here set forth also draws insight from neo-Marxist work, although it is not itself a neo-Marxist theory.

Let me return to the notion of philosophy as being engaged in clarifying purposes. I take it that all philosophical thinking is directly or indirectly linked to the achievement of some human purpose. This insight has important ramifications. Let me provide a few examples to illustrate this point. Let us suppose that my car won't start. I immediately proceed to remedy the problem, doing what I can, given my understanding of how automobile engines work. The intellectual work I do in trying to fix the problem is conducted within the framework of my purpose, namely to get my car running. Thus, the actions that I take related to getting my car started make sense only in terms of my purpose, in relation to what I am doing. If I conclude that my car's battery is dead, I may attempt to jump the battery. Or, if I conclude that the spark plugs are bad, I may call the tow service to come and take my car to the service garage to get the spark plugs replaced. All of this makes sense in terms of my purpose. However, if instead of doing these sorts of things, I go and turn on the water hose and start watering my yard, one could understandably ask, what in the world does watering my yard have to do with getting my car started? If I say, "Nothing," but I decided to water my yard while waiting for the tow service to pick up my car, I give an answer not related to doing something to start my car. Watering the yard in that situation is an action linked to another purpose, presumably keeping my grass from dying for lack of water. However, if I were to explain in response to the question as to why am I watering the yard that I think that a good yard wetting may get my car going, one would rightfully wonder about my sanity. This action is not reasonably related to my purpose.

So far we are on safe ground. I do not think that many people would disagree with my observation that we engage in thinking to clarify and accomplish purposes. However, there is another aspect of this kind of thinking that may not be as evident; namely, that purposive action entails value commitments. To have a purpose in mind is to assume that something is desirable or of value. To engage in purposive action is to realize a value. For example, in the case of my nonoperative car, I want to get it started. I value or desire having a car that will run.

One may reply that, yes, values are involved with purposive actions, but as in the case of my car, they are often fairly mundane values. Admittedly, the situation referred to here is mundane; nevertheless, the conceptual point is that values are involved. If I am correct in arguing that all purposive action entails values in this way, then all thinking that is involved in clarifying and achieving purposes must be thinking that is done in the context of values. This, I submit, is not mundane. For it is a point with important implications for philosophizing.

We must, of course, distinguish practical thinking from philosophical thinking. The car situation is an example of practical thinking. Philosophical thinking involves conceptual analysis. But from the point of view of praxis-based philosophy, conceptual analysis bears some relationship to action, or purpose that informs action. And this is the point that I need to clarify.

All concepts serve certain purposes and are held for certain purposes, with some purposes being more intentional than others. For example, let us take the concept of "empirical truth." Most philosophers subscribe to some concept of empirical verifiability as a condition of assertability, although I hasten to add there is disagreement over specifics, such as what counts as verifiability and what the grounds are for claiming that this is a condition of assertability. In terms of my thesis, I would want to know what *purpose* this concept serves. Why are we concerned about the necessary conditions of assertability? I submit our interest lies in the purpose not only to be clear about conditions of assertability as a matter of intellectual interest about the uses of language but also to distinguish between utterances that pretend to be assertions, such as "God exists," but are not really, and true assertions. The desire to possibly exclude metaphysical utterances from counting as assertions presumably is motivated not by some kind of an antireligious sentiment but by a desire to secure what belongs to the world as comprehensible within factual language and, at the same time, possibly disencumbering religious utterance from the artificial burden of proof that comes with a claim to assertability. For it certainly does not follow from the recognition that "God exists" is not an assertion that it is a meaningless utterance. It is just not the kind of utterance we characterize as being an assertion.

So our purpose for examining the conditions of assertability is to understand both what is world-determined and what is not of the world. As Wittgenstein said, "It is not *how* things are in the world that is mystical, but *that* it exists" (1922/1961: 149). I may be incorrect with regard to what motivates some people's interest in empirical truth, but this broad stroke is accurate enough to make my point: The purpose of developing and maintaining a concept such as empirical truth is to strengthen our understanding of certain ways that we can relate to the world. It almost goes without saying that this purpose implies a value, something that we regard as desirable. We consider it desirable to be clear about what can be factually said and what cannot be factually said. We want to be able to determine why some putative assertions really are not assertions at all. And in so doing, some would agree that we manage to restore religious faith to its rightful sense of evocation of the mysterious.

This is not all there is to the story of the relationship of philosophical concept to purpose. To be sure that we have, broadly speaking, secured an essential understanding of the conditions of assertability, we must not only think carefully about counterexamples and potential weaknesses in the analysis but also test the concept by experience. And how do you test such a concept by experience? I should think that, at the very least, we would try out a variety of putative assertions to see whether the conditions of their use correspond to this interpretation. Also, we would want to reflect upon religious experience, moral experience, and aesthetic experience to see whether we can still make sense of such experiences denuded of a factual way of regarding these experiences. In a more comprehensive effort, we should, of course, like to arrive at an analysis of the logic of these other kinds of utterances. But the important point is that we test the overall analysis not merely by reflecting on language usage but by seeing if our religious and ethical experiences are affected by this analysis.

One of the ways that this kind of examination can be done effectively is through being more alert to the purposes that propel our conceptual path. One possibly less personally threatening way to do this is by linking action with purpose. We should ask not only what purposes underlie our philosophical commitments but also what actions are required by our purposes or as means to realize our purposes. A maxim, I think, safe to enunciate is that in the absence of any discernible concept of actions or ways to realize a purpose, then the purpose is in a basic sense meaningless.

Let us test the putative purpose behind this preference for an empirical verifiability notion of assertability. Above I have said that our interest is to secure what belongs to the world as comprehensible within factual language and to disencumber religious utterance from the, for if artificial, burden of proof that comes with assertability. What "actions" serve this purpose? For one thing, the linguistic effort to clarify the conditions of assertability is clearly linked to this purpose. Also, I would think that efforts we take to secure our factual understanding of the world by a process of empirical confirmation are further general actions connected to our purpose. In terms of our religious commitment, practicing our religion or faith in nonempirical ways also is an example of carrying out this purpose. However, if a person were to declare an interest in this kind of factual verification theory of assertability but proceed in life to treat religious utterances as if they were utterances, and, in effect, recognize no difference between the factual and nonfactual, I would wonder if this person really had a serious purpose in mind.

Having made a case for the idea that concepts are linked to broad purposes, I would also like to make some observations about the general relationship of concepts to purposes. First, concepts can illuminate or embellish purposes just as actions linked to more concrete purposes help illuminate and clarify our more concrete purposes. This insight is captured by the adage "the proof's in the pudding." Suppose someone says that he or she has always wanted to become a teacher. When presented with a realistic opportunity to become a teacher, should this person turn down the opportunity, we would question whether this person was sincere about wanting to become a teacher. Similarly, one of the best ways that this person can come to a better understanding and appreciation of his or her purpose is by becoming a teacher. Through becoming a teacher, the person gains a validation of his or her purpose. It also is likely that the new teacher will gain a deeper appreciation of this profession. Purpose is clarified through action.

Turning to a philosophical example of purpose clarified through intellectual action, let us consider aesthetics. I assume one's concept of beauty may affect how one interprets experience and how one acts on experience. In any case, I assume that a possible underlying purpose for clarifying one's concept of beauty is to understand and more fully appreciate experiences of beauty, whether in nature or in art. If one adopts the Platonic view that beauty is not inherent in things but emanates from a supersensible form, and that what we should be doing is to increase our capacity to appreciate "beauty in itself," then the effect on our experience of beauty would be rather different from a view that says that beauty is inherent in objects themselves. The latter view may encourage one to spend more time enjoying concrete things rather than seeing concrete experiences of beauty as an occasion to attempt to commune with beauty itself. So certainly our purpose is clarified through this kind of intellectual action of attempting to deepen our understanding of the concept of beauty.

Second, concepts reciprocally can clarify purposes. I do not think that I need to spend too much on this observation, since widespread agreement exists pertaining to the clarifying role of concepts themselves. In practical decision making, being clear about the means we have available to achieve a purpose is part of a realizable purpose. For example, if someone is tone deaf, it may not make sense for that person to have a goal of becoming a jazz musician. Philosophically, conceptual clarity helps us better understand and achieve purposes. For example, being clear about the justification for physician-assisted death will provide guidance to implementing such a policy.

Third, concepts serve ideological purposes. Consider, for the purposes of illustration, a philosopher who is a defender of the procedural republic, that is, the notion that society should be organized in a way that maximizes individual freedom. This viewpoint is associated with a certain view of the self as finding or making meaning in a very individualized way. Part of the difficulty in criticizing the concept of philosophical liberalism or the procedural republican view is that its adherents feel that if they were to abandon this viewpoint, they would have to abandon certain deeply held values, such as the right of self-determination. The evidence that ideological investment in certain concepts is great is found among philosophers who often are loathe to abandon a position in the face of trenchant and convincing criticism.

Given our ideological rigidity, we may object that it is not helpful to dwell on ideology in relation to philosophical investigation. But such an objection is, I believe, misguided. We should serve philosophers the same medicine they proffer others, namely, that in the spirit of commitment of intellectual integrity (another ideology?), philosophers must be willing to examine critically their most basic assumptions about life.

## Dewey on Theory and Practice

Before proceeding further, I should acknowledge my affinity with John Dewey, who also was concerned with bridging the gap between theory and practice. Dewey attempted to show, as Rorty (1979) has, that many of our philosophical problems are due to the influence of idealism and rationalism — theories that seek to found knowledge on immutable truths (Dewey 1929). Dewey believed that the traditional philosophical disdain for the practical was rooted in this search for immutable truth.

Dewey also rejected empiricism, the view that all knowledge is derived from sense experience. He maintained that we must distinguish between empirical experiences and experimental ones, the latter of which he endorsed (1929: 81). The first kind of experience is concerned with uncontrollable change, the latter with directed and regulated change (83). Dewey attempted to address the skepticism that has traditionally challenged the validity of all sense experience by claiming that knowledge is not concerned with direct experiences themselves but with the conditions that give rise to the kinds of experiences we have (104). For him, skepticism would be appropriate only if we were really trying to get at immutable truths. But this is not possible. Since experience is a given, our intellectual task can only be that of understanding how, in fact, we view and appropriate objects of experience.

Dewey believed that the scientific method was the key to finding solutions to practical problems, and making intellectual and social progress. For him, this scientific method was virtually the same as practical problem solving, a position not dissimilar to the view I outlined above. "Intelligence" is "directed inquiry" — a matter of the human organism's providing methods by which the problematic aspects of experience can be controlled and understood in a systematic way. Dewey attempted to bridge the gap between thinking and experience by calling thinking "deferred action" and identifying such action as "present exploratory action" (223). It is primarily through action that problematic situations are resolved. Clearly a congruence exists between Dewey's concept of action and my own view of *praxis*.

## Countering Ideological Rigidity

One of the ways that progress can be made in countering ideological rigidity is through a more praxis-informed philosophy. Let me outline how I see this.

I have argued above that conceptual analysis can in some respects be viewed as a form of "action" — intellectual action aimed at serving a particular purpose. Second, I have argued that purposes are normative: To have a purpose is to regard something as desirable, and actions are intelligible only in light of the purpose the action is attempting to realize. From this it follows that conceptual analysis, insofar as it is a form of intellectual action, is necessarily carried out in terms of serving some goal that is held to be desirable. This being the case, some scrutiny of our value-laden intentions is helpful.

Many of our purposes are very ideological. To say that a purpose is ideological is to say that the purpose is realized in the context of a set of interrelated beliefs and values essential to our self-esteem. We need to think about ways by which we may effect a change in our ideologies. The way that this can come about is through the recognition that having an ideologically laden goal is, in effect, to be "emotionally invested" in a goal.

Thus, we come upon an interesting recognition, namely, that goals or purposes, especially ideological ones, are not merely normative, but are normative interests in which we have strong emotional investment. If we can effect a change in our emotional investment in our basic concepts or beliefs, we may be able to alter our purpose, or at the very least be a little more clearheaded about our goal or purpose. How might we effect such a change in our emotional state?

## The Role of the Cognitive Theory of Emotions

It is here that I think the cognitive theory of emotions is very useful as a tool. According to the cognitive theory of emotions, emotions are highly self-involved appraisals (Solomon 1983/1976). Let me illustrate with an example. Suppose I walk out to the parking lot and see Mary, a friend of mine, driving out of the lot in my car. I am instantly angry. Mary has taken my car! I feel that I have been wronged. In this case, the emotional response of anger is one of judging or making an appraisal that Mary has wronged me by taking my car without my permission.

The cognitive theory of emotions is opposed to the more traditional view of the emotions that considers emotions to consist primarily of inner feelings. According to this theory, our emotions are not subject to rational appraisal. Indeed, they often cause us to behave in ways that run counter to our rational judgment. For example, in the traditional view, anger is a concept that refers to an inner episode that can "well up within us" and require "release" or "expression." So my response to Mary from the traditional view is one of my bursting inside with feelings of anger at what has happened.

The cognitive theory of emotions would counter that although certain inner sensations are associated with a particular emotional state, the emotion is not constituted by the inner state. Clearly, my anger with Mary involves my chest's tightening, a tightening in my temples, a rush of adrenaline, etc. But there is more to my emotional response than this. From the perspective of the cognitive theory of emotions, the other central ingredient is my judgment or appraisal that I have been wronged. This is a moral judgment or appraisal not only that someone has done something wrong but that I am the object of the wrongdoing. This latter aspect of the emotional response emphasizes the highly self-involved nature of our emotional responses.

Take the example of another emotion, feeling guilty over something. To acknowledge that one has done something blameworthy is not the same as to experience an emotion of guilt. The emotion of guilt is extreme self-reproach or blame for having done something wrong (Solomon 1983/1976: 319). The appropriate appraisal here is not that one acknowledges wrongdoing but that one considers oneself to be blameworthy for having done something wrong.

One of the interesting aspects of our emotional life is that often our emotions are in some sense in conflict with our intellectual beliefs. For example, a person might intellectually believe that all ethnic groups are socially equal, but at the same time still possess racist feelings, such as the feeling that members of other ethnic groups are inferior in some sense to his or her own. The emotion here may be a sense of dislike of other ethnic groups. Granted that liking and disliking are more generic emotions than anger or guilt, they nevertheless still seem to be emotional responses involving self-involved appraisals. In the case of prejudice, a person feels that in some sense the people who are the objects of one's prejudice are not only inferior but in some, often ill-defined, sense threatening to a person's well-being.

While in many cases there is a close alignment between emotionally relevant belief and our intellectual beliefs, in the case of prejudice, there well may be an inconsistency between the emotionally relevant belief and the intellectual belief. A few comments about emotionally relevant belief are important. This kind of belief is perhaps best characterized as an example of "experience as" rather than an "experience that." Emotionally relevant beliefs are forms of "experiencing as" in which we experience the significance of something as being of a particular sort. In a situation where there is no tension between an emotionally relevant belief and an intellectual belief, no disjunction exists. For example, if I am an opponent of capital punishment and experience particular offenders, who might otherwise legally merit capital punishment, as objects of sympathy and concern, a convergence exists between my intellectually held belief and my emotionally relevant belief.

However, in the case of racist feelings, a disjunction presumably exists between one's intellectual belief that all members of ethnic groups are socially equal and one's racist feelings. The racist individual, in this case, intellectually believes that prejudice is wrong but experiences ethnically different individuals in a negative way.

The solution to such a disjunction is for the racist individual to work at bringing the intellectually held belief and emotionally relevant belief into line. Perhaps such an individual should become personally involved with people about whom she or he has racist feelings. Maybe this person needs to socialize or become involved in some way with such people. By becoming more involved with people who are potential objects of the individual's racist feelings and carefully reflecting on those experiences, he or she may begin to experience them in ways that are more convergent with the individual's intellectual belief that all ethnic members are socially equal. The potential solution to the racist individual's inner contradiction, then, is to engage in those relevant forms of actions that will enable him or her to bring his or her emotionally relevant belief into alignment with his or her intellectually held belief. The racist individual needs not only to believe that all people are socially equal but to experience individuals in accordance with this belief. Such an individual needs to experience them as having the same fundamental sense of dignity that he or she attributes to himself or herself.

Now we can see the importance of praxis, of the role of action in effecting a change in our purposes. Our philosophical purposes are expressions of our ideologies, our highly self-involved beliefs and values in which our self-esteem is at stake. Sometimes, the set of intellectual beliefs that is at the heart of an ideology converges with our self-involved ways of experiencing the significance of whatever are the objects of our beliefs. Other times, our intellectual beliefs are at odds with our ways of experiencing the significance of the world. If our set of intellectual beliefs is in need of transformation, then engaging in those actions that will enable us to experience the world in a way that challenges those beliefs may be the most powerful "argument" against our beliefs. In fact, we may never change our ideology in the face of strong argument. Rather, we must experience the shortcomings of our ideology. Also, while we may have intellectually arrived at a fairly reasonable point of view, we still may be experiencing irrational emotions. We may still experience the significance of the world in alignment with another, earlier-held set of intellectual beliefs. Our intellectually relevant beliefs may have changed, but not our emotionally relevant ones.

Let me take one example that has great significance for service-learning, namely, the debate between philosophical liberalism and liberal communitarianism. The philosophical liberal believes, among other things, that individuals are sufficient unto themselves, that we are the maker of our own values. In contrast, the liberal communitarian believes that individuals cannot find complete fulfillment independent of community. Let us suppose, for the sake of argument, that the philosophical liberal will not accept any criticism leveled against this theory. The philosophical liberal continues to assert that it just seems right that we are the creators of our own individual sense of value. However, suppose we convince this person to become involved in activities, to put himself or herself at the mercy of others through assisting others in a time of need. It may be that through this experience the philosophical liberal comes to recognize emotionally what the liberal communitarian has been maintaining all along, namely, that we find full human meaning and significance only in the context of community; we can find complete self-fulfillment only in relationship with others. Withdrawing into our own private worlds may be important as a way to regenerate our exhausted selves from demanding work with others. But the withdrawal is at best only a temporary suspension. We are drawn into the world to mingle and be with others. Community is the place where we truly discover our individual authenticity.

It is in this way that a praxis-informed philosophy can perhaps help us clarify and deepen philosophical thinking. We need to be more intentional about the purposes our conceptual investigation serves. And when we detect a lack of convergence between the intellectual aspect of our purpose and our feelings about the way things should be, perhaps we can clarify our purpose, and thereby our concepts, through adopting those forms of action that bring our intellectually relevant beliefs into accordance with our emotionally relevant beliefs, or conversely.

## References

Dewey, J. (1929). *The Quest for Certainty*. New York, NY: G.P. Putnam.

Rorty, R. (1979). *Philosophy and the Mirror of Nature*. Princeton, NJ: Princeton University Press.

Solomon, R.C. (1983/1976). *The Passions: The Myth and Nature of Human Emotion*. Notre Dame, IN: University of Notre Dame Press.

Wittgenstein, L. (1922/1961). *Tractatus Logico-Philosophicus,* translated by D.F. Pears and B.F. McGuinness. London, Eng.: Routledge & Kegan Paul.

# Fluid Boundaries:
## Service-Learning and the Experience of Community

by Cathy Ludlum Foos

In a 1994 article in the journal *Ethics,* Will Kymlicka and Wayne Norman note over the past decade an increased interest in the concept of citizenship in discussions of political philosophy. A major impetus for this growing interest, they claim, is the fact that widespread egoism and cynicism with regard to politics have made it clear that the health and stability of a modern democracy depend not only on the justice of its "basic structure" but also on the qualities and attitudes of its citizens: for example, their ability to tolerate and work together with those who are different from them; their desire to participate in the political process in order to promote the public good and hold political authorities accountable; their willingness to show self-restraint and exercise personal responsibility in their economic demands and in personal choices that affect their health and the environment. Without citizens who possess these qualities, democracies become difficult to govern, even unstable (352-353).

Kymlicka and Norman describe the major competing contemporary theories regarding citizenship and how it is learned, discussing along the way flaws in each of the theories. Their conclusion is that, despite the touted importance of good citizenship, political thinkers in particular and we as a society in general have not identified the best means or the best forum for teaching and promoting citizenship. In this paper, I will discuss an approach to civic education that, while certainly not unheard of, is not sufficiently mainstream to have received any mention in a survey article on the topic of citizenship. That approach is service-learning.

One major university defines service-learning as:

> A *course-based, credit-bearing educational experience in which students*
> • *participate in an organized service activity that meets identified community needs [and]*
> • *reflect on the service activity in such a way as to gain further understanding of course content, a broader appreciation of the discipline, and an enhanced sense of civic responsibility. (IUPUI 1994)*

Not every institution defines service-learning in quite this way, and some of the elements of the definition are controversial. What is basic to service-learning, however, is that students engage in meaningful community service combined with some form of directed reflection activity that assists them in putting their experience into a larger context and thus learning something from that experience.

There are two parts to this paper. The first section is theoretical. It begins with a brief sketch of my reasons for taking an essentially liberal position on the role of public schools in the teaching of ethics, followed by a survey of several criticisms of the liberal approach to moral education. The common thread linking the various criticisms is that each accuses liberalism of being destructive of community by placing undue emphasis on the importance of the individual. Plausible responses to these criticisms have been offered by defenders of liberalism, but, as I will argue, there is a gap between the theory and practice. Liberal moral education may well have some of the negative consequences critics note if it is not carefully undertaken. Thus, the second part of the paper is practical. I will discuss how the pedagogy of service-learning can be used by teachers to promote the goals of liberal moral education while warding against the negative aspects of individualism.

## Defending a Liberal Position

When it comes to education, we as philosophers are at a disadvantage relative to those in other fields. One of my colleagues recently attended a conference on teaching mathematics. He told me there are some interesting new ideas about how to teach calculus, and he is going to experiment with some of these ideas in his classes. He does not yet know whether these ideas will in fact improve math education, but that is really the only question at issue. He is not plagued by the question of whether math should be taught, or by the question of just what math is, anyway. Analogous questions, however, are an issue for those of us who aspire to teach ethics. Needless to say, I cannot adequately address these questions in this paper. I will, however, begin by indicating some answers to them.

The question of whether ethics should be taught arises only in the context of public schools. No one disputes the role of the family and the religious community in the teaching of ethics. However, there are those who argue that the family and the church (or synagogue, or whatever) are the only institutions that should teach ethics. Public schools, so the argument goes, will teach the prevailing political ideology, which will certainly conflict with the moral values of the parents of some of the students. The state does not have the right, say the critics, to teach values, because when the values taught conflict with the values taught at home, the student will become at least confused and at worst will rebel against her or his parents' authority.

There is certainly something to this argument. When values are taught, they are more than likely at some point to conflict with what some of the students are learning at home. However, that is not sufficient reason to proscribe the teaching of values in public schools. As Amy Gutmann (1987) argues, parents do not have absolute say over the values their children will be taught. To say that they do implies that children are the exclusive property of their parents. Parents have a unique role to play in the lives of their children and certainly should have considerable discretion over what will happen in their children's lives. However, that discretion is not absolute. "Because children are members of both families and states, the educational authority of parents and of polities has to be partial to be justified" (30). Since ethical views have an impact on behavior, and since the behavior of its citizens has a direct impact on the state, the state certainly has the right to have some say as to what ethical views its citizens ought to be taught.

Having answered in the affirmative the question of whether ethics should be taught, we come up against the question of what exactly it is we should teach. If we ask what teaching mathematics is, we might get the answer, "Teaching how to add and subtract, multiply and divide." When we ask what addition or multiplication is, we get a straightforward, uncontroversial answer. If, by contrast, we ask what teaching ethics is, we get the answer, "Teaching how to distinguish right from wrong." So far, so good, until we ask what is right and what is wrong. How can the state presume to teach children how to distinguish right from wrong when there is no uncontroversial answer to the question "What is right, and what is wrong?"

To answer this question, I turn to John Rawls's distinction between a political conception of ethics and a comprehensive doctrine (1993). A comprehensive doctrine is a view that includes not only rules for conduct but also a conception of what is most worth pursuing in life and an image of what sort of character individuals should cultivate. The Catholic Church, for example, provides its members with a comprehensive doctrine. Along with the basic rules against murder and stealing are rules about things such as premarital sex, gay sex, birth control. There is a value placed on a particular tradition, and there are models within that tradition who represent the ideal of a truly worthwhile life. The Amish similarly possess a comprehensive doctrine. Their doctrine, however, differs in significant ways from the Catholic one. The Muslim faith provides yet another comprehensive doctrine, which conflicts at some points with each of the others. The important point to note is that in a pluralistic society, there will be many such conflicting comprehensive doctrines, no one of which is demonstrably superior to the others.

While there is no one comprehensive guide to behavior and values that all members of our society will accept, we nonetheless have to establish guidelines for behavior. This is where the political conception of ethics comes in. A political conception is more restricted than is a comprehensive doctrine. It provides simply the rules of conduct and the forms of association that are necessary for the fair ordering of a pluralistic society (Rawls 1993: 13). Much of the objection to teaching ethics in public schools may stem from a failure to distinguish between these different conceptions of ethics. It is indeed up to the family or religion, *not* the public schools, to teach young people a particular comprehensive doctrine, to instill in them a sense of what is most valuable in life. It is very much the role of public schools, however, to teach the basics of a political conception of ethics — to promote in students an understanding of and appreciation for justice and the virtues of a good citizen. As Gutmann (1987) has argued, it is not the job of the schools to teach children how to lead a good life; rather, it is the more modest one of "conscious social reproduction."

As citizens, we aspire to a set of educational practices and authorities of which the following can be said: These are the practices and authorities to which we, acting collectively as a society, have consciously agreed. It follows that a society that supports conscious social reproduction must educate all educable children to be capable of participating in collectively shaping their society (39).

This in turn means educating children to allow others to participate equally in shaping society, which is to say, teaching children to acknowledge and listen to points of view other than those with which they were raised. Thus, the specifically liberal approach to teaching citizenship involves educating young people to engage in what Stephen Macedo (1990) calls "public reasonableness" and "public justification." The core of these ideas is the necessity to show a genuine respect for all individuals by requiring that any policy that is to become coercive law be justifiable with reasons "that are widely acceptable to reasonable people with a broad range of moral and philosophical commitments and interests" (44).

The liberal emphasis on the individual, however, has come under heavy fire from more than one direction. The most interesting and, I believe, noteworthy criticisms have come from communitarians. Gutmann (1992) argues that communitarian criticisms of liberalism fail to make the case for abandoning liberalism as a social and political theory but still goes on to point out, I believe correctly, that liberals can nonetheless learn much from communitarian observations about individuality and community.

Thus, even if the communitarian critics have not given sufficient reasons for abandoning liberalism, they have usefully challenged its defenders. One should welcome their work if for no other reason than this. But there is, in fact, another reason. Communitarianism has the potential to help us discover a politics that combines community with a commitment to basic liberal values (Gutmann 1992: 133). To put the case a bit more strongly, I would maintain that there are a number of concerns raised by communitarians for which liberal theory has a good answer but that remain genuine and pressing concerns because in practice theory can often be distorted. In the rest of this section, I will discuss two related concerns about the way in which an emphasis on individualism can contribute to an unhealthy social climate.

One such concern is that giving greater priority to individual rights and choice than to the common good will lead to a society of increasingly self-centered people. Critics point to our distressing crime rates, and to incidents such as youths' shooting other youths for their jackets or shoes, and say that indeed liberalism has rendered us a dangerously self-centered society. However, liberalism does not advocate a selfish disregard of others. On the contrary, it stresses the need to be clear on the difference between having a concern for *my* individual rights and having a concern for the rights of *every* individual. This is not a new insight but one that seems to need rediscovery every so often. Over a century ago, John Dewey noted, "There is an individualism in democracy . . . but it is an ethical, not a numerical individualism; it is an individualism of freedom, of responsibility, of initiative to and for the ethical ideal, not an individualism of lawlessness" (1993: 61).

Liberal values do not imply, or unavoidably lead to, self-centeredness. Nonetheless, the current social environment vividly demonstrates that if we are not careful how we *teach* the value of individualism, it is possible to fail to promote the ethical side of individualism of which Dewey speaks. Thus, a liberal approach to teaching ethics must balance the emphasis on individualism with a sense of social responsibility.

Another criticism made of liberalism is its failure to take seriously enough the value of community. Here the focus is not on whether we will end up with a society of selfish people but on whether we will fail our citizens in a crucial way if we lead them to think of the individual, not the community, as primary. Communitarians argue that liberalism fundamentally misdescribes people when it makes the individual primary and contends that individuals must be free to choose their own conception of the good — in Rawls's terms, that they must be free to adopt whatever "comprehensive doctrine" of value they choose. Michael Sandel (1984) characterizes the debate in the following terms:

> On the rights-based ethic it is precisely because we are essentially separate, independent selves that we need a neutral framework, a framework of rights that refuses to choose among competing purposes and ends. . . . Communitarian critics of rights-based liberalism say we cannot conceive ourselves as independent in this way, as bearers of selves wholly detached from our aims and attachments. They say that certain of our roles are partly constitutive of the persons we are. . . . But if we are partly defined by the communities we inhabit, then we must also be implicated in the purposes and ends characteristic of those communities. (223)

His point is that since we always find ourselves already existing as members of a community, steeped in its traditions and values, our identity is not wholly separable from that of the community. As Alasdair MacIntyre (1981) puts it, "We all approach our own circumstances as bearers of a particular social identity. . . . Hence what is good for me has to be the good for one who inhabits these roles" (204-205). To teach otherwise, communitarians claim, is to teach falsely.

According to communitarians, one of the chief problems with presenting a false image of the self as separable from its context is that when people attempt to make such a separation, they end up not free but uprooted, not empowered but impoverished. Thus, for instance, Sandel (1984) notes that "the totalitarian impulse has sprung less from the convictions of confidently situated selves than from the confusions of atomized, dislocated, frustrated selves, at sea in a world where common meanings have lost their force" (224). Human beings, he argues, are not essentially individual but essentially social, and a satisfying, fulfilling life requires participation in a community that provides a context for that life.

The liberal response is that community is indeed important but that liberalism properly conceived does not imply "atomized, dislocated, frustrated selves." Liberalism acknowledges the importance community plays in people's lives, but it also acknowledges that every community has its misfits, its malcontents, its pariahs. If individualism is not given sufficient priority, those who are not at home in a particular community will suffer. Most of us are better off in a community, but it must be up to the individual to decide whether the community into which she or he was born is the community in which she or he can flourish. For example, a gay male born into a fundamentalist Christian community that is unequivocally opposed to his living out his sexual orientation is not likely to agree that "what is good for me has to be the good for one who inhabits these roles." Liberalism does not advocate de-situating the individual from the community but emphasizes the importance of being able, if desirable, to re-situate from one community to another, more congenial one. It is commonly alleged that liberals fail to recognize that people are naturally social or communal beings. But there is a sense in which the opposite is true: Liberals believe that people naturally form and join social relations and forums in which they come to understand and pursue the good. The question is not whether individuals' values and autonomy need to be situated in social relations but whether the relevant relations are necessarily or desirably political ones (Kymlicka 1989: 904-905). A political emphasis on individualism does not necessarily entail a social emphasis on individualism.

Critics might point out, however, that we are living in a society where people are in fact becoming increasingly fragmented, lonely, and insecure. But since, as was noted above, a theory that emphasizes the individual can easily be distorted in antisocial ways, such distortion is the fault not of the theory but of the way in which it is presented. What needs to be communicated to students is the value of community as such, including, but not limited to, the community into which one was born. Hence the title of my paper.

Liberals acknowledge that the boundaries that a community establishes for its members are important insofar as they provide the necessary context for individual flourishing. Those boundaries, however, need to be fluid rather than rigid. They should allow for the community we identify with to shift, expand, sometimes change radically, but never to become a prison that keeps people in against their will.

## Service-Learning in the Service of Promoting the Goals of Liberal Moral Education

In this second section of my paper, I will explain why I think service-learning is a valuable approach to teaching civic virtue. I will respond to each of the main arguments of the first section of the paper, showing how service-learning can provide a means to address the concerns raised by critics. The claims I make on behalf of service-learning are based primarily on anecdotal evidence from faculty members, myself included, who employ service-learning as part of their pedagogy.

I began by arguing that the teaching of ethics in public schools must be limited to teaching the (Rawlsian) political conception of ethics. Since the hallmark of this conception of ethics is fairness to all (reasonable) comprehensive life views, what must be taught is an ability to deal critically with one's experience and assumptions. How, then, do we accomplish that? Classroom discussions of abstract ethical theory, or of hypothetical cases such as Kohlberg's Heinz Dilemma, or even discussions of actual current events are of limited value. So long as they are issues upon which no action the student can take will have an effect, there is no need for the student to reach a decision about how to act. Insofar as no decision with real consequences is called for, the learning process is incomplete. Consider, for example, the following position espoused by Stephen Macedo (1990). According to Macedo, the prime characteristic of the good liberal citizen is autonomy: "A crucial feature in the move . . . to autonomy is the development of the capacity critically to assess and even actively shape not simply one's actions, but one's character itself . . . " (216). The resources for developing this capacity are the various aspects of a pluralistic culture — art, religion, history, philosophy: "Autonomous liberals are immanent, interpretive critics of themselves, others, and their culture" (226). That sounds all well and good, but if students are getting their resources for critical reflection largely at second hand, they are likely to consider much, if not all, of what they encounter as so many intellectual curiosities, especially when what is being read or discussed does not jibe with the student's own experience. (How often do we hear, "Well, that's *his* opinion."?)

Real critical reflection, especially in those areas most in need of critical assessment, often requires immediate experience.

> *The idea that dispositions and attitudes can be altered by merely "moral" means conceived of as something that goes on wholly inside of persons is itself one of the old patterns that has to be changed. Thought, desire and purpose exist in a constant give and take of interaction with environing conditions. (Dewey 1963: 61-62)*

When students find themselves involved with an actual community issue, working with people with whom they can sympathize, and in a position to make a real difference in a situation, thought, desire, and purpose come together. Thus, for example, teachers of composition who have their students do their writing as a service to a community agency rather than as an in-class assignment quite often note a significant improvement in the quality of writing, including critical thinking, their students produce.

Service-learning, as a form of experiential learning, is a valuable way to promote learning and critical thinking. It is my contention that service-learning can also serve as a practical means of addressing the concerns communitarians have raised regarding liberal values. The communitarian criticisms discussed above focused on the tendency of individualism to lead to self-centeredness and/or to promote an environment in which people's ties to their communities are weakened to the point that they feel isolated and insecure. Needless to say, these social ills are the result of a highly complex interplay of numerous factors, and it would be a gross oversimplification to suggest that they are solely the result of liberal individualism. Likewise, it would be hopelessly naive to suppose that service-learning could even come close to solving these problems. Nonetheless, it is plausible to suppose that a distorted perception of the liberal emphasis on the individual contributes to a climate that fosters egoism and isolation. Service-learning can mitigate against this tendency by providing a communitarian counterweight to lessons about individual rights and freedom of choice.

With regard to the fear of promoting a self-centered society, service-learning can provide students with a firsthand view of some of the consequences of self-centered action. Of course, the potential for any part of the school curriculum to influence students' moral character is limited. However, in my experience, many people who advocate an egoistic morality are not genuinely cruel or hard-hearted. They simply have been bombarded with the rhetoric of individual rights (understood as *my* rights) and freedom of choice without having sufficiently reflected on how each person's freedom to choose affects others. Being directly confronted with people, in many ways like themselves, who are on the losing end of the self-centered actions of others can be a sobering experience. I have observed this, for example, with almost every one of my students who have volunteered at a nursing home. They are simply amazed at the lives some elderly people live, neglected by family and society at large. If these service experiences are accompanied by directed reflection on the notion that individual rights apply to *everyone* and that the thoughtless pursuit of one's own good often has serious implications for the lives of others, the chances of liberal values' promoting self-centeredness are likely to be significantly diminished.

The greatest benefit I see from service-learning is that service projects can provide for students a valuable experience of community that may serve to counteract the tendency toward isolation. This is not unrelated to the previous discussion of the role service-learning may play in offsetting self-centeredness. The more isolated one feels from community, the more self-centered one is likely to be; the more connected one feels to a community, the more likely one is to make one's choices from the perspective of the good of the group. One way in which this can happen is through working with people with whom one might have thought one had little in common. Students often express diffidence about working with people who are "different" from them. However, once their service work has been completed (or even just begun), they often note surprise at their ability to communicate with these people and to identify with many of their experiences and/or feelings. One of my students admitted that she began her service at a nursing home with great hesitation, and even fear. After having worked there for only 10 hours, she acknowledged that she had actually enjoyed talking with many of the people she had met and now felt noticeably less uncomfortable around elderly people.

Relatedly, service-learning can strengthen students' sense of being vital members of a community rather than isolated individuals. When students feel that even trying to solve social problems is pointless, this is often because they believe there is nothing they, as individuals, can do. Thus, they feel isolated insofar as they feel ineffective; it is difficult *not* to feel isolated from a community when one feels as if one's actions will have no measurable impact on that community. Service-learning provides an opportunity for students to see firsthand that they *can* have an impact.

A dramatic way to give students a sense of effectiveness is placements with large-scale projects such as Habitat for Humanity. In a service experience such as this, students can gain an appreciation of the power of community when they see what the multiplication of individual efforts in a cooperative venture can accomplish. On a smaller scale, students can work on small group projects. A colleague of mine in the psychology department has his students do group projects for the local mental health association. At the end of the semester, each group has a concrete product that they present to the agency (for example, one group produced an orientation videotape, which has decreased considerably the amount of time agency staff must spend orienting new volunteers). My colleague speaks movingly of the sense of satisfaction his students express when they hand over the results of their work, knowing that they have, in some clearly identifiable way, enhanced the ability of the agency to carry out its mission. In each of these examples, the experience of community service has provided a counterweight to our society's tendency to generate feelings of isolation from community.

A final example will, I hope, pull together the various points I have made in this section. One of my students recently did her service project with our local AIDS task force, helping to serve food and provide fellowship at a couple of monthly dinners for people with AIDS and their families and/or caretakers. This student indicated in her paper that she had chosen this particular service because the plight of people with AIDS in our society was something that had bothered her for some time. She had already seen the problem, but up until this point she had done nothing about it. There were several reasons she gave for her lack of action. One was that she already had a very busy schedule, and since this issue was not one that directly affected her life, she had no compelling motivation to get involved. Another was that she lives in a community that is hostile to gays and associates AIDS with gays. Since her husband holds a prominent position in town, she felt that getting involved in this issue could be harmful to her husband and, by extension, herself. And her third reason? She didn't get involved because she couldn't see any way in which she could really make any difference. Why give of her precious time in order to get involved in an issue concerning people she didn't know, and that could have adverse consequences for her husband and her, when she could see no clear evidence that her action would do any good? Such points were not trivial. Her perception that taking action on behalf of people with AIDS could be detrimental to her own interest was a very realistic one. Her sense that this population was not *her* community was understandable. And, in a town such as hers, her belief that any action she might take would not make a real difference was entirely justified. This student is not a particularly self-centered person, but her account demonstrates how easy it is, when setting priorities, to choose the narrower, more individualistic, course over the more community-oriented course.

Her experience of attending several dinners, however, had such an impact on her that it started a chain of events that resulted in an invitation from the openly homophobic community's Ministerial Association to the director of the AIDS task force and the county health nurse to come to one of the Association's meetings and educate its members about AIDS and the plight of people with AIDS. This meeting, in turn, resulted in conversations about the feasibility of using a local parsonage as an AIDS hospice. In her paper, the student talked about having gained an increased sense of self-worth as a result of having taken action on her beliefs. She took that action because talking with AIDS-infected people at the dinners had expanded her sense of community. She went from thinking of AIDS patients as vague others for whom she had some sympathy but with whom she had no real identification, to thinking of them as vital members of her own community whose welfare she no longer thought of as in opposition to her own but as a part of her own. Thus, her experience of service-learning (in a course that was presenting a liberal version of social ethics) both expanded and strengthened her sense of belonging to a community, not in a merely abstract manner but in a manner that expressed itself in action. The final comment in her paper was, "I feel it has been a privilege to be a part of the community service that I performed. I appreciate that we were given an opportunity to take our learning into the world. . . . " My remark to her was that it appeared that she also had taken the world into her learning.

## Conclusion

I have argued that civic virtue can and should be promoted in the public schools through the teaching of a liberal conception of limited, political morality. The chief features of this morality are a commitment to the autonomy of individuals with regard to choosing their own comprehensive conception of the good life, a correlative emphasis on individual rights, and a capacity for "public reasonableness" that includes the ability to assess one's own values and assumptions critically. I have addressed several criticisms of the liberal approach, and have indicated why I think the criticisms point not to genuine problems in the liberal position but to ways in which liberalism can be (and has been) distorted. Finally, I have indicated briefly why I believe service-learning can help to guard against these distortions. However, I should also note that one or two isolated service-learning experiences are likely to have only limited impact. The only way in which the benefits I have described can be reasonably expected to have a lasting effect is if students are exposed to numerous and varied service-learning experiences throughout their academic careers.

### References

Dewey, J. (1963). *Liberalism and Social Action*. New York, NY: Capricorn.

———. (1993). "The Ethics of Democracy." In *The Political Writings*, edited by D. Morris and I. Shapiro, pp. 59-65. Indianapolis, IN: Hackett. (Orig. published 1888)

Gutmann, A. (1987). *Democratic Education*. Princeton, NJ: Princeton University Press.

———. (1992). "Communitarian Critics of Liberalism." In *Communitarianism and*

*Individualism*, edited by S. Avineri and A. de-Shalit, pp. 120-136. Oxford, Eng.: Oxford University Press.

Indiana University Purdue University Indianapolis (IUPUI),Office of Service-Learning. (1994). "Definition of Service-Learning." (Available from Robert Bringle, Director, Office of Service-Learning, AO 138, IUPUI, 355 N. Lansing Street, Indianapolis, IN 46202-2896)

Kymlicka, W. (1989). "Liberal Individualism and Liberal Neutrality." *Ethics: An International Journal of Social, Political, and Legal Philosophy* 99: 883-905.

————— , and W. Norman. (1994). "Return of the Citizen: A Survey of Recent Work on Citizenship Theory." *Ethics: An International Journal of Social, Political, and Legal Philosophy* 104: 352-381.

Macedo, S. (1990). *Liberal Virtues: Citizenship, Virtue, and Community*. Oxford, Eng.: Oxford University Press.

MacIntyre, A. (1981). *After Virtue*. Notre Dame, IN: University of Notre Dame Press.

Rawls, J. (1993). *Political Liberalism*. New York, NY: Columbia University Press.

Sandel, M. (1984). "Morality and the Liberal Ideal." In *Justice: Alternative Political Perspectives*, edited by J. Sterba, pp. 219-224. Belmont, CA: Wadsworth.

# Service-Learning, Citizenship, and the Philosophy of Law

by Stephen L. Esquith

## Citizenship

Advocates of service-learning long have argued that service-learning makes students better democratic citizens. By serving at a nonprofit organization or public agency for several hours each week in an area related to a course they are taking, they become more skilled in the arts of communication, more aware of the political institutions that govern their society, more inclined to participate in public life, and most of all more committed to advancing common goods over private interests. The goal of citizenship, one service-learning advocate writes, "does not mean mastering all the facts or having answers to all the questions. Rather, it means that when one assumes the role of citizen, 'I' becomes 'we'" (Morse 1989: 25).

What is missing in this defense of service-learning as a form of political education is precisely what is most important for democratic citizenship, that is, the ability to discern the reflexivity and chameleon-like qualities of power in a democratic society and the capacity to sustain democratic dialogue with imagination and poise. To the extent that service-learning neglects these phenomena, it suffers from the same kind of romantic view of politics that other communitarian and republican doctrines have been criticized for in recent years (Bellah et al. 1985). Unless students who participate in service-learning are taught how to reflect critically on power's effects on them as active participants and passive subjects, they will oscillate between feeling intoxicated with power and alienated from it. They will feel the rush that comes from being part of a communitarian experiment that rejects politics as usual, and then just as quickly they will feel frustrated when the experiment takes an unexpected turn, is co-opted, or fails. They will too quickly imitate the powerful accents in the voices they are contesting, and then just as quickly lose their balance when they miss their mark. Without a political education in power, service-learning students will not have the poise to hear how power resonates in their own voices and then limit it to local purposes. In some cases, their experience in service-learning may even weaken their resolve to participate in democratic politics rather than strengthen it.

My goal in this essay is to sketch an alternative conception of service-learning that places an education in power at the center of democratic citizenship. I begin with an observation of Tocqueville's about the pervasiveness and power of legal categories of thinking in American democracy, and I suggest that educated democratic citizens should be mindful of this aspect of legal power. Drawing on Dewey and Emerson, I explain what it means to grasp through reflective experience the discursive as well as the coercive power of the law. The argument begins with political theory and ends with a philosophical interpretation of experience, imagination, and poise.

## Law's Powers

In *Democracy in America* (1969), Alexis de Tocqueville argues that the aristocratic "temper" of the legal profession was "the most powerful and, so today, the only counterbalance to democracy" (263). The law limits the excesses of majority rule in America for two reasons. First, lawyers "form the political upper class and the most intellectual section of society" (268). Because of their adherence to the formal rule of precedent, they have more respect than most democratic citizens for order and historical traditions (267). Second, this "upper-class" temperament is disseminated through popular institutions such as jury trial and inhibits democratic citizens from giving in too quickly to their passion for political and economic equality.

According to Tocqueville, "There is hardly a political question in the United States [that] does not sooner or later turn into a judicial one." Legal language "infiltrates" society from top to bottom. However, this litigiousness is almost invisible. The law's discursive power "enwraps the whole of society, penetrating each component class and constantly working in secret upon its unconscious patient, till in the end it has molded it to its desire" (270).

It is this "little dreaded and hardly noticed" power of the law to "counterbalance democracy" that I believe should be a major topic in a course on the philosophy of law and that service-learning is particularly well suited to address. If democracy means that power should originate with and remain under the control of the people as a whole, then a legal culture in which power operates "in secret" must be understood critically by democratic citizens, not just absorbed "unconsciously." Democratic citizens should be able to recognize how the law in a democracy "enwraps the whole of society" and then critically assess this and other forms of power.

Courses in the philosophy of law should not simply teach students how to make arguments based on precedents and analogies, and use terms such as *punishment, responsibility*, and *causation* with logical precision. They should help students understand how finely woven legal doctrines in criminal law, tort law, property law, and constitutional law work on citizens in the subtle ways Tocqueville suggests. Service-learning can give students a feel for the "desire" of the law and an understanding of how the law works its way into the lives of democratic citizens, and so enable students to meet the challenges the law poses to a fuller, more active democratic citizenship. By incorporating service-learning into a philosophy of law course, the discursive power of the law can be brought into focus. By reflecting on their own experiences working, for example, with public interest law firms specializing in environmental issues, legal advocacy programs for disadvantaged minorities, tenant rights organizations, parole and probation departments, student legal services organizations, and shelters for battered women and the homeless, students have an opportunity to assess how the doctrinal language of the law infiltrates, penetrates, and molds "its unconscious patient."

This discursive power is not always a matter of unwanted manipulation; sometimes it has immediate benefits. Coercive state power by itself may not be enough to remove an architectural barrier, vacate an unlawful eviction order, or compensate families for the damages done by corporate negligence. Wrongdoers may be coerced into following the letter of the law but still subvert its spirit. Technically in compliance, they may behave so grudgingly that the coercive power of the law must be coupled with more discursive strategies such as negotiations, conferences, and public hearings before access is really available, housing affordable, and innocent victim vindicated.

But the discursive power of the law is not always so benign and easily reconcilable with democratic procedural norms. When it "enwraps the whole of society" so that every political question seems naturally to "sooner or later turn into a judicial one," the law may turn citizens into clients, consumers, and spectators in their own lives, excessively dependent upon professionals and drained of the confidence and composure they need to make their own case in public (Harr 1995). They may mimic legal language and some may even prevail in court. But they may also find that the experience has left them strangely disconnected from their friends, neighbors, and fellow citizens. Just as a bitter divorce and child custody battle may sour parent-child relations, so too may legally resolved disputes over wetlands use and the place of religion in public education short-circuit democratic deliberation and deepen resentment on all sides. Many political disputes such as those that have occurred over the drawing up of legislative voting districts may ultimately have to be decided in court. But even in these cases, a premature reliance on legal remedies (court-ordered busing is another example) may exacerbate the problem and strip citizens of the skills and habits they need to discuss their differences imaginatively. The skills of democratic citizenship (meeting one's opponent halfway and playing the role of the loyal opposition) do not translate very well into adversarial legal language. What is needed is the poise to resist seeking legal remedies too often and too soon so that political imaginations can be creatively engaged together.

Where does this poise and imagination come from? My claim is that one place it may be cultivated is in the reflective experience of service-learning in a course on the philosophy of law. Not surprisingly, the inspiration for the notion of reflective experience developed here is John Dewey. After examining Dewey's notion of experience (and imagination), I will compare his optimistic views with Ralph Waldo Emerson's famous essay "Experience," in which Emerson introduces the notion of poise.

## Experience and Imagination

In *Democracy and Education* (1966), Dewey makes the bold claim that "an ounce of experience is better than a ton of theory simply because it is only in experience that any theory has vital and verifiable significance." Theories without experience, Dewey continues, become mere "catchwords" that actually "render thinking, or genuine theorizing, unnecessary and impossible" (144).

Theories — "genuine" theories for Dewey — do not exist apart from the experience that verifies or falsifies them, and experience, fully reflective experience, does not exist apart from theory. Rather it is an integral part of the "trying" and "undergoing" that connects what has gone before with what is likely to follow. All human experiences, it seems, have some reflective element, and fully reflective experience, Dewey argues, is informed by theoretical hypotheses that "bind together cause and effect, activity and consequence" (145).

The most fully reflective experience, the experience of thinking, begins with the identification and clarification of a problem in its context (e.g., how should parking be regulated on an urban university campus?), then considers a hypothesis in answer to the problem (e.g., if distributive justice is the goal, then distribute scarce parking places according to the relative social values of the drivers' purposes), and finally tests the hypothesis in practice. This model of reflective experience, Dewey argues, should guide education in a liberal democratic society. We should not assume that students carry with them a supply of experiences that can be examined, and we should not assume that they can easily identify what the problem is in the new experiences they are introduced to. But with help, these new problematic experiences can be analyzed and connected to others in an explanatory way. This kind of reflective experience is what education should strive for (152-163).

Educational experiences in general, according to Dewey, should be neither completely passive nor frantically active. Even though there are moments in an educational experience when the student must step back and take certain things in without trying to change them, education should never be merely a process of exposure or absorption. The necessarily active dimension of experience is best captured, according to Dewey, in aesthetic experiences where there is a concentrated effort to grasp the whole.

In *Art as Experience*, Dewey emphasizes the important way in which aesthetic experience forms a bounded whole as the artist moves back and forth between doing and undergoing:

> *The doing may be energetic, and the undergoing may be acute and intense. But unless they are related to each other to form a whole in perception, the thing done is not fully esthetic. The making for example may be a display of technical virtuosity, and the undergoing a gush of sentiment or a [reverie]. If the artist does not perfect a new vision in his process of doing, he acts mechanically and repeats some old model fixed like a blue print in his mind. (1980: 50)*

According to Dewey, this conception of aesthetic experience in which the doing and undergoing alternate within a single vision is not unrelated to other forms of experience. Aesthetic experience is "the clarified and intensified development of traits that belong to every normally complete experience" (1980: 46; 1994: 314).

What constitutes, then, a "complete" experience? Dewey suggests that it is one that is neither overly receptive nor overly energetic, and therefore one that permits both the doer and those who see or hear the experience from the outside the time to reflect back upon its genesis and its possible consequences and thus to give it unity.

Overly receptive experiences are like daydreams that allow more and more to rush in, but no effort is made to cultivate any of the moments so that they can be used as the basis for action. On the other hand, overly energetic experiences are like frantic searches; the experiences are so "dispersed and miscellaneous as hardly to deserve the name" (Dewey 1980: 44-45). In contrast to both, a complete experience is one in which the rhythms of doing and undergoing are not allowed to overwhelm each other. "What is done and what is undergone are thus reciprocally, and cumulatively, and continuously instrumental to each other" (50).

How is this reciprocity between doing and undergoing achieved in a legal-political experience? I suggest that in order to resist the temptations to daydream about power's utopian possibilities or to frantically search out new opportunities for control, a person must have a certain kind of poise and focused imagination. She (or he) must be able to hear how her own encounter with the language of power has affected her "unconscious" attitudes toward others. She must be able to recognize the hint of superiority as well as the guilt in her voice after she has mimicked prisoners and guards or wrongly shared a confidence with a judge in chambers. And she must then have the honesty to admit this is happening to her without retreating to utopian fantasies of perfect solidarity. Dewey does not discuss this element of reflective experience explicitly, and I will return to it in the next section on Emerson.

Dewey does, however, recognize how important the imaginative element is in reflective experience. Our hypothetical service-learner must also be able to imagine how in her academic voice, with its new accents and hesitations, she still might cooperate with others. This act of creativity and imagination is perhaps the most difficult task of democratic citizenship and, says Dewey, its "most priceless addition to life." In his short essay "Creative Democracy: The Task Before Us" (1981), he describes imaginative cooperation this way:

> *A genuinely democratic faith in peace is faith in the possibility of conducting disputes, controversies, and conflicts as co-operative undertakings in which both parties learn by giving the other a chance to express itself. (226)*

In imagining how we sound to others and might possibly interact with them, we rehearse the conditions for the kind of interaction and sought-after cooperation Dewey has in mind. Only after we have heard the tones of ridicule and intimidation in our legal voice, even when it pretends to be just presenting the stark, seemingly incontrovertible legal facts of the matter, can we feel that perhaps it is possible to enrich our own lives through cooperative discussion and compromise with those with whom we strongly disagree. The opposite danger, to repeat, is that we will be overly receptive to the voices of these others, and this attitude is no less destructive of the structured companionship of democratic politics than is an overly energetic, yet condescending and controlling attitude.

This self-conscious interplay between receptivity and energetic action is also a balance between the old and the new, the academic voice and practical experience. The imaginative acts of democratic citizenship take self-control and composure, and also require the capacity to represent older ways of sharing and cooperating. Even in a democracy, citizens get locked into a certain way of seeing and thinking. They like to be reminded of those things that they find familiar, not strange. For this reason, imaginative and creative acts of citizenship often encounter great initial opposition. To overcome this opposition, acts of democratic imagination self-consciously must carry forward some elements of the old political order as building blocks for the new. Speaking of aesthetic experience, he notes, "Imagination is the only gateway through which these meanings [derived from prior experiences] can find their way into a present interaction; or, rather as we have just seen, the conscious adjustment of the new and old is imagination" (Dewey 1980: 272). In law, the judicial doctrine of *stare decisis* attests to the need to construct a bridge between new laws and old.

There is, however, a danger of confusing the imaginative with the imaginary. What distinguishes the two, according to Dewey, is that the latter passes away, in some cases, because it is "arbitrary," while the former, after initial strong resistance, endures. The imaginary only "toys" fancifully with new political forms; the imaginative grounds them in common experiences and "nature," and so gains a hearing for them (268-269).

## Poise

These skills of democratic participation, at least as I have been able to extrapolate them from Dewey's conception of experience, still need work. One can easily anticipate the dangers facing philosophy students thrust into politically charged and unfamiliar service-learning placements. While some degree of composure and respect for the voices and past practices of others would help them get through the day, there is a degree of political optimism in Dewey's call for "creative democracy" — stemming from his faith in our ability to align imaginative democratic practices with "nature" — that service-learning students should be wary of. The imagination Dewey expects of democratic citizens will encounter a human limitation that Emerson describes in his essay "Experience" (1981): "Though we have health and reason, yet we have no superfluity of spirit for new creation" (267). Nature, including human nature, remains partially inaccessible to philosophy and art. All we can hope for, Emerson suggests, are "relations to each other" that are "oblique and casual" (269).

Having mourned our transient existence, however, Emerson does offer two consolations. Even though art and artists are as rigid and inelastic as the rest of us, there is something we can do to reflect the light. "There is no adaptation or universal applicability in men, but each has his special talent, and the mastery of successful men consists in adroitly keeping themselves where and when that turn shall be oftenest to be practiced" (273). And while all of us are "superfluous" most of the time, together "we are always of the gaining party" (273-274).

Second, in addition to this argument from the division of labor, Emerson suggests another source of earthly redemption. We live in a mixed world of "Illusion, Temperament, Succession, Surface, Surprise, Reality, and Subjectiveness" (288). The best we can do is to keep our eyes on the road: "We live amid surfaces, and the true art of life is to skate well on them." To do this, he argues, we must attend closely to the moment, to the land directly under our feet, and to those with whom we share this fate: "Let us be poised and wise, and our own, to-day. Let us treat the men and women well; treat them as if they were real; perhaps they are" (275). The poise we need to "skate well" on the shifting surfaces of political life is not the poise and imagination of the artist or poet who can grasp the unity of the whole and see how, following Tocqueville, the law "enwraps all of society." This is too much to ask, cautions Emerson.

## Political Education

Dewey had great admiration for Emerson. "When democracy has articulated itself," he wrote, "it will have no difficulty finding itself already proposed in Emerson" (1929: 76). It is not obvious what Dewey means by this. I want to suggest a common purpose they share that might explain Dewey's high regard for Emerson.

The purpose Emerson and Dewey hold in common is the education of citizens so that they can respond cooperatively to the unpredictable, shifting patterns of power in their lives. Emerson, writing in an earlier age, refers to the powers of Nature, trade, and language itself. While power does indeed follow certain regular compensatory and circular paths, he argues, the variations are infinite and elude any grand historical theory (Esquith 1994: 249-262). For Dewey, the powers of concentrated industries and the state are more important. To the extent that liberal democratic theory remains tied to the 19th-century ideal of individualism, he argues, it will not be able to control the overt and covert forms of violence that modern society now contains: "When, then, I say that the first object of a renascent liberalism is education, I mean that its task is to aid in producing the habits of mind and character, the intellectual and moral patterns, that are somewhere near even with the actual movements of events." These "actual movements" he described as the "realities of production enforced by an era of machinery and power" (1963: 61).

These new realities are not, according to Dewey, simply technological or economic. Corporatism is a larger cultural phenomenon, and, if it is to be brought under democratic control, it requires a new conception of individualism, not the "earlier pioneer individualism" (1962: 36). Twentieth-century corporatist organization has transformed political life, not just the structure of business. It has led to a schizophrenic citizenry — apathetic in the face of the power of big business and spasmodic when corporate control falters: "Political apathy broken by recurrent sensations and spasms is the natural outcome" (59-60). As difficult as it sometimes may be, Dewey urges that we put our trust in the deliberative capacities of common citizens and their potential to grow and keep up with these shifting forms of corporatist power. He has faith that ordinary citizens, if given the right language and enough experiences to use and refine it, can create a new democratic culture. Emerson is less sanguine, but sees no other way to cope with power and still remain faithful to the ideal of democratic participation. In this sense, both are theorists of democratic political education.

This kind of democratic political education is especially important for prelaw undergraduates. At large universities in the United States, philosophy of law courses, along with other prelaw courses, are usually heavily enrolled. These prelaw students often seek internships with private law firms. Later in law school, a shrinking number participate in public-interest law clinics, and, after graduation, most pursue a career in private practice, where they become either overly energetic in Dewey's sense or demoralized. In either case, they will likely overlook the discursive power of the law they traffic in. A service-learning component in an undergraduate philosophy of law course may be the best way to inoculate some, though by no means all, students against these dangers.

## References

Bellah, Robert, et al. (1985). *Habits of the Heart: Individualism and Commitment in American Life.* Berkeley, CA: University of California Press.

Dewey, John. (1929). *Characters and Events: Popular Essays in Social and Political Philosophy.* Vol. 1. New York, NY: Henry Holt.

———. (1962). *Individualism Old and New.* New York, NY: Capricorn Books.

———. (1963). *Liberalism and Social Action.* New York, NY: G.P. Putnam.

———. (1966). *Democracy and Education.* New York, NY: The Free Press.

———. (1980). *Art as Experience.* New York, NY: Perigree Books.

———. (1981). *The Later Works of John Dewey.* Vol. 14, 1939-41, edited by Jo Ann Boydston. Carbondale, IL: Southern Illinois University Press.

———. (1994). *Experience and Nature.* Chicago, IL: Open Court.

Emerson, Ralph Waldo. (1981). *The Portable Emerson,* edited by Carl Bode. New York, NY: Penguin Books.

Esquith, Stephen L. (1994). *Intimacy and Spectacle: Liberal Theory as Political Education.* Ithaca, NY: Cornell University Press.

Harr, Jonathan. (1995). *A Civil Action.* New York, NY: Random House.

Morse, Suzanne W. (1989). *Renewing Civic Capacity: Preparing College Students for Service and Citizenship.* ASHE-ERIC Higher Education Report No. 8. Washington, DC: School of Human Development, The George Washington University.

Tocqueville, Alexis de. (1969). *Democracy in America.* Vol. 1, translated by George Lawrence, edited by J.P. Mayer. Garden City, NY: Anchor Books.

# Deepening Democratic Participation Through Deweyan Pragmatism

## by Judith M. Green

Increasingly throughout the 20th century, localized problems that have given birth to grass-roots movements for social transformation worldwide have reflected the globalization of our lived human situations. Trade, transportation, communication, the production of goods and services, the growth of knowledge and technologies, the arts, and the processes of education, imagination, and conflict have become increasingly globalized, interactively yielding both great gains and great problems for humanity. Our kitchens reflect the rich bounty of the world's diverse lands, waters, and cultures. The Internet now allows school children to communicate with their peers on the opposite side of the planet, deepening their understanding and broadening their imaginative horizons in the process.

And a hunger for better possibilities growing out of an increasingly detailed sense of how other people live seems to have fueled a global movement toward democracy, building in waves throughout the 20th century to the strength of a tsunami in 1989, when courageous citizens with sledge hammers destroyed the Berlin Wall separating them from their dreams, and their counterparts in Russia and throughout Eastern Europe swept aside the particular form of nationalist totalitarianism known as "Soviet Communism." Soon thereafter, the end of apartheid in South Africa followed by peaceful elections to shape a multicultural democracy established a high-water mark that continues to inspire the world, even as the resurgence of violent cultural imperialism in Bosnia and Rwanda horrifies all, perhaps especially those who saw historical progress toward democracy as linear and inevitable.

In addition to these "setbacks" to the growth of a global democratic civilization, we also face loss of local control to powerful forces of international capital, a related global environmental crisis with already devastating implications for the quality of life in poor and relatively powerless locales, and raging epidemics sweeping across every continent. Even many citizens who reside in "formally democratic" nations, and who should count as "winners" in our globalized economic struggles, find their lives hollowed out by ontological rootlessness and existential nihilism. In America's forgotten central cities, many who are doubly excluded by poverty and racism experience a near-total lack of meaning, purpose, and love in their lives, so that alcohol, addictive drugs, meaningless sex, and mindless violence seem like acceptable substitutes.[1]

Perhaps the combination of these gains and these losses, these new problems and new opportunities arising out of the ongoing globalization process, explains why the contemporary urge toward social transformation is so widespread and so deep. But why democracy? John Dewey's answer, in light of the turbulent transformations of the first half of the 20th century, is that an immanent impulse toward democracy is part of our evolved human nature as modern persons. To some extent, we share a reflective sense that only democratic forms of life can overcome the experienced problems of humanity's past and allow each and all of us to experience the fullness of our own particular variety of growth within a necessarily and desirably cooperative network of human flourishing.[2] Perhaps Dewey is right that modern people share such an immanent impulse toward a dimly envisioned democratic ideal. Or perhaps "democracy" has been seized upon as a panacea by Western-educated leaders of grass-roots social transformation movements in other parts of the world who hope that the West's "formally democratic" political, legal, and economic institutions will cure their own country's economic, social, environmental, and health crises.[3] Certainly these Western nations, the powerful international organizations they control, and the gigantic transnational firms that currently regard them as home have exerted considerable influence to ensure that "formally democratic" institutions modeled on and readily compatible with their own are adopted as solutions world-wide.[4]

Yet if we look closely and compare grass-roots social transformation movements in South Africa, Poland, Mexico's southernmost state of Chiapas, and the United States, among other examples, we see significant differences, not only in the specific problems they seek to overcome but also in their ways of approaching transformation and in their guiding conceptions of the democratic ideal. This suggests that if, in fact, a movement toward democracy is sweeping the world, we must understand the meaning of democracy contextually and in terms of Wittgensteinian "family resemblances" instead of as an already existing institutional form with a set of uniform, necessary, and sufficient characteristics.[5] Moreover, this wave of democracy-hungry transformative efforts includes grass-roots movements toward fuller citizen participation in governance within long-term, well-established, economically and militarily successful countries such as the United States. Or, to take a different kind of example, we find many from Poland's world-historic Solidarity Movement now asking, "What was our revolution for?" — even as Western-style economic, political, and legal institutions are being put into place with such rapidity and such "success" that their nation is widely viewed as a model of posttotalitarian transition to democracy.[6] Examples such as these suggest that "formal democracy" itself has problems and deficiencies as a transformative goal for our global era.

"The cure for the problems of democracy," John Dewey often said, "is more democracy" — or as we might say now, *a deeper democracy* that calls upon the dispersed knowledge and hopes of a diverse citizenry, that invites them into partnership in designing solutions and in making them work, and that transforms the participating citizens themselves as the key to transforming their political, legal, and economic institutions as well as the quality of their daily lives.[7] Active citizen participation in the process of deepening democracy has tremendous potential for transforming our globally interlinked problems and for increasing human flourishing worldwide in the 21st century. Deweyan pragmatism offers us helpful guidance in realizing that potential through citizen participation in social inquiry, through cross-difference cooperation in community building, and through citizen-guided processes of policy development and evaluation. As Dewey suggested, the key to effectiveness in all three of these aspects of democratic citizen participation is education for democracy, in which community-based service-learning can play an invaluable role.

## Overcoming Critics' Concerns About Democratic Citizen Participation

Sometimes criticism of the feasibility of active citizen participation masks an unrealistic belief that democracy can be more effectively achieved through some other transformation process, e.g., revolution. However, as Tanzania's first postcolonial president, Julius Nyerere, pointed out in the 1960s, even when revolution is effective in changing a country's leaders and in reshaping its institutions, the deeper challenge remains: changing the hearts and minds of the people, the attitudes and habits of daily life.[8] Likewise, writing 10 years after the Bolshevik revolution of 1917, Dewey offered a related but more detailed diagnosis as to why such expectations are unrealistic — as unrealistic as had been those of radically democratic proponents of the American and French Revolutions:

> *These facts explain why the more things changed, the more they were the same; they account, that is, for the fact that instead of the sweeping revolution [that] was expected to result from democratic political machinery, there was in the main but a transfer of vested power from one class to another. . . . In spite of sudden and catastrophic revolutions, the essential continuity of history is doubly guaranteed. Not only are personal desire and belief functions of habit and custom, but the objective conditions [that] provide the resources and tools of action, together with its limitations, obstructions and traps, are precipitates of the past, perpetuating, willy-nilly, its hold and power. The creation of a* tabula rasa *in order to permit the cre-*

*ation of a new order is so impossible as to set at naught both the hope of buoyant revolutionaries and the timidity of scared conservatives. Nevertheless, changes take place and are cumulative in character. Observation of them in the light of their recognized consequences arouses reflection, discovery, invention, experimentation. When a certain state of accumulated knowledge, of techniques and instrumentalities, is attained, the process of change is so accelerated that, as [today], it appears externally to be the dominant trait. But there is a marked lag in any corresponding change of ideas and desires. Habits of opinion are the toughest of all habits. (1927: 336-337)*

If a deeper democracy is the goal of social change processes, we must realize that it cannot be achieved by revolutionary fiat, but requires personality-reformative experience gained through democratic participation in progressively reshaping a shared way of life.

Sometimes criticisms of participatory democracy amount to a counsel of despair or an expression of smug cynicism, suggesting that there is nothing that ordinary people can do to fulfill their own deep impulses to end their own and others' misery, to share their values and experience, and to participate in shaping the future terms of social life. Instead, they suggest that one becomes somehow superior, or escapes the hoodwinked herd at least to some extent, if one refuses to be taken in, either by the rationales for coercive concentrations of power or by empty gestures that invite pacifying but ultimately meaningless citizen participation. Given the seriousness of humanly caused or cooperatively avoidable suffering in many parts of the world today, such despair and cynicism represent immoral responses, in that they suggest that our shared responsibility to play a transformative role in relief of suffering can be eluded simply by adopting a certain attitude toward it. Even if it were true that nothing could be done by ordinary citizens to effectively oppose overwhelming, immiserating power in a certain context, it would be nobler, and might communicate a profound message to the future, to act defiantly in the face of such a context, as did the Jews in the Warsaw ghetto, rather than to wait passively to be consumed by flames.

Various critics have argued that, while seemingly desirable in theory, active citizen participation cannot fulfill its democratic potential for redirecting social life because of nearly insuperable history-born impediments and practically ineradicable human flaws, including ignorance, selfishness, animosities from the past, incommensurable cultural differences, the unwillingness of many to participate in projects that do not serve their immediate self-interest, the Herculean difficulties of gaining consensus, and the necessarily coercive character of processes that seek to enforce social agreements. Each of these traits is indeed a serious concern that must be factored into realistic strategies for overcoming obstacles to effective, democratic citizen participation. Nonetheless, we have three kinds of reasons for believing active citizen participation can actually help to optimize human flourishing within the complex, interlinked problem situations of our global millennial era. These kinds of reasons are epistemic, political, and moral.

## Epistemic Reasons

If, as Dewey argued, the ideal goal of human action in general is to promote growth toward human flourishing, then every social action, whether individual or collaborative, has a moral dimension; and if every situation of choice and action that has a moral dimension is unique, calling for its own particular solution, as Dewey further argued, then "local" knowledge — intelligent, experience-based appreciation of the process of development, of the current characteristics, and of the values at stake in a particular situation — will always be relevant and necessary to a fully adequate solution.[9] To be sure, in times of war, natural disaster, or other urgent crisis, a shared sense of urgency about immediate and decisive action often prompts people to look to their leaders and those who have general knowledge about broadly similar kinds of problems to propose and to impose some kind of intervention. But something is always overlooked or lost in such top-down approaches to problem solving, and often the general solution that fails to take into account the peculiarly relevant particulars of a situation is disastrously wrong, sooner or later.

In normal contexts of social decision making, and in crises, too, fully adequate solutions require local knowledge. And since relevant local knowledge is broadly dispersed, there are good epistemic grounds for regarding broadly inclusive citizen participation as necessary to processes of social inquiry that can be reasonably expected to optimize human flourishing in a given context at a given time. As to why citizen participation in optimally effective social inquiry must be active, as opposed to the now-dominant model in which experts simply aggregate the opinions of otherwise passive individuals, an active role allows bearers of local knowledge to weigh, to correct interactively, and to enhance cooperatively the quality of expressions of local experience and values. This is necessarily an interactive, transformative epistemic process that expert outsiders simply are not in the proper epistemic position to undertake, though experts may facilitate and contribute to this process by proposing alternative ways of framing issues, by seeking clarifications, and by suggesting comparisons with situations elsewhere.

## Political Reasons

The important political reasons for favoring active citizen participation in social inquiry are more closely related to such epistemic reasons than is generally acknowledged. If citizens have not actively participated in the process of inquiry that leads to selection of public policy, they may have good epistemic reasons for opposition to proposed changes, given well-remembered historical abuses of power even within "formally democratic" institutions and well-founded distrust of experts who fail to include local knowledge in their policy recommendations. Of course, sometimes citizens' opposition to public policy proposals is based on narrow self-interest, as when a NIMBY (not in my back yard) group forms to block a development they agree would promote the general good, but would require their neighborhood to experience some adverse consequence. However, there is good empirical evidence to suggest that active citizen participation in decision processes about hard-to-site public developments decreases the likelihood of such NIMBY groups' forming, and that active citizen participation in public policy formation tends to increase its ease of adoption by representative bodies, as well as its ease of implementation.[10] But the seldom-emphasized point is that citizens may have good epistemic reasons for their distrust of imposed or purely expert-generated public policies, to the extent that they realize the importance of widely dispersed, interactively formulated local knowledge within the processes of social inquiry that can create contextually optimal outcomes.

## Moral Reasons

Likewise, this good political reason for favoring active citizen participation in inquiry that leads to public policy is closely related to good moral reasons. Since citizens can potentially contribute to policy formulation their own interactively refined sense of values as well as their experience-based local knowledge, and since their appreciation of their life context can be deepened and enriched by interactive participation, forcing them to accept a passive role would be to contribute to their own moral infantilization. Also, if participating in cross-difference public processes helps to avoid or undo intergroup biases based on ignorance and past patterns of exclusion, such participation can also contribute to the moral improvement of citizens' intellects and characters. Finally, if it helps them to become skillful in cooperative processes and accustomed to taking shared responsibility for their shared future, it can help them to ensure a more respectful, more peaceful, and more desirable quality of community life than can the all-too-common current alternatives.[11]

The aspects of human flourishing that active citizen participation can help to optimize include both "objective" improvements in social outcomes and "subjective" improvements in life satisfaction, fuller development of human potentials, and contextual support for the formation of desirable habits and character tendencies.[12] In general, better-thought-out public policies implemented with fuller public support from a better-informed, more responsible citizenry should lead to progressive improvements over time in such "objective" aspects of human flourishing as environmental protection, disease control, literacy, and economic development — especially if our measures of them reflect localized distributions and not just national aggregates. As long as we continue to express economic welfare in terms of gross domestic product, suboptimal local outcomes and even worsening local situations are masked; at the same time, the importance of the human flourishing of those worse-off citizens is downplayed. On the "subjective" side, we can expect active citizen participation to lead to improvements in the now-virulent problems of existential nihilism and ontological rootlessness, as well as the development of those desirable aspects of human intelligence and character that generally receive little stimulation within "formally democratic" but bureaucratically administered societies. We can expect to see changes in the kind of life people imagine and desire as their lived experience of cooperative participatory responsibility teaches them a more deeply democratic relational awareness of other persons and of our shared ecosystem.

# Overcoming the Obstacles to Effective, Democratic Citizen Participation

In order for these "objective" and "subjective" improvements in human flourishing to occur within the complex contexts of democratic transformative struggle, sets of obstacles that frequently occur within democratic transformative struggles in our present era must be overcome. These theoretical and practical obstacles, which reflect the democratic deficiencies of existing institutions, processes, and mindsets, include (1) obstacles created by concentrations of power, by existing bureaucratic-hierarchical models of decision making, and by prevailing expert models of inquiry; (2) problems created by a lack of citizen preparation for and experience within active participatory processes of social inquiry and decision, especially when they require collaboration in contexts involving historically based patterns of oppression; and (3) problems in conceptualizing and progressively reevaluating goals, objectives, and strategies within ongoing processes of democratic struggle. Deweyan pragmatism offers rich resources for overcoming each of these kinds of obstacles and problems.

## Obstacles Created by Concentrations of Power

Some critics overemphasize the first set of obstacles in arguing that, however desirable active democratic participation may seem in theory, anti-democratic concentrations of power in bureaucratic national governments and transnational capitalist corporations, as well as prevailing expert models of inquiry, make meaningful employment of such participation unrealistic in practice. Ironically, such criticism sometimes involves an unwitting fetishization of economic and political institutions and processes very like that of some proponents of "formal democracy," who treasure and trust a set of peculiar, historically emergent institutions while distrusting humanity. It is important to remember the lessons of *The Wizard of Oz* and *The Merchant of Venice:* There are human beings operating all that machinery, and they bleed like the rest of us. Though an occasional sociopath such as Hitler or Stalin gains coercive control for a time, most of the wielders of bureaucratic and economic power wish to be well thought of by their neighbors, and thus are susceptible to public opinion and organized opposition. A recent example is the influence of large-scale prodemocracy demonstrations in Indonesia in helping to end the long-term autocracy of President Suharto, not only because he was moved by them and concerned about his place in history but also because they aroused concerns among potential international investors.

In considering how to overcome this first set of obstacles, it is important not to overlook the real efficacy citizen participation has demonstrated in recent times in helping to bring about democratic change in various parts of the world. For example, the persistent and united efforts of workers and intellectuals in the Solidarity Movement in Poland to open up democratic processes, as well as those of South Africa's multicultural African National Congress to end apartheid, have made significant contributions to an international current of progressive social transformation, increasing the likelihood and the effectiveness of emergent citizen activism in other places. Moreover, in the United States, recent federal and state growth management legislation has included a requirement that active citizen participation be part of the process of adopting comprehensive plans on state, regional, and local levels, and it has opened up a whole new realm of opportunities for experimentation and learning. Even the World Bank has recently begun to require that applicants demonstrate that society-wide benefits will result from its loans. Thus, one of the important background conditions for the rapid evolution of active citizen participation processes — an at least minimally supportive legal framework — is increasingly being met. However, it would be dangerously unrealistic to minimize the obstacles, to overlook other accompanying conditions that must be achieved, if active citizen participation is to be both effective and democratic in its impact.

## Problems Created by a Lack of Citizen Preparation

One of the most important sets of problems to be overcome is that created by lack of citizen preparation for and experience within active participatory processes of social inquiry and decision making, especially when these require cross-difference collaboration. As Dewey argued, the key to solving these problems is democratic education, not only of the formal kind structured by schools but also of the less formal kind one gains through community-based service and through working within transformative democratic coalitions and existing citizen participation processes.

> *The best guarantee of collective efficiency and power is liberation and use of the diversity of individual capacities in initiative, planning, foresight, vigor and endurance. Personality must be educated, and personality cannot be educated by confining its operations to technical and specialized things, or to the less important relationships of life. Full education comes only when there is a responsible share on the part of each person, in proportion to capacity, in shaping the aims and policies of the social groups to which he belongs. This fact fixes the significance of democracy. It cannot be conceived as a sectarian or racial thing nor as a consecration of some form of government [that] has already attained constitutional sanction. It is but a name for the fact that human nature is developed only when its elements take part in directing things [that] are common, things for the sake of which men and women form groups — families, industrial companies, governments, churches, scientific associations and so on. The principle holds as much of one form of association, say in industry and commerce, as it does in government. (Dewey 1920: 199-200)*

Education is so important because it can transform character as well as overcome ignorance; it can help people to see why a better future for all requires cooperation instead of animosity and separation. Schools must foster recognition of cross-difference commonalities (not identities) as well as respect for democratically tolerable differences as important learning objectives.

> *A curriculum [that] acknowledges the social responsibilities of education must present situations where problems are relevant to the problems of living together, and where observation and information are calculated to develop social insight and interest. (Dewey 1916: 226)*

To be effective in cultivating the skills, experience, and understanding that will allow citizens to be effective participants in active processes of social inquiry and democratic decision making, ongoing educational processes must be critically multicultural, enhance capacities to gather and to evaluate information, and develop skills in cross-difference collaborative conversations. It is these conversations that can help participants to bring out areas of common interests, values, and goals while respectfully expressing, hearing, and responding to disagreements.[13]

But education for democracy must go beyond the critically multicultural classroom if it is to be effective. Service-learning can help students move beyond the abstract, theoretical stage of understanding that so often reflects their lack of broader life experience. It can help them to discover real human needs and better cooperative possibilities within the wider community. It can help them to discover and to ground a personal impulse toward lifelong, active citizen participation in meeting those needs and in realizing those possibilities — Dewey's democratic impulse. And it can help them to appreciate their present level of developed efficacy relative to that inner impulse and to focus their aspirations for further growth in knowledge, skills, relationships, and transformative achievements into a meaningful, purposive life plan.

Similarly, active participation in democratic change-focused, cross-difference coalitions can make an important contribution within a lifelong educational process, helping to change biases and to overcome resentments from the past. Over time, cooperative educational experience in such cross-difference coalitions can also help to build the habits and the relationships that form the basis for more deeply democratic communities of daily life that themselves meet certain basic human needs and become the focus of interpersonal loyalties and shared hopes.

> *Associated or joint activity is a condition of the creation of a community. But association itself is physical and organic, while communal life is moral, that is, emotionally, intellectually, consciously sustained. . . . "We" and "our" exist only when the consequences of combined action are perceived and become an object of desire and effort, just as "I" and "mine" appear on the scene when a distinctive share in mutual action is consciously asserted or claimed. (Dewey 1927: 330)*

Unlike short-term, narrowly focused coalitions, such communities of commitment can stabilize the struggle over the long period of time deeply democratic change can be expected to take, especially in the face of organized and powerful opposition.

As Dewey's analysis of the democratic ideal suggests, such an analytic of the transformative potential of lifelong democratic education is not utopian, in that it grows out of the best of contemporary experience, even in our era of globalized mass institutions.

> *Regarded as an idea, democracy is not an alternative to other principles of associated life. It is the ideal of community life itself. It is an ideal in the only intelligible sense of an ideal: namely, the tendency and movement of some thing [that] exists carried to its final limit, viewed as completed, perfected. Since things do not attain such fulfillment but are in actuality distracted and interfered with, democracy in this sense is not a fact and never will be. But neither in this sense is there or has there ever been anything [that] is a community in its full measure, a community unalloyed by alien elements. The idea or ideal of a community presents, however, actual phases of associated life as they are freed from restrictive and disturbing*

*elements, and are contemplated as having attained their limit of develop-
ment. Wherever there is conjoint activity whose consequences are appreciated as good by all singular persons who take part in it, and where the
realization of the good is such as to effect an energetic desire and effort to
sustain it in being just because it is a good shared by all, there is so far a
community. The clear consciousness of a communal life, in all its implications, constitutes the ideal of democracy. (Dewey 1927: 328)*

Active participation of citizens in ongoing processes of deepening democracy within their particular local communities, as well as within the translocal
movements that link these efforts, is desirable because it has the potential
to educate character, as well as to help citizens develop the knowledge and
the shared will to cooperatively solve real and imperative problems.

## Problems in Reevaluating Goals

Whether such democratic citizen participation occurs within hostile,
antidemocratic contexts of transformative struggle, within cross-difference
change coalitions that are generally accepted as legitimate in "formally
democratic" societies, or within emerging institutionalized processes of a
more deeply democratic character, problems in conceptualizing and progressively reevaluating goals, objectives, and strategies within particular,
dynamic contexts must be effectively addressed. Here again, Deweyan pragmatism offers invaluable guidance. First, it leads participants to expect that
there is no cookbook solution to the problems that activate their transformative efforts, but rather that they must undertake a process of collaborative inquiry to find the solution that is uniquely most effective in meeting
their needs.

*Morals is not a catalogue of acts nor a set of rules to be applied like drug-
store prescriptions or cook-book recipes. The need in morals is for specific
methods of inquiry and of contrivance: Methods of inquiry to locate difficulties and evils; methods of contrivance to form plans to be used as working hypotheses in dealing with them. And the pragmatic import of the logic
of individualized situations, each having its own irreplaceable good and
principle, is to transfer the attention of theory from preoccupation with general conceptions to the problem of developing effective methods of inquiry.
(Dewey 1920: 177)*

Instead of supporting the unrealistic expectation that some generic quick fix
is available if citizen participants simply consult the right expert, Deweyan
pragmatism guides them to cooperatively create rolling "experimental"
processes of analyzing a problem, formulating an operating hypothesis,
agreeing upon a shared objective, acting together, evaluating the consequences, and formulating new hypotheses for the next stage of their ongo-

ing collaborative transformation effort.

> Let us . . . follow the pragmatic rule, and in order to discover the meaning of the idea ask for its consequences. Then it surprisingly turns out that the primary significance of the unique and morally ultimate character of the concrete situation is to transfer the weight and burden of morality to intelligence. It does not destroy responsibility; it only locates it. A moral situation is one in which judgment and choice are required antecedently to overt action. The practical meaning of the situation — that is to say the action needed to satisfy it — is not self-evident. It has to be searched for. There are conflicting desires and alternative apparent goods. What is needed is to find the right course of action, the right good. Hence, inquiry is exacted: observation of the detailed makeup of the situation; analysis into its diverse factors; clarification of what is obscure; discounting of the more insistent and vivid traits; tracing the consequences of the various modes of action that suggest themselves; regarding the decision reached as hypothetical and tentative until the anticipated or supposed consequences [that] led to its adoption have been squared with actual consequences. This inquiry is intelligence. (Dewey 1920: 173)

Clarifying its larger purposes as well as the practical meaning of the democratic ideal is one of the important outcomes a community of active citizen participants will achieve if it employs Dewey's approach effectively; thus, it will progressively broaden its unavoidably limited initial vision and understanding.

> Progress is sometimes thought of as consisting in getting nearer to ends already sought. But this is a minor form of progress, for it requires only improvement of the means of action or technical advance. More important modes of progress consist in enriching prior purposes and in forming new ones. (Dewey 1916: 231)

Given that active citizen participants cannot know in advance what resources they may need at some future point, Dewey wisely advises them to make choices that do not preclude future desirable choices.

> Every condition that has to be brought into existence in order to serve as means is, in that connection, an object of desire and an end-in-view, while the end actually reached is a means to future ends as well as a test of valuations previously made. Since the end attained is a condition of further existential occurrences, it must be appraised as a potential obstacle and potential resource. (1938: 229)

Here again, realism about the unpredictable challenges of democratic participation in effective direction of change, not only within local constraints but also within those created by our democratically deficient global "super-context," requires us to use wisdom and care with our own and others' time, energies, resources, and hope. It requires that we always choose for sustainability — social, existential, environmental.

## Conclusion

All of these considerations suggest not only that the ongoing, active participation of citizens in shaping the terms of their shared social life is required by the meaning of th? now globally significant ideal of democracy but also that it is feasible in a wide variety of interlinked contexts of struggle to transform past-born problem situations in ways that promise all a fuller experience of human flourishing in the future. Deweyan pragmatism offers valuable lessons and general guidance for ensuring that such active citizen participation is both democratic and effective in a wide variety of contexts. But it also reminds us that, in the end, the challenges of social inquiry and choice in shaping a preferable future must rest as much as possible on the shoulders of those who will bear the consequences. This is why service-learning and the lifelong democratic impulse to active citizen participation service-learning may help to awaken is so important: It offers those shoulders of the future invaluable opportunities for developing a democratic character, an appreciation of real diversity, an imagination that can discover the better possibilities within what is, and the will to make a difference.

### Notes

1. "Ontological rootlessness" is my own term for the uneasy experience of lacking deep, lasting, valued connections to any particular place on the planet and to any particular network of human persons, a situation in which modern people often find themselves due to repeatedly relocating for higher education and job opportunities. Cornel West develops the concept of "existential nihilism," especially as many people experience it in America's central cities, in his Race Matters (1993).

2. Dewey discusses the democratic impulse in many of his writings. Two of his most accessible books that, taken together, develop Dewey's conception of the democratic impulse roughly as I have described it are The Public and Its Problems (1927) and Theory of Valuation (1939).

3. In his last book, Where Do We Go From Here: Chaos or Community? (1967), Martin Luther King, Jr., suggested that part of the impulse toward what he called "the worldwide freedom revolution" came from the experience in higher education at Western universities of future leaders of less powerful societies, including both their classroom studies of democratic theory and their experience of daily life in the West, with its democratic strengths and its deficiencies.

4. I refer in particular to recent heavy-handed efforts by the International Monetary Fund to reshape government as well as banking practices and institutions throughout posttotalitarian Eastern Europe and in several economically troubled Asian countries in conformity with Western "formally democratic" and capitalistic models. One of the most influential economic theorists leading this effort who sees Western models as historically validated universal ideals and localized experimentation involving citizen participants as dangerous is Harvard economist Jeffrey Sachs; see, for example, his *Poland's Jump to the Market Economy* (1993).

5. See Ludwig Wittgenstein's *Philosophical Investigations* (1953), in which he analyzes the concept "game," discovering that there is no single set of necessary and sufficient universal characteristics that all of the activities we call games share, but rather that they are interrelated like the faces of members of a family in a photograph, in which some share a type of nose, others a type of chin, and others a general way of looking at the camera. My claim here is that like games, the various versions of the democratic ideal and of cooperative processes and institutions guided by it share no universal characteristics, but are interlinked instead by what Wittgenstein called patterns of "family resemblance."

6. At a recent conference on "Democracy and the Post-Totalitarian Experience" in Karpacz, Poland (May 1998), in which I had the honor of participating, and from which I learned a great deal, Leszek Koczanowicz of the University of Opole, Opole/Lower Silesian University College of Education, Wroclaw, Poland, presented a persuasive paper entitled "In the Name of the Nation . . . In the Name of the Market: What Was Our Revolution For?" In it he discussed widespread discontent among many of the Solidarity Movement's original participants with the lack of citizen participation in shaping Poland's way forward toward democracy, and with an associated lack of a deeper transformation in attitudes and norms of community life. Koczanowicz's paper and others presented at that conference will be published in a forthcoming volume of *Central European Value Studies* from Editions Rodopi of Amsterdam and Atlanta. The contrasting sense that Poland's "transition to democracy" is a model for other posttotalitarian societies in Eastern Europe is expressed by Jeffrey Sachs (1993) and many other neoclassical capitalist economists.

7. For one among many locations in which Dewey expresses his confidence that "the cure for the problems of democracy is more democracy," see *The Public and Its Problems* (1927). For my own more detailed discussion of what "a deeper democracy" entails and how it can be fostered, see my *Deep Democracy: Community, Diversity, and Transformation* (1999).

8. See Julius Nyerere's experience-based insights about the limitations of revolution as a method of changing hearts and minds in his *Freedom and Unity* (1968).

9. Dewey discusses this uniqueness of moral situation that makes intelligent, situational problem solving necessary in many places, including in *Reconstruction in Philosophy* (1920), *Experience and Nature* (1925), *The Public and Its Problems* (1927), *The Quest for Certainty* (1929), and *Theory of Valuation* (1939).

10. For empirical evidence for my claim that active citizen participation throughout public planning processes helps to prevent the formation of NIMBY groups, and also eases adoption and implementation of new public policies, see David Woods's "Lynnwood Legacy: A Collaborative Planning Model for the 1990s" (1993).

11. For a thoughtful theoretical discussion of case studies of adversarial blocking in public policy development and of cooperative participatory alternatives, see Daniel Kemmis's *Community and the Politics of Place* (1992).

12. I do not use "objective" and "subjective" in this discussion as dualistic polar opposites, but rather, following Dewey, as interlinked poles within a larger whole approach to inquiry about human flourishing.

13. For a fuller discussion of my views on the rationale and methods of critical multiculturalism in education, see my "Educational Multiculturalism, Critical Pluralism, and Deep Democracy" (1998).

## References

Dewey, John. (1916). *Democracy and Education*. Republished in a critical edition in *John Dewey: The Middle Works, Vol. 9*, edited by Jo Ann Boydston. Carbondale, IL: Southern Illinois University Press, 1985.

—————. (1920). *Reconstruction in Philosophy*. Republished in a critical edition in *John Dewey: The Middle Works, Vol. 12*, edited by Jo Ann Boydston. Carbondale, IL: Southern Illinois University Press, 1988.

—————. (1925). *Experience and Nature*. Republished in a critical edition in *John Dewey: The Later Works, Vol. 1*, edited by Jo Ann Boydston. Carbondale, IL: Southern Illinois University Press, 1981.

—————. (1927). *The Public and Its Problems*. Republished in a critical edition in *John Dewey: The Later Works, Vol. 2*, edited by Jo Ann Boydston. Carbondale, IL: Southern Illinois University Press, 1988.

—————. (1929). *The Quest for Certainty*. Republished in a critical edition in *John Dewey: The Later Works, Vol. 4*, edited by Jo Ann Boydston. Carbondale, IL: Southern Illinois University Press, 1988.

—————. (1939). *Theory of Valuation*. Republished in a critical edition in *John Dewey: The Middle Works, Vol. 13*, edited by Jo Ann Boydston. Carbondale, IL: Southern Illinois University Press, 1991.

Green, Judith M. (1998). "Educational Multiculturalism, Critical Pluralism, and Deep Democracy." In *Theorizing Multiculturalism: A Guide to the Current Debate*, edited by Cynthia Willett, pp. 422-448. New York, NY: Blackwell Publishers.

—————. (1999). *Deep Democracy: Community, Diversity, and Transformation*. Lanham, MD: Rowman & Littlefield.

Kemmis, Daniel. (1990). *Community and the Politics of Place*. Norman, OK: University of Oklahoma Press.

King, Martin Luther, Jr. (1967). *Where Do We Go From Here: Chaos or Community?* New York, NY: Harper & Row.

Nyerere, Julius. (1968). *Freedom and Unity.* New York, NY: Oxford University Press.

Sachs, Jeffrey. (1993). *Poland's Jump to the Market Economy.* Cambridge, MA: MIT Press.

West, Cornel. (1993). *Race Matters.* New York, NY: Vintage.

Wittgenstein, Ludwig. (1953). *Philosophical Investigations.* New York, NY: Macmillan.

Woods, David. (June 1993). "Lynnwood Legacy: A Collaborative Planning Model for the 1990s." *Urban Design and Planning* 7: 13-16.

# Service-Learning as a Vehicle for Teaching Philosophy

by Eugene J. Valentine

In what follows, I will share some thoughts on service-learning as a vehicle for teaching philosophy. By "service-learning," I mean integrating service and academic study into a unified learning experience. By "teaching philosophy," I mean teaching concepts, dispositions, and skills that will enable students to better acquire wisdom. By "wisdom," I mean the intelligence to live well.[1]

To the extent that we view living well, or the well-lived life, as a life of contemplation, we will strive to teach our students the concepts, dispositions, and skills that will enable them to acquire theoretical wisdom. In a logic course, for example, we might have our students serve as tutors in logic to persons who are in need of tutoring, as this would be an excellent vehicle to help those students to acquire theoretical wisdom in this area.

To the extent that we view living well, or the well-lived life, as a life of action, we will strive to teach our students the concepts, dispositions, and skills that will enable them to acquire practical wisdom. In a logic course, for example, we might have our students serve as referees for debates in primary or secondary school civics classes, as this would be an excellent vehicle for helping our students to acquire what might rightly be called practical wisdom in logic.

Whatever combination of theoretical and practical wisdom we are trying to imbue, however, we will want our students to serve others whose lives, or whose ways of being in the world, are such that serving them will inform, reinforce, or enhance our students' efforts to acquire a desired wisdom.

In a philosophy of sport course, our students might serve injured athletes or athletes with special needs. In a feminist philosophy course, our students might serve residents of a domestic violence shelter. In an environmental philosophy course, our students might serve a group of endangered animals or a polluted stream. In a philosophy of law course, our students might serve clients of a legal services program. In an existentialism course, our students might serve persons who are physically disabled or homeless, whereas in a course on Marx, our students might serve both wealthy residents of nursing homes and poor residents of nursing homes. In an ethics course, where students enter into a moral dialogue with views other than their own, our students might perform interracial or interfaith service at a community center.

In a philosophy course on the relationship between the well-lived life and the good community, students might perform any of the services above, and many more, so long as the service performed would inform, reinforce, or enhance their efforts to acquire that combination of theoretical and practical wisdom that would count as civic wisdom (see "Possible Service Opportunities" on pages 162-163 for a partial list of service options). Such a course would at once be a philosophy course, a civic education course, and a service-learning course. It is on such a philosophy/civic education/service-learning course that I will focus the remainder of my remarks in exploring service-learning as a vehicle for teaching philosophy.[2]

## Philosophical Framework of the Course

A highly effective way to use service-learning as a vehicle for teaching philosophy is to construct an explicit philosophical framework for students to think about service-learning as they serve. Students should be encouraged to raise philosophical questions about this framework and, upon completion of their service, should be encouraged to produce reasoned arguments as to why this framework should be expanded, modified, or abandoned. This exercise in philosophical criticism provides students with a valuable philosophical learning experience.[3]

At the first meeting of my philosophy/civic education/service-learning course, I introduce students to Aristotle's distinction between intellectual virtues (the disposition or habit of thinking well) and moral virtues (the disposition or habit of acting well). I try to explicate this distinction by drawing an analogous distinction between the disposition to "reflect well" and the disposition to "connect well."

I then argue that what we should first and foremost try to accomplish in civic education/service-learning courses in public institutions of higher education is the acquisition of intellectual virtues, whereas what we should first and foremost try to accomplish in a civic education/service-learning course in public institutions of primary or secondary education is the acquisition of moral virtues. I argue that institutions of higher education are institutions where students are considered to be intellectually "of age" or capable of acquiring theoretical and practical wisdom. The primary goal of a civic education/service-learning course at a public institution of higher education should be to develop the disposition to reflect well on the relationship between a well-lived life and a good community. Its goal should be to educate citizens to participate in civic dialogue concerning how we should connect our lives to the lives of others. This dialogue would include a discussion of what moral virtues we should teach primary and secondary school students. We may well acquire moral virtues in such a course (e.g., a sense of connectedness with those we serve), but it is not necessary to the success of the course that we do. Students in our civic education/service-learning courses are generally relieved when they are informed that they will not be graded on their acquisition of moral virtues, and that a complete and consistent libertarian or feminist separatist analysis of their service experience, for example, could conceivably earn them an A.[4]

The following is an example of how a student came to a fuller understanding of the distinction between intellectual and moral virtues because the distinction was explicitly built into the philosophical framework of the course. The student was, by her own account, an evangelical Christian from a dysfunctional family. She was also a 4.0 business major. She did her service with residents in a nursing home. One of the residents was a terminally ill man who was the father of her best friend from childhood. She felt a special obligation to sit down and talk to him about the positive role he had played in her life when she was a child. She did not, however, make time in her busy schedule to do so before he died.

At the end of the quarter, the student analyzed her service experience in a term paper using concepts of Kant and Hobbes. She was very clear in her own mind it was her Kantian obligation to make time to talk with her friend's father. She was equally clear, however, that her highest priority had been the Hobbesian priority to maximize the satisfaction of her passions over time. She concluded not only that she had treated her friend's father as a means to an end but that she had also treated her own parents, boyfriend, and her college education as a means to an end only. Her "real goal," she went on, was to "get north of I-70," where there were good-paying jobs with an opportunity for advancement. She recognized there was a "contradiction" between what she truly believed she ought to do and how she was actually living her life, but that if she were honest with herself, she did not see anything changing in the foreseeable future. Her use of the concepts and views of Hobbes and Kant was superb throughout her analysis of her service experience, and she received an A.

The student later told me that it was the most difficult paper that she had ever written and, to apply Aristotle's distinction, that she would have written her paper "much differently" had she thought she would be graded on her acquisition of moral virtue. It was her remarks that led me to have students evaluate the philosophic framework for the course in their term papers.

I also build into the framework of the course a distinction between service-learning experiences and traditional academic internships, as well as a characterization of the service-learning relationship I would like students to try to establish (see "Roles of Service-Learning in Civic Education" and "A Service-Learning Taxonomy" on page 164). I have students think of service-learning as an experience that has as its goal *serving* rather than *observing*. I then introduce them to what I call the "paradox" of service-learning, to wit, that "we may well learn more about ourselves and others through *serving* than through *observing*." This "paradox" helps students to think of the unique ways in which they engage themselves and others when they serve.

I characterize the particular service-learning relationship that I would have students try to establish as an I-Thou relationship, where the server tries to view the person served as a Thou, or human subject capable of moral integrity and deserving of respect. I then have them read Martin Buber on the I-Thou relationship, and have them attempt to establish such a relationship with those whom they serve. Students also try to ascertain whether it is indeed possible to establish such a relationship, and whether or not what Buber has to say about such a relationship holds true. Is it possible to relate to a resident of a nursing home who is incontinent and senile as a Thou? Is it possible to establish such a relationship with anyone? What should I do in an I-Thou relationship if the Thou asks me to pray for her to die? Is it true that I can only speak with my "whole being" in an I-Thou relationship? In short, the students use their service experiences to philosophically evaluate the very philosophical framework that guides them in their service-learning efforts.[5]

Finally, I build into the philosophical framework of the course clear guidelines for the students to follow (see "Guidelines for Service-Learning" on page 165). The first guideline is that we serve others who are "in need" as opposed to others who simply "have a need," on the grounds that the challenge of connecting our lives to the lives of other human beings across the differences created by need provides us with a greater opportunity to inform, reinforce, and enhance our efforts to acquire civic wisdom.

In discussing this guideline in class, I make a distinction between objective needs, or needs that we have by virtue of who we are (e.g., Marx's needs of humankind or species needs); and subjective needs, or needs that we in fact experience as needs (e.g., Marx's actually experienced needs or dispositional desires). We then discuss what we should do if the persons whom we serve have an objective need that they do not, in fact, experience as a need. Should we act as a Kantian "political moralist" and use coercion or manipulation to get these persons to meet their objective need, or should we act as a Kantian "moral politician" and limit ourselves to rational persuasion in our efforts to get them to meet their objective need? I then stipulate, for the purposes of trying to establish an I-Thou relationship, that we will act as moral politicians toward those whom we serve, with the provision that we may critique this stipulation in our term papers after we have completed our service.[6]

The second guideline is that we serve others in as "direct" a manner as possible, whether it be direct interpersonal service to a person or persons in need or direct "internatural" service to a herd of animals or stand of trees in need. What lies behind this guideline is the belief that direct service, while not morally superior to indirect service (fundraising, clerical work, or lab analysis), provides us with experiences that better inform, reinforce, and enhance our efforts to acquire civic wisdom.[7]

In discussing this second guideline, I make note of Nietzsche's call for us to become an "artistic Socrates" — one who marries aesthetic nuance with rational analysis — and I argue that it is through direct interpersonal or inter-natural service that we can best acquire the skills of an artistic Socrates. It is not uncommon to find in term papers at the end of the quarter references to this marriage of nuance and analysis by both liberal and conservative students who have served youth at risk. Liberal students, who are predisposed to see social issues in terms of a lack of opportunities, find themselves wrestling with the issue of values. Conservative students, who are predisposed to see social issues in terms of a lack of values, find themselves wrestling with the issue of opportunities. In both cases, students leave the course with a more nuanced analysis of social issues, often weaving together quantitative and qualitative characterizations of their service experience.

The third guideline is that we serve others, whenever possible, who are not members of our "immediate" communities. This guideline is put forth on two separate grounds. The first is the pragmatic ground that it works against the fragmentation of human beings along the lines of race, gender, class, and religion.[8]

The second is the philosophical ground that it provides students with richer experiences with which to evaluate postmodern depictions of reason as pervasively racial, gendered, or ethnocentric in character. A case in point would be the service experiences of an African-American student who served as a tutor and mentor to a 17-year-old European-American girl living in "The Bottoms," an area of shacks, junk cars, and confederate flags located in a floodplain of the Scioto River about 15 miles from campus. The girl lived in a foster home and was a client of Children's Services. She had dropped out of school, and in less than a year she would be on her own. My student spent 40 hours tutoring her in English and math at her home or at a local pizza parlor up on the highway.

The student wrote in her term paper that she had chosen Children's Services as a service option because she knew she should try to serve persons outside her immediate community and few, if any, African-American teenagers were clients of the agency. She also wrote of the trepidation she felt when she first drove out to where the girl lived and of her wish that she had stayed "a little closer to home." She soon discovered that the girl was functionally illiterate. She then shared with the girl the fact that when this student was 17, she too could not read, and she spoke of the ways in which this had caused her great pain and embarrassment. The recognition that they had something very significant in common led to an openness and trust between them. This in turn facilitated their efforts to work together to get the girl on the road to literacy.

This openness and trust, however, also facilitated what the African-American student characterized as a "meeting of the minds" on the subject of the confederate flag. She wrote:

> We didn't agree on everything. She convinced me that for most white people the flag was not about the slave times, but about feeling good about themselves. I convinced her that there would be no Confederate flag without the slave times. I also think I convinced her that not just black people, but anyone who really thought about it, would have to agree that waving that particular flag is not the best way for people to feel good about [themselves]. She might still date a guy with a flag, but I don't think that she would ever personally have one.[9]

It is a little more than four years ago that the student wrote the above. This fall she encountered the girl she had served. The girl is now a young woman and an LPN, and she continues to eschew the Confederate flag. This student's experience is typical of the approximately 100 African-American and European-American students who have performed interracial service at Shawnee State over the past eight years. The journals, term papers, and classroom comments of these students indicate that such "meetings of the mind" as reported above are far more frequent than many postmodern thinkers would have us believe.

For example, an African-American Hebrew Pentecostal who helped elderly European-American Christians prepare their income tax returns at a senior citizens center commented, "I believe my religion is closer to the truth than theirs, but when you stop to think about it, we mostly believe in the same thing." Similarly, an African-American female student who served a European-American male student with cerebral palsy as a note taker/mentor, remarked that the two of them had a number of disagreements on issues having to do with physical disability and race. She continued, "These disagreements did not always get resolved, but through them we came to see the human being in each other." A European-American male, who performed his service at the 14th Street Community Center, wrote of being cast as a whip-wielding slave overseer in a play commemorating Black History Month: "Even without the whip, it would have been a very difficult part for me to play. For the first time, the words about the slave owner degrading himself more than he degrades the slave really hit home." A European-American female student who performed her service at the center wrote of a "lock-in" she helped to chaperone:

> Kids come in with their sleeping gear. They dance and socialize. Pizza gets delivered around 11 pm and then the doors are locked. The kids get into their sleeping bags and blankets and talk late into the night. As they get

tired, they let their defenses down. I remember three young boys in the third or fourth grade talking about whether their fathers really loved them. None of the fathers had ever lived with [his son], or did things with [him] on a regular basis. Each of the boys, in turn, raised the possibility that his father did love him, but one or both of the other boys reminded him of the fact that his father almost never came around.

There is a lot of talk about how the black community is different from the white community because black children have a male presence in their lives through their uncles, grandfathers, and ministers. I've thought a lot about this and I think black kids miss their fathers just as much as white kids miss theirs. And I don't have any problem sharing this view with black people.

The service-learning experiences recorded above by no means provide us with a "crucial experiment" for the refutation of postmodern theories of racial or ethnic inter⌐ubjective agreement in favor of philosophical essentialism, or even Wittgenstein's notion of family resemblances. These experiences do, however, inform, reinforce, and enhance our students' efforts to acquire wisdom concerning the role that is played by our race, gender, or ethnicity when we reason. If William James is right, and sport can serve as the moral equivalent of war, service-learning can serve as the moral equivalent of multicultural war.

## Philosophical Content of the Course

As stated above, the philosophical content of the course being discussed here is the relationship between a well-lived life and a good community. I will now turn to discussion of how the service experiences of students enrolled in this course inform, reinforce, or enhance their efforts to achieve civic wisdom concerning this relationship.

In the course, we study four philosophical paradigms for reflecting upon the relationship between a well-lived life and a good community. Two of them are the premodern paradigms of Plato and Aristotle, and two are the modern paradigms of Hobbes and Kant.

As we perform our service, we examine the various concepts with which Plato and Aristotle, and subsequently Hobbes and Kant, think through the relationship between the well-lived life and the good community. A short list of these concepts would include natural capacities, virtues (including self-discipline), virtue ethics, final causes, natural predispositions, self-realization, passions (including self-esteem), ethical relativism, opportunities, values, moral reason, autonomy, and self-respect.

We begin by noting that the efforts of Plato and Aristotle to think through the relationship between a well-lived life and a good community were inspired by the efforts of Socrates to revitalize the Athenian *polis* through a rational examination of the nature of virtue and the virtuous life. We also note that the process by which Socrates examined the nature of virtue was analogous to the process of service-learning. Socrates "served" his fellow Athenians by disabusing them of the notion that they knew what virtue was when, in reality, they did not. Having helped them remove this obstacle to their thinking about virtue, Socrates then worked together with them on a joint effort to learn about the nature of virtue or the virtuous life.

Book I of the *Republic* begins with a casual conversation between Socrates and Cephalus in which Plato introduces the concept of passion and argues that we are never more pathological or passive than when we are passionate. In Book IX, the last book of the *Republic,* Plato argues that we should never make the satisfaction of our passions our highest priority in life. If we are to live well, we must put our passions to sleep. At this point, we begin to record in our journals our thoughts about the respective priorities that we and the persons whom we serve place upon satisfying our passions.

We then juxtapose the views of Plato on the passions with the views of Socrates's contemporary Thucydides. Thucydides, like his modern translator Hobbes, holds that our passions set the agenda for our lives whether we like it or not. Whereas Socrates, Plato, and Aristotle all try to rationally examine the nature of virtue and the well-lived life, Thucydides and Hobbes hold that any effort to examine the nature of virtue or the well-lived life can be reduced to an examination of the passions of the parties making the effort. Finally, we remark that the role of our passions in living a well-lived life and in building a good community is a perennial issue in non-Western traditions as well.[10]

We then turn our attention to Plato's arguments in Book II for a division of labor, and note that Plato argues for this division on the grounds that people have different natural capacities. Indeed, it is Plato's position that we are radically different by nature, with some of us hardly fit by nature for human companionship. Is it possible that the reason some of us are servers and some of us are in need of service is that we are different by nature? To what extent can we explain the differences that we observe in the wealth, power, and status of members of our community in terms of their having different natural capacities? (See "Some Remarks on Writing Our Term Papers" on page 166 for a partial list of questions that students might ask themselves in the course.)

Service-learning students who serve learning-disabled students, students who have failed the state ninth grade proficiency exam, and GED and Adult Basic Education students are particularly engaged by questions concerning natural capacities. As one of the students who was a tutor in a learning-disabled class wrote:

> There are all sorts of kids in the class. Some are truly disabled by nature, but others are simply discipline problems, and some of the minority kids seem to be in the class because it is the path of least resistance for them and for their teachers. I think we make too much out of kids being different by nature, but at least some of the time they are.

Another student served several Adult Basic Education students who were recovering alcoholics. When asked whether these students might be different from him by nature because of a genetic predisposition to alcoholism, he replied:

> My father and my uncle are alcoholics, and when they drink things can get pretty bad. When I was 12 my mother sat me down and told me that alcoholism runs in families and that if I tried to drink, I might become an alcoholic too. She asked me if that was the kind of person that I wanted to be. I have never taken a drink. The main difference between me and the students I tutor is the values that my mother taught me.[11]

This young man's response provided us with a timely introduction to Plato's own views on the centrality of virtues, dispositions, or character traits in a well-lived life. For Plato, natural capacities represent our first nature, but virtues or character traits represent our second nature. Virtues are the key to living the well-lived life and forming the good community, as they determine how well we employ our natural capacities.

Through reading further in Book II of the *Republic*, we determine that, for Plato, the primary role of the *polis* is to constitute the second nature of its citizens through the teaching of virtues. For one student, the issue of constituting citizens through the teaching of virtues was raised by the service that he performed at the 14th Street Community Center, which serves a low-income, historically African-American community.

The student was a European-American male whose steelworker father and homemaker mother had taught him, as he grew up, that people should not be judged by the color of their skin. While he was driving a van load of youth down to Shawnee State to see a basketball game, a seven-year-old African-American youth called him a "fat honky." The student was shocked and a little angry, but he did not let his emotions get the best of him. He asked the youth in a civil tone to take a seat, which the youth initially refused to do. Later, at the game, the student took the youth aside and explained to him that what he said was wrong and that he could not take any more trips on the van unless he was respectful and obeyed the rules. The youth feigned indifference, but obeyed the rules on the return trip.

The next day in class, the student explained the incident with the youth in the following words: "That don't come from a kid. That comes from what a kid sees and hears around him, starting with the adults. What *does* come from a kid is trying to get a reaction, and that is how I am trying to deal with it." Over the course of the next 10 weeks, the student insisted that the youth abide by the rules of the center. At the same time, he was civil and helpful to the youth, even on those occasions when the antics of the youth and his friends caught the student "off guard." At the end of his service, the student wrote in his journal about how his parents had raised him not to be a racist, and followed it with the words "I am not a racist!!!"

The student shared the above journal entry with the class, and a discussion took place regarding what it means to be a racist. Although a number of students argued that a racist was anyone who had any racist thoughts or feelings, a slight majority of students, black and white, came to the conclusion that if it is our second nature to treat persons of other races with respect and dignity, then we are not racists. I responded by asserting that we had just had an introduction to virtue ethics.

When we read Plato on virtue ethics, we invariably have a discussion as to whether the family or the community plays a greater role in constituting the character of the young. The majority of the students usually conclude that even if the family plays the greatest role, the values taught within the family must be reinforced in the community to ensure that these values will "take." One class characterized this position as a "partial" victory for Plato.

Students whose service involves issues of teen pregnancy and drug use most often argue that the values taught at home must be reinforced outside the home. An African-American student who served at the Community Center directing a Christmas play, for example, told the class of a conversation she had had with a 40-year-old drug addict who dropped by to watch rehearsals. He stated that it had always been possible to buy drugs on the street corner outside the center, but that what had changed in the last 20 years was the fact that people in the community no longer remonstrated with youth who bought from, or hung out with, drug dealers.

A student who mentored secondary school students who were already parents similarly juxtaposed the roles of the home and the community in her term paper:

> Parents are important, but Plato is right when he says that the community plays an important part in shaping our children. This reminds me of a line from the movie **True Lies**, where a friend consoles a father who found out that his little girl was stealing. The friend tells him that he and his wife are not her parents anymore, that now her parents are "Axel Rose and Madonna."

Finally, a student who served women at the Domestic Violence Task Force Shelter brought out some of the subtle ways our community "teaches values." Drawing upon a supplemental reading on community-oriented policing (i.e., the role of the police is to assist the community in its efforts to inculcate and reinforce the community's values) the student wrote:

> As far as the community is concerned, I think we need to adopt the Platonic concept of community policing. All too often we say, "we shouldn't get involved" or "it's not my problem." I think the community needs to stand up to the abusers to let them know that their actions are unacceptable. Friends, neighbors, coworkers, even strangers need to get involved. I think this would help the women themselves to see that the actions of the abuser are not acceptable, and perhaps make them more apt to leave. Many of the women I dealt with have said it was their fault. Perhaps if more people stepped in, men and women would both get the message that abuse is not acceptable.

We conclude our discussion of Plato's view that virtues matter most by asking ourselves questions such as the following: To what extent can we characterize the differences that exist between ourselves and the persons we serve, or more generally, the differences that exist in health, wealth, power, and status among members of our community in terms of the values or virtues of individuals? What role do the values or virtues of our workforce play in global economic competition? What role do our own values play in how we respond to negative service experiences? More generally, what role do the values or virtues of our fellow citizens play in determining how they respond to negative experiences in their lives? As one student asked, "Why is it that Americans are increasingly 'going postal'?"

Our discussion of Aristotle's views on the well-lived life and the good community focuses on the concepts of final cause, natural predisposition, and self-realization that he uses to argue for his thesis that we are *polis* animals. To help students understand Aristotle's thesis that we are predisposed by nature to live in political communities and do the good of these communities, we draw a number of philosophical distinctions. We distinguish between a natural predisposition and a Platonic virtue (Aristotle would claim that a biological predisposition or tendency is experienced differently from a characterlogical disposition or habit), a Hobbesian passion (a genetic predisposition does not necessarily have pleasure as its end, goal, or purpose), and a Kantian duty (a predisposition is not something we consciously will). To make the strongest case that we can in support of Aristotle's thesis, we read the work of E.O. Wilson on the sociobiology of reciprocal altruism (Wilson 1978).

It is the students' own service experiences, however, that prove pivotal to their understanding and evaluation of Aristotle's thesis. When we discuss how we might best characterize Aristotle's thesis in terms of their service experience, students usually gravitate toward the notion of "belonging."

Thus, they ask themselves whether they, or the persons they served, experienced a predisposition to "belong" to a political community. I, in turn, encourage their use of this notion by pointing out that the Greek term for citizen is *polites*, which literally means one who belongs to a *polis*. One sports studies student served in the summer recreation program at Happy Hearts, a local school for mentally retarded children. She noted in her journal that the children seemed to have a strong drive to be "accepted," which, when it came to forming teams, became a strong drive to "contribute." She then quoted from the Walt Disney video *The Mighty Ducks*, in which the coach (who happens to be performing court-mandated community service) states, "A team isn't a bunch of kids out to win. A team is something you belong to. It's something you feel. It's something you have to earn."

Another student who served at the community center ran headlong into the issue of gang wannabes, an inclination he tried to characterize in terms of a natural predisposition to belong to a political community. Portsmouth does not have street gangs per se, but the student encountered shifting constellations of youth who identified themselves with a drug enterprise or a sector of public housing. These constellations of youth called themselves "gangs" and engaged in gang-like behavior. The student witnessed a 16-year-old boy in one of these self-proclaimed gangs order a 12-year-old boy in the same gang to beat up another 12-year-old who was the boy's classmate and friend, but who was not a member of the gang. With tears in his eyes, the boy set out to pummel his friend but, due to the intervention of the student, allowed his friend to leave relatively unscathed. The student wrote that what he had witnessed was a political predisposition "unperfected by virtue." To support his characterization, he quoted a *Time* magazine article on Stanley "tookie" Williams, a cofounder of the Crips, the nation's largest, and arguably most violent, street gang. On death row, Williams has written a series of children's books against gang violence, one of which is entitled *Gangs and Wanting to Belong*. In the book, he writes, "As much as you might want to fit in, don't join a gang. You won't find what you are looking for. All you will find is trouble, pain, and sadness. I know. I did" (Willwerth 1996: 58).

We conclude our discussion of Aristotle by asking ourselves questions such as the following: Were the people we served in need because of biological predispositions that had not been perfected by virtues? Were we able to act appropriately toward those whom we served, even though our service experience was frustrating and unpleasant, because of a biological predisposition to do the good of our community?[12]

Our discussion of Hobbes and the modern scientific conception of the well-lived life and the good community begins with Hobbes's assertion that "good" is that which is the object of our appetites, and "evil" is that which is the object of our aversions. Thus, the moral philosophies of Plato and

Aristotle, Hobbes tells us, are but descriptions of their particular passions. When it comes to reflecting on the nature of the virtuous life, our reason is but a scout or spy for our passions.

As physical beings in a physical world, our reason instructs us how to move toward the objects of our appetites and desires, and how to move "fromward" the objects of our hates and aversions. The well-lived life is one in which we maximize the satisfaction of our passions over time, and the good community is one that provides us with the opportunity to do so. This introduction to the modern scientific worldview, with its attendant ethical relativism, is both theoretically appealing and practically repugnant to many students, and their service experiences provide an arena in which to grapple with this tension.

One student, who served in a nursing home, wrote the following in her term paper:

> Hobbes was right about our appetites and aversions. I wanted to move fromward the smell of feces and fromward the company of a man with Alzheimer's. But I didn't. Nor do I believe that I stayed because my reason told me that that was the best way to satisfy my passions over time. I stayed because of the values that my parents taught me growing up. You don't walk away just because something is unpleasant. You don't quit.
>
> Being virtuous isn't always pleasant. Didn't Aristotle say that courage was a painful virtue?

Another student, who served as an Adult Basic Education tutor, wrote how he dealt with the fear and anger he experienced serving persons who were there only because it was required of them to receive public assistance:

> I didn't avoid them, and I didn't blow up at them. The reason was simple. I wanted to complete this course with a good grade. I am almost 30 years old, and I am beginning to feel a little foolish about not having my college degree.
>
> I had combat tours in Panama and Iraq when I was in the service. It is not easy to walk off into a situation where you think that your life, whatever you've made of it, could be over. I am sorry to say, however, that satisfying my passions is what got me through. The reason that I would not quit or desert is that I knew I would be unable to face my comrades, or my family or friends again. It was a classic case of death before dishonor, but it was a dishonor based on the judgment of others. Our self-esteem is based mostly upon what other people think of us.

These two students, although characterizing their service experiences in different manners, are giving serious thought to what factors motivate our actions. Are values something separate from passions? Can values lead us to act independent of, and possibly contrary to, our passions? Can passions be used to inculcate values? To what extent can we characterize the differences that exist between members of our community in terms of their ability to satisfy their passions prudently? The first student, although she wrote about her values' playing an independent role in motivating her actions, also wrote, "I was surprised to learn to what degree I am a Hobbesian thinker. Most of the time I did things, not because of the values I was raised with, but because I wanted my passions or needs to be met." The second student, although he wrote about overcoming adversity in terms of maximizing the satisfaction of his passions over time, also wrote, "As I evolve, I think that I am learning that the satisfaction of my passions, including feeling good about what other people think of me, is not as much of a priority in my life as it once was. I now realize what Cephalus was speaking of."

A concomitant issue raised by Plato and Aristotle, on the one hand, and by Hobbes, on the other, is whether the persons we serve, and by extension our community as a whole, are more in need of values or opportunities. This issue has, to a great extent, informed the debate between conservatives and liberals over the last 20 years. One student, a swarthy ex-Marine who was raised on a farm, weighed in heavily on the side of values until he performed his service as a life guard at the McKinley Memorial Swimming Pool. This historically African-American pool was built by the city of Portsmouth after two McKinley brothers drowned while swimming in the Ohio River at a time when the only swimming pool in town was a private "whites only" pool. One day when the student was vacuuming the pool prior to its opening, a carload of whites drove by and shouted "nigger" at him. He recorded the experience in his journal as follows:

> At first, I thought it was funny. I used to get in fights with blacks when I was growing up. Then I started to get angry. Finally, I started to think what it must feel like to be black. The majority of people in town are white, and they have almost all of the power. There are fewer opportunities for blacks, including the opportunity to feel good about themselves.

Another student, who was a beauty pageant winner from a wealthy suburban high school, was primarily drawn to the notion of opportunities before she performed her service in our rust-belt town tutoring high school students who had not yet passed their state-mandated ninth grade proficiency exam. She wrote the following in her term paper:

> For every student who did try, five or six didn't try. They wanted you to do their exercises for them, and they did not do any exercises at home. Some of these students have been in this tutoring program for three years now. These students have roofs over their heads and food to eat. Many of them have their own cars. Several of them might be slow, or poor test takers, but

*most of them just don't try. They have poor work habits. They have a poor work ethic, as the Greeks would say. They have the opportunity to feel good about themselves by passing the exam, but they won't work at it.*

*It's not a question of self-esteem, it's a question of self-discipline. When I competed in pageants, I spent almost two hours a day on the stairmaster and in the weight room. I always placed well in bathing suit competitions. I had no self-esteem problem. If they worked as hard as I did, they would-n't have any self-esteem problem either.*

This student gave additional voice to her views in the classroom after our local school board announced that no students would be allowed to take part in high school graduation ceremonies unless they passed their ninth grade proficiency exam. She strongly supported the school board's decision. A discussion ensued among members of our class about the decision, and it was informed by the personal, yet nonegoistic experiences of the students. It was also characterized by both a passion and a lucidity not usually found in classroom discussions. What follows is a paraphrase of the discussion.

*The proficiency tutor began by pointing out that we had to take into consideration the symbolic effect of the board's decision on the sophomores and juniors whom she tutored as well.*

*"How else do we get them to become more self-disciplined in their studies?" she asked.*

*One of her classmates, who served some of the same youth in an after-school program sponsored by Community Action, asserted, "It may be too late for them. Like Plato said, values are best taught when children are young."*

*The tutor replied, "But if we are going to teach the value of self-discipline to the young, we have to make an example of the older youth who do not have any. When you teach values, your target is much broader than the persons who are being penalized or being made an example."*

*"But what about the youth who did try," responded a classmate who served at-risk youth in a substance-abuse prevention program sponsored by the counseling center. "Aren't they being penalized unfairly?"*

*The tutor thought for a minute and replied that they probably were getting the short end of the stick, but they were few in number in comparison with the youth who simply did not try. After some verbal sparring, members of the class who had served at-risk youth agreed there was a significant "values problem" with most of these youths. They also agreed it was probably not possible to send a values message to youth without at least some kids' being unfairly denied an opportunity to feel good about themselves. They concluded that we should support the board's decision and let the chips fall where they may, providing we redoubled our efforts on behalf of students who try hard but are a little slow, and we devised new test-tak-ing procedures for students who try hard but are simply poor test takers.*

Members of the class were invigorated by the fact they had made some "real progress on a moral issue." I reminded them that our course was designed to teach intellectual virtues, including the disposition to reflect well practically. If it is successful in this respect, maybe we won't have to settle for ethical relativism.

This provided me with my introduction to Kant. I represent the work of Kant as an effort to provide a secular defense of many of the central tenets of the Judeo/Christian/Islamic worldview against attacks by proponents of the modern scientific worldview of Hobbes. I do so because most students' lives are informed either directly or indirectly by concepts embodied in these three religions, and these concepts are primarily responsible for the practical reservations they have about the modern scientific worldview.

Our discussion of Kant's conception of the well-lived life and the good community focuses on his concept of pure practical reason, or moral reason. Common reason, Kant tells us, gives us the capacity to transcend our moral particularity. It enables us to act independently of, and possibly contrary to, both our Hobbesian passions and our Platonic or Aristotelian virtues.

As this is a civic education course, I do not dwell on the epistemological or metaphysical underpinnings of Kant's view, nor do I delve into the logical intricacies of the categorical imperative. I do, however, share my own view that Kant's later writings on history can be read as opening the door to historically progressive categorical imperatives, and I introduce students to the arguments put forth by natural law theologians to the effect that the history of moral thought represents a "broadening and deepening" of our understanding of human nature and human community. I also introduce them to the argument, most recently put forth by Thomas Nagel, to the effect that if we think at all about right and wrong, we must think of ourselves as submitting to moral reasoning rather than creating it (Nagel 1997).

Service-learning is admirably suited to help students determine the cash value of these arguments for the acquisition of civic wisdom. The experience of serving others puts students in a unique position to evaluate to what extent, if any, our moral reason is, or can be, free from prejudice or error. More specifically, it puts students in a unique position to evaluate to what extent, if any, our reason enables us to transcend our particular passions or values.

One student, for example, who was a single mother of three, did her service with a Head Start program in which her youngest child was enrolled. She found that her service awakened painful feelings from her own childhood when she was "poor and constantly made fun of in school." She wrote of having to transcend these feelings, or Hobbesian passions, in order to discipline a poor and marginalized child named "Mason," who had repeatedly ignored her instructions to stay in line during a graduation ceremony.

> To say the least, I became quite frustrated. I ended up sitting on the floor holding Mason while he screamed, kicked, and cried. Considering my past childhood experiences of being publicly humiliated in school, I could understand how my actions might be humiliating him. To avoid reviving the old pain from my childhood, I wanted to release him. Yet a Kantian view of the situation took hold in my mind. Kant would reason that even though I didn't enjoy holding Mason, I had a duty to do so, not only for his own growth as an individual but for the good of the class as a whole.
>
> I think Kant would agree with Mary Chapin-Carpenter. We have two lives — the one that we are given, and the one that we make. The pain that I felt holding Mason was a fact from my childhood. But I was not dependent on that pain. I acted independently of it.

The above student performed her service during the spring quarter of 1993. Since then Mary Chapin-Carpenter has twice been voted female country vocalist of the year, and I now make reference to her in a handout on Kant.

During the same quarter, I had a "service-learning" experience that informed, reinforced, and enhanced my own efforts to acquire wisdom regarding the role, if any, moral reason can play in helping us to transcend our particular passions. I was asked by a member of the Ohio General Assembly to testify before its Education Committee on behalf of House Bill 396 that would require every school district and institution of higher education in Ohio to provide opportunities for students to participate in "community service education programs." A committee member who represented an inner-city district in Cleveland asked me, "You are a philosopher, so you must be familiar with the work of Maslow on the hierarchy of needs. Do these poor kids have a need to serve? Shouldn't they be the ones who are being served?" I replied that I thought the work of Dr. Martin Luther King, Jr., was more convincing than the work of Maslow, and that Dr. King was correct when he asserted that we can all be great because we can all serve. I asserted that one of the most psychologically damaging things that we could do to any American would be to have that person grow up thinking of herself or himself as either a server or servee. I often think back to that exchange when I reflect upon the role that moral reason, as opposed to actually experienced needs or regularly experienced passions, can play in the lives of particular persons, including my own.

This brings us to a topic of discussion that regularly arises in the classroom at Shawnee State, and that is the issue of public assistance. More than one-third of our students receive AFDC. In the spring of 1995, almost two years before state or national welfare reform came to Ohio, one of our AFDC students served an HIV-positive resident of Scioto County named "Ted." Ted was a former street hustler in Los Angeles, where he became infected. He returned home and was receiving welfare benefits as well as additional assistance through the AIDS Task Force.

The student wanted to "help him to feel better" but was put off by Ted's attitude that "the world owed him a home and money simply because he was born into it." She wrote:

> I think at times I contributed to Ted's attitude by helping him to get as much assistance as possible from as many organizations as he could. Portsmouth probably has a lot of people who feel [that] the world owes them a living, and that they do not owe their community anything. I knew there was a welfare dependency problem, but I had never experienced it firsthand. I myself receive AFDC, but I am grateful for the help. There is a difference between gratitude and feeling like something is your due.

To try to make sense out of her service experiences, the student drew upon an assertion made by Kant in his *Fundamental Principles of the Metaphysics of Morals*: "To secure one's own happiness is a duty, at least indirectly; for discontent with one's condition, under a pressure of many anxieties and amidst unsatisfied wants, might easily become a great *temptation to transgression of duty*" [emphasis added] (1988: 23). She continued:

> Kant is saying that we need to meet some of our needs some of the time if we are to have the psychological strength to act from duty on a regular basis. Kant is also assuming that it is possible for us to meet our needs. This is where public assistance comes in. There is no way that I could be working toward my degree without AFDC. This isn't just true for me; it is true for other people as well. If we are to treat others as ends, we have an obligation to make it possible for them to meet some of their needs some of the time.
>
> But we should not meet their needs for them. That is where welfare dependency comes in. If we meet their needs for them, we are not treating them as ends, or as moral agents capable of acting from duty. We might make people like Ted happy that way, but happiness is not an end in itself for Kant. If [people receive] public assistance, they should do some kind of work, or go to school, even if it doesn't make them happy. Kant would say we are within our rights to require this. I would agree.

When students discuss the extent, if any, to which moral reason enables us to transcend particular virtues or values, they often do so in terms of their personal efforts to act contrary to the values with which they were raised. One student served in a Head Start program where she encountered a teacher who regularly made fun of a young boy in front of the class assistants and the other children, all of whom seemed to go along with it. The student was "shocked," but she had been raised to be "nonconfrontational" and a "peacemaker." She wrote:

> In accordance with my nature, I tried to stop the teasing by openly giving attention and affection to the boy. But if anything, it made matters worse. I thought about retreating into my shell, but I knew that would not help the boy either. Finally, I decided I had to tell the teacher to her face that what she was doing was really hurting the boy and giving the wrong message to her assistants and the children. This was very hard for me to do because I was raised to believe that nothing good came out of confrontation. I believe Kant says it best. I acted against the values I was raised with because I knew I had to do the right thing.

When this student read what she had written to the class, a classmate questioned whether she had accurately characterized her service experience. He suggested that the primary reason she found it difficult to talk to the teacher was that she experienced fear, or a passion to move fromward the teacher. She, in turn, responded by citing another classmate for whom it was second nature to "let people know where he stood," but who reluctantly "bit his tongue" during his service because his reason "told him" that to be forthcoming would "do more harm than good."

Finally, one nontraditional student, a high-level hospital administrator who performed his service in a nursing home, wrote about the capacity of moral reason to transcend values or virtues on a societal level:

> The residents are good people who for the most part have lived the "well-lived life" without formal education or a course like this one. Their lives and philosophies are predicated on the teachings of the Bible and their loyalty to God and country. They were raised in "Pericles's time," a golden age when there was a values consensus and a House Un-American Activities Committee. But even when we had a values consensus, it included things like segregation of the races, which is still second nature to many of the residents.
>
> We now live in "Socrates's time," when we no longer have a values consensus and everyone asks "whose values?" We need to go beyond some of the old values and come up with a new set of values that everyone, black and white, men and women, can get behind. To do this, we have to talk to each other and reflect. This is where a course like this one comes in.
>
> If we can't reason beyond our own particular values on things like race and gender, then we are lost. But I think we can. This is a big part of what we did during the civil rights movement. It wasn't second nature or "authentic" for blacks and whites to work side by side or rub shoulders socially, but we did it. The "we" in "we shall overcome" was based more on Kant's moral reason than on the values that I or the residents in the nursing home were raised with.

These remarks, made by the student in his term paper, illustrate how his service experience informed, reinforced, and enhanced his efforts to reflect upon the potential of reason to emancipate us from repressive social constraints.[13]

## Summary

The writings and discussions of the service-learning students cited above indicate that such students develop a facility and disposition for using philosophical concepts to reflect upon the well-lived life and the good community that they might not develop in other philosophy courses. Their writings and discussions also indicate that they develop an appreciation for the theoretical implications and practical ramifications of using these concepts that they well might not develop in other courses. In short, they indicate that this service-learning course is an excellent vehicle for teaching our students the concepts, dispositions, and skills that enable them to acquire both theoretical and practical wisdom concerning the relationship between a well-lived life and a good community. They indicate that such a service-learning course is an excellent course for acquiring civic wisdom.

### Notes

1. I am deliberately leaving the relationship between intelligence and will open to Aristotelian, Humean, Kantian, or other interpretations. I do not believe that what I have to say about philosophy and service-learning requires me to be more specific. Indeed, I believe that service-learning can be an important vehicle for teaching students how to think both theoretically and practically about this relationship.

A central mission of members of Alcoholics Anonymous is to serve one another in their respective efforts to stay sober. I believe that it is because of their practical engagement through service that members of AA who have taken our philosophy service-learning course invariably come to the course with insightful things to say about the relationship between intelligence and will.

2. Shawnee State University was one of 15 colleges and universities to attend the first Institute on Integrating Service With Academic Study sponsored by Campus Compact. Shawnee State offers civic education/service-learning courses in ecology, engineering technologies, philosophy, and political science. Our philosophy service-learning course is considered to be our "generic" service-learning course. Our civic education/service-learning courses satisfy an ethical reasoning graduation requirement, and we currently enroll between 75 and 100 students per year in these courses.

3. Students in *any* service-learning course should be provided with a philosophical framework for thinking about what they should be trying to achieve in the course. I suspect, however, that students in service-learning courses often do not have a reasonably specific, if provisional, idea of what it is that they are trying to achieve. At a

plenary session of the winter 1991 Michigan Campus Compact meeting, only three of the more than 50 attendees chose to discuss what service-learning is, while the majority of those in attendance chose to discuss how to measure what service-learning accomplishes. More recently, at the fall 1996 Ohio Campus Compact meeting, I presented a philosophical framework for understanding what we should be trying to accomplish with service-learning courses in higher education. I received an evaluation in which the evaluator agreed with what I had to say but had a problem with the fact that I said it, because it "excluded" what some people in the service-learning movement were trying to do.

4. Many private institutions of higher education, especially religiously affiliated institutions of higher learning, have the institutional mission to teach moral virtues, including the virtue of connecting well. It may be the case that at some of these institutions the mission of teaching intellectual virtues, including the virtue of reflecting well on the relationship between the well-lived life and the good community, does not take precedence over the teaching of moral virtues.

5. How we characterize the service-learning relationship that we would have our students try to establish has much to do with our own views on the well-lived life. As Heideggerians, for example, we might characterize this service-learning relationship in terms of Heidegger's notion of "conscience," i.e., as the call of the self to authenticity in its relationship to other "selves."

6. At a session on interracial service-learning at the 1997 AAC&U conference, "Community Service and Service-Learning: Working for Democracy, Diversity, and Citizenship," the question was raised about whether it was paternalistic to talk of service in terms of service to a person or persons "in need." Several participants believed that it was, and stated that they chose to characterize service in terms of helping persons or communities to "manage their resources." This, of course, begs the question as to why we choose to help certain persons or communities manage their resources and not others.

I believe that if we conscientiously commit ourselves to acting as Kantian moral politicians in addressing the objective need/subjective need conundrum, then we will not fall into the trap of paternalism.

7. Whether the concept of community can be extended beyond the human community to include those whom Black Elk (1972) refers to as the two-legged, the four-legged, and "the wings of the air and all green things" is one of the fundamental questions that we can raise in a philosophy/civic education course. It has been my experience, however, that any in-depth effort to answer this question is best reserved for a separate ecology service-learning course.

8. In an excellent op ed piece entitled "Islands of Quality, Sea of Decay" that appeared in the March 16, 1991, issue of *The New York Times*, Joshua Freeman and Katha Pollitt argue that community service that is oriented only toward the server's own immediate community can have a very deleterious effect on the community as a whole by widening the gap between the haves and have-nots. The case that they cite concerns a group of civic-minded residents of the Upper East Side of Manhattan who raise a considerable sum of money to refurbish and improve their local city playground. The authors point out that the net result of their efforts is to increase the difference in quality between the recreational facilities available to the youth of the affluent Upper East Side and those available to the youth in most of the other neighborhoods of Manhattan.

Their solution to the problem is ingenious, and it involves the civic-minded residents of the Upper East Side's serving, in part, those who are not residents of their own immediate community. They propose that 50% of the donations made by residents of more affluent neighborhoods for the improvement of their local city facilities be channeled by a municipal agency to poorer neighborhoods for comparable purposes. Although the authors point out that their proposal risks some major problems, it is hard to argue with their concern that community service not become a vehicle for further dividing communities.

9. To encourage honest reflection on the part of our students, and to protect the right to privacy of those who are served, all journals and papers in the course are guaranteed confidentiality. Quotations from these sources will be treated as anonymous personal communications.

10. Service-learning courses can incorporate efforts made in non-Western traditions to deal with this issue. The Buddhist notion of attachments, for example, can be fruitfully compared and contrasted with the Western notion of passions. Service-learning courses can also provide a forum for comparing and contrasting Confucius and Aristotle on social virtues. Lao Tzu's notion of power *(Te)* as virtue could also be introduced in a service-learning course, as could his writings on the forces of yin and yang and their implications for gender relations, political authority, and service itself.

11. The term "value" used by the young man and the term "virtue" used by Plato are not, strictly speaking, synonymous. "Value" is a modern term that goes back to Hobbes when he argues that the value of a man is as of all things his price. By the 19th century, however, the term became distinguished from the term "fact" and came to mean what ought to be. Teaching values, in turn, came to mean teaching what ought to be, but without the focus on regular practice that induces dispositions, habits, or virtues.

12. Female students characterize their service experiences in terms of a predisposition to belong to a political community less frequently than do male students, although female students tend to agree with Aristotle that we have natural predispositions to procreate, to leave likenesses of ourselves behind, and to form households. We once discussed this phenomenon in class, and the class was split evenly on whether this might be due to women's having been historically excluded from the public sphere or to women's and men's having different natural predispositions.

13. There is a sense in which we have come full circle from the days of Socrates to today. At the heart of the contemporary conflict between the intolerance of moral absolutists and religious fundamentalists on the one hand, and the solipsism of moral relativists and postmodernists, on the other, lies a philosophical conflict over what role, if any, our reason can play in enabling us to transcend our moral particularity. In an attempt to get to the bottom of this conflict in the course discussed here, we ask ourselves such questions as whether our service experiences suggest that modern philosophical criticisms of the power of reason to transcend our moral particularity have become self-fulfilling prophecies on a societal level.

## References

Black Elk. (1972). *Black Elk Speaks*. New York, NY: Simon & Schuster.

Kant, I. (1988). *Fundamental Principles of the Metaphysics of Morals*. Buffalo, NY: Prometheus Books.

Nagel, T. (1997). *The Last Word*. New York, NY: Oxford University Press.

Willwerth, J. (September 23, 1996). "Lessons Learned on Death Row." *Time*: 58.

Wilson, E.O. (1978). *On Human Nature*. Cambridge, MA: Harvard University Press.

## Possible Service Opportunities
## Reflections on Community Involvement 485S

You may also select a service option of your choice. It must be interpersonal service to a person or persons in need. It cannot be service that we have regularly performed, nor can it be something that we have done for pay. It also cannot be service that will prevent someone else from receiving pay. Our service must be supervised by someone who is not a relative or individual with whom we have a personal relationship (friend, family friend, neighbor, colleague, et. al.). Service options must be approved by the instructor.

The following is a list of service options that have been previously selected by Shawnee State students. The asterisk indicates that the instructor should make the initial contact.

\*1.     Crisis hotline volunteer. Must serve during hours with high call-in rate. An average of ten hours of training is required; up to seven of which will count toward service.

\*2.     Serving victims of domestic violence in South Central Ohio. Volunteer should be female and should have some life experience.

\*3.     Serving HIV positive residents of Southern Ohio through the AIDS Task Force.

\*4.     Serving as a peer mentor to secondary school students who are parents. (GRADS Program).

5.     Mentoring a foster child. Call Ms. Faye Weddington at Children's Services (456-4164). Students must be willing to follow through on this option, and must have own vehicle and auto insurance.

6.     Being a visitor/companion to persons in a nursing home or serving as an "activities aid" with persons in a nursing home. Contact the person responsible for volunteers at the nursing home where you wish to serve.

7.     Students may serve as volunteers with the Adult Basic Education or GED programs at SSU, helping adults to learn how read or do math. Students may also do work with Adult Basic Education or GED programs at centers near their homes. Volunteers must be willing to take the initiative in engaging these students. Students wishing to serve with programs other than SSU's should contact the supervisor of their program of choice. On campus, contact Ms. Carolyn Gross (Ext. 2452).

8.     Serving as a tutor for students who are "academically at risk" in area high schools, including tutoring students whom have failed the 9th grade proficiency test. Volunteers should contact the appropriate vice principal or teacher at their high school of choice.

9.     Volunteering as a tutor/mentor/computer instructor at the 14th Street Community Center, (Lincoln Elementary), or Church of God (Wilson Elementary) After School Drop-In Programs weekday afternoons, 3-6pm. Contact a VISTA volunteer (354-5837). Volunteering as a tutor/mentor/activities aid at Farley Square as part of the Counseling Center's Substance Abuse Prevention Outreach Program. Contact Mr. Clarence Parker (353 -1802). Volunteering as a mentor/tutor/activities aid with CAO Youth Services Bureau. Contact Ms. Judy Carver (354 -7541).

10.     Serving mentally retarded adults at Star Workshop (Portsmouth) or Good Shepherd Manor (Piketon). Contact Mr. Fred Nelson, Portsmouth, (354-1517) or Mr. Norm Trembloy, Piketon, (614-289-2861).

11.     Serving mentally retarded students at the Vern Riffe School (formerly Happy Hearts) (Portsmouth) or Carousel Center (Portsmouth). Contact Mr. Tony Miller (353-1876) or Ms. Brenda Benson (354-3995).

12.     Serving as a volunteer in a child care facility that primarily cares for disadvantaged children (approximately 2/3rd of the children must be documented as socio-economically disadvantaged). West End Day Care is one such facility. Contact the supervisor at the facility of your choice. Must serve children no younger than four years of age, and must be willing to take initiative.

13. Serving with the Meals on Wheels Program that delivers meals to people's homes. Must be able to volunteer between 11am and 1:30pm, must be able to drive one's own vehicle, and must be covered by one's own auto insurance. Contact Ms. Jean Sheets (353-7606).

14. Serving as a volunteer with psychiatric inpatients at River Valley Health System. (Formerly Portsmouth Receiving) Contact Ms. Barbara Pratt (354-2804).

15. Serving as a volunteer with outpatients of the Scioto Paint Valley Mental Health Center in Waverly. Monday and Thursday from 10:30 to 1pm. Contact Ms. Melissa Hirn-Pulliam (614-947-7783).

16. Working as a volunteer at the SOMC Cancer Center with both patients and their families. Contact Ms. Sandra Hall (354-5000). Must serve with Dr. Inoshita's practice.

17. Volunteering at a Drop-In Center for clients of Shawnee Mental Health (Portsmouth, Ironton, West Union, Ohio). Contact Ms. Anita Brown, Portsmouth, (354-7702), Ms. Katrina Miller, West Union, (513-544-2782), or Ms. Glenda Marting, Ironton, (614-533-9500).

18. Visiting Veterans on Long Term Care Wards of a Veterans Administration Hospital. Huntington, (304-429-6741) Chillicothe, (614-772-7052).

19. Teaching a "business basics" course to junior high school students. Training and teaching materials are provided by Junior Achievement (Portsmouth, Ironton, and South Shore, Kentucky). A good option for business majors. Contact Ms. Debne Marlette (606-329-1699).

20. Serving as a teacher's assistant for physically disabled students: grades 9-12 at Clay High School, contact Ms. Carolyn Redden 12pm weekdays (354-6644); grades 6-8 at Valley Middle School, contact Ms. Jill Hickman 12pm weekdays (259-2651).

21. Serving as a volunteer with inmates of a county jail. Either male or female volunteers. For Scioto County call Sheriff Doninni (354-7566). Must show initiative.

22. Serving as a volunteer with the VITA program (Volunteer in Tax Assistance). Contact Mr. Rod Millhuff (353-3328). Up to 14 hours of training are required seven of which count toward one's service.

23. Serving an SSU student who has a disability (as a note taker/tutor/mentor). Contact Mr. Eustace Matthews (355-2276).

24. Serving as a volunteer with Head Start. Must be a Head Start parent, or have a recent physical and undergo a criminal background check. Serving as a volunteer with a KEEP (Kindergarten Enrichment Program). Contact the school of your choice to see if it has such a program.

25. Serving as a volunteer in a homeless shelter. In Portsmouth, contact Ms. Maureen Cadogan (353-4085).

26. Serving as a volunteer in a learning disabled or developmentally delayed class. Contact the school of your choice to see if it has such a class. In Portsmouth, Lincoln Elementary has such a class.

27. Serving as a life guard at the McKinley Pool. Red Cross/ CPR training will be provided. Contact Mr. Orville Ferguson (355-2448). Serving as a youth activities aide at Mound Park. Contact Ms. Alison Kalb (354-5753)   or (354-5951). These are summer options only. Mound Park: June 10th - Aug 16th, M-F, 11am - 5pm; McKinley Pool: June 15th - Aug 7th, M-S, 1 pm B 6 pm.

28. Serving as an intake assistant at Southeastern Ohio Legal Services. Contact Mr. Mark Cardosi at 354-7563.

## Roles of Service-Learning in Civic Education

1. To promote the capacity and disposition to *reflect*, especially on the role of human connectedness in the life of a community. This is first and foremost the role of service-learning in higher education.

2. To promote the capacity and disposition to *connect*, especially to those who are not family, friends or neighbors. This is first and foremost the role of service-learning in primary and secondary education.

3. To become aware of possible vocational/avocational opportunities.

## A Service-Learning Taxonomy

### Active Learning

| | | | |
|---|---|---|---|
| Students encouraged to ask questions | Classroom time devoted to discussion | Students do role playing, put on trials, hold town meetings, actually teach a class | Experiential Learning, or learning outside of the classroom |

### Experiential Learning

| | | | |
|---|---|---|---|
| Field Studies e.g. field trips, semesters abroad | On-the-Job Training, e.g. government internships, business internships, practice teaching | Traditional Academic Internships, e.g. psychology or sociology internships where we, as learning subjects learn *about* others who are objects of observation | Service-Learning Internships where we, as learning subjects, also learn *from* others who are themselves learning subjects. Service-Learning Internships are a laboratory or practicum in human connectedness. |

### Guidelines for Service-Learning

I.    We serve others who are in need--who have a true deficit that needs to be addressed.  The challenge of connecting with another human being across the difference created by need enhances service-learning.

II.    We serve others in as direct a manner as possible--direct interpersonal service to the person or persons who are in need, or direct inter-natural service to others in nature who are in need (e.g. developing a caring relationship with a river bank).  Direct service is not in itself morally superior to indirect service (e.g. fundraising, filing, or lab analysis) but it provides the server with experiences that better promote reflection on the nature of the well-lived life and the good community.

III.    When possible we serve others who are not members of our immediate community.  This not only works against the fragmentation of human beings along the lines of class, race, ethnicity, or gender, it  provides the server with a richer experience of community upon which to reflect.

## Some Remarks on Writing Our Term Papers

In our term papers we will try to analyze, characterize, or make sense out of our noteworthy service experiences, both objective and subjective. To do so, we will use the concepts of Plato, Aristotle, Hobbes and Kant (we may also use other concepts in addition to these). We will use these concepts to try to characterize what we experienced, and to try to determine what we *ought to do* about what we experienced. We must use the concepts of all four thinkers, even if it is only to argue that they are not relevant to the particular experience in question.

We will want to analyze, or make sense out of, the positive experiences we had. Are they experiences of enjoyment (Hobbes), experiences of authenticity (Plato), experiences of self-realization (Aristotle) or experiences of self respect (Kant)?

How can we *best* make sense out of our negative experiences? How, can we *best* use the concepts of our thinkers to characterize how we able to act appropriately toward those whom we served despite having these negative experiences? Did we simply calculate that it would be in our long term self-interest to do so (Hobbes)? Did we fall back on the values with which we were raised (Plato)? Were our actions guided by a natural instinct or predisposition (Aristotle)? Did we exercise moral will power to act independently of our passions and/or even of our values (Kant)? In short, what did we learn about ourselves as we served?

In what ways were the persons whom we served in need? Are they in need in terms of natural capacities (Plato), in terms of a weak or unperfected social predisposition (Aristotle), in terms of opportunities to satisfy their basic passions (Hobbes), in terms of the virtues that were or were not inculcated in them (Plato and Aristotle), in terms of the strength of their moral will (Kant)? How can we *best* use the concepts of our thinkers to explain the differences that we observed among people whom we served.

How can we best characterize the way that members of the agency or institutional staff related to the persons we served? Using the concepts of Plato, Aristotle, Hobbes and Kant, what *recommendations* would we make for improving the service given by the agency or institution? What *recommendations* would we make for improving our community in respect to the better meet needs of the persons we served?

Finally, drawing upon our noteworthy service experiences, please evaluate or critique the philosophical framework of our service-learning course.

Our analysis, or characterization, of our noteworthy service experience should reach a *conclusion* as to which concepts of Plato, Aristotle, Hobbes or Kant (or which combination of their concepts) *best* enables us to analyze or characterize our service experience.

# Service-Learning in Perspectives on Poverty

by Carolyn H. Magid

## Background on the Course and My Objectives

Perspectives on Poverty is an upper-level philosophy course designed to integrate a substantial service-learning project with study of both contemporary normative moral/political theories and current public policies dealing with poverty. In creating this course I had several guiding ideas. I wanted to involve students in evaluating public policy about poverty. Public debate about poverty policy usually relies on but avoids reference to philosophical theories of justice, rights, and obligation. I saw the course as a chance to use study of philosophical theories to illuminate the debates. I expected that a service-learning project that places students in a major community institution that serves poor people (an inner-city school) would greatly increase their opportunities to understand both poor people and the impact of actual and proposed policies. I hoped that the course, and its service-learning component, would encourage students to care about poor people and poverty policies, and would energize and empower them to engage in solving problems as they saw them.

Over the last few years, poverty policy has emerged in the United States as a major focus of public debate and government action. The prominence of the debate on poverty policy coincides with a major bipartisan shift on policy. After years with a "safety net," which has in fact supported less and less, policymakers are poised officially to abandon it altogether. The country has given up all pretense to real equality of opportunity through public education in favor of a two-tier system based on social class and race. The losers in this policy change have been closed out of mainstream society's opportunities and separated from the rest of us by locale, by experience, and by resources, as well as by prospects. Despite the widely publicized increase in the numbers of people in poverty and the increasing income gap between rich and poor, many in the mainstream seem prepared to support or at least go along with these policy changes.

Support for these changes rests in part on questionable, unexamined, and/or undefended approaches to issues about justice, rights, and obligation. Policymakers and those in the mainstream are also often uninformed about and disconnected from the people impacted by their policies. Those deciding for poor people know little about the poor and are opting for policies that will cut off decision makers even further from those whose futures they decide. Even people who do care tend to see problems as intractable and believe that relatively recent downturns (such as increasing numbers of long-term homeless families) are inevitable.

In developing Perspectives on Poverty, I wanted to work with a small group of students to begin to do with them some of what was lacking in the public arena — to position them to approach poverty problems and policies as thoughtful, informed, engaged, and empowered problem solvers. Because the public debate involves issues about justice, rights, and obligation, I felt philosophy had a claim to a role here. Work in an inner-city school would give students direct (if brief) experience with poor people in their own community. Whatever conclusions about policy the students came to would at least be more authentic and more grounded in moral and political theory than much of what goes on in the public arena.

In offering the course at Bentley College, I had the advantage of working at an institution that has made a major commitment to incorporating service-learning throughout the curriculum. Because there is a strong service-learning program, I expected that students who came to my course (mostly seniors) would come with prior experience in service-learning with poor people, and that some would come with questions about justice, rights, and obligation based on their previous service experiences. Because Bentley is a business school, I also expected that students would be oriented to using their skills to solve problems. I saw the course as providing them with compelling real-world cases and problems to whose solutions they could and would want to contribute.

With these objectives in mind, I developed Perspectives on Poverty (see pages 177-183) and first taught it as an experimental course in 1993. The course is now a permanent part of the philosophy curriculum. I have now taught it four times. Each time the course has been offered, student demand has far exceeded class capacity. Students have been uniformly enthusiastic about their experience working in an inner-city school, and have given the course as a whole high evaluations. Although there are *many* ways the course could be improved, I have been impressed by its relative success in accomplishing the objectives I had in developing it. In what follows, I will describe course structure and content and the service-learning project. I will also discuss what I think the course (especially the service-learning project) has accomplished, drawing on student experience and work.

## Course Structure and Content

The course has three major components. First, it involves a study of current philosophical theories of obligation, rights, and justice with discussion of their application to questions about poverty. They include: What do specific theories say about the moral obligations of government, other institutions, and individuals in dealing with poverty? Should we distinguish between deserving and undeserving poor, and on what basis? Do people have the right to have their basic needs met? Can a just society allow tremendous inequalities in resources and opportunities? How should we deal with conflicting claims about justice, rights, needs, freedom, and equality?

Second, the course utilizes a service-learning project and course texts to explore the experiences of poor people in the context of the institutions that impact their lives and life prospects. As I will describe more fully below, students have worked as assistants to teachers at a Boston public elementary school. I am currently supplementing the service work with reading and discussion of two texts — Alex Kotlowitz's *There Are No Children Here* (1991) and Jonathan Kozol's *Savage Inequalities* (1991). The texts were chosen to build on the service-learning experience in different ways. The Kozol text provides a broader (and more dramatic) set of descriptions of public schools in poor (and advantaged) communities, as well as offers some moral argument about equity in education. The Kotlowitz text profiles two low-income youths in the context of their family and the many broader institutions that shape their lives, allowing students to consider ways that different institutions and family circumstances impact their educational experiences.

The third and final component of the course involves an evaluation of current policy and policy proposals about ways to deal with poverty in the United States. Here students study specific current policy issues and are expected to draw and make a case for conclusions about them that integrate the philosophical theories with their experiential and textual investigations earlier in the course. I have selected a few policies/policy proposals for study each year based on important current controversies, and use current reporting and opinion pieces as texts. Policies discussed have included proposals for increased funding or funding equity in education, school choice across district and city lines, school-assignment programs that distribute students based on income as well as race, changing state policies on homeless shelter eligibility, and welfare reform.

I want to acknowledge here that the course's crowded agenda comes at the cost of detailed and more inclusive consideration of major philosophical theories. I will try to suggest that there are gains that offset this loss. The chance to put theories to use and an interest in doing so based on the service-learning project give students a more connected and grounded view of those theories. In evaluating them, students bring to bear a new and different set of experiences; they can explore the implications, for the children and the public schools, of adopting different theories. Usually colleges, including Bentley, offer several general courses in ethics and social/political philosophy. Students interested in further exploring theories they encounter here can go on to these other courses.

It should also be obvious that this single course does not provide students with the information and skills to do thoroughgoing assessments of specific policies. My hope is to start students on that process, to give them a sense of what would be needed to do a more comprehensive assessment, and to motivate them to want to do more.

## The Service-Learning Assignment

The centerpiece of the course (and clearly the most exciting part for the students) has been a service-learning assignment as assistants to teachers at a Boston public elementary school. I have been fortunate to be able to establish an ongoing relationship with the Alexander Hamilton School, one of Boston's more sought-after schools. As with other schools in the Boston Public School system, many of this school's students come from low-income families, both new arrivals to this country and long-term residents. The school has limited material resources. Its very old building has no real gym or large assembly room. The tiny cafeteria does not prepare food and serves only small groups at a time. The schoolyard is also the parking lot and, until a few hoops were installed this year, had no resources for children at recess. The school does have teachers and a principal who are talented and dedicated. It also has an exceptionally diverse group of students whose friendships and schoolwork relationships transcend differences in culture, ethnicity, and language. The success of my course has depended on the school's cooperation and goodwill as teachers and the principal have taken the time to incorporate my students and to evaluate course outcomes.

Each student works at the school six hours (four visits) over a month. Students travel together at a time that includes a scheduled class meeting time; many choose to add in another three-hour visit that entitles them to write a final essay focusing on the school. Students are assigned to a specific class and project for the duration of their work. Projects, determined by classroom teachers, vary depending on classroom needs. Some have not required advance planning (tutoring in reading and writing, computer work, individual work with children learning English). Others have required considerable advance effort, e.g., a series of interactive presentations on college and careers that included role-playing with children about getting jobs and setting goals. Many teachers want our students to help teach sportsmanship and cooperative play through sports and games. In the first year, we worked with six teachers, in subsequent years with as many as 10. Our group experience has covered work with children at each grade level K-5, with a multigrade special-needs classroom, and with the resource room and the computer science laboratory.

## Opportunities for Reflection

During the month students are at the school, I use remaining class meetings to discuss the service experience and to integrate it with what they are learning from the Kozol and Kotlowitz texts. Students are required to keep a journal, for which I typically assign topics to keep their multifaceted experience focused on relevant issues. I often read and comment on material from their journals as a starting point for broader discussions.

The schoolchildren and their school become a major focus of subsequent discussions of policy. We look at how actual and proposed policies would and should impact this institution and these children and their families. At the request of students, I have also usually provided a final essay option that allows them to present and assess proposals for improvements at the Hamilton School. In this context, one important topic is the use and limits of their own service.

## Results

With regard to service, I feel my students perform a useful and greatly appreciated function at the Hamilton School. Our work has been extremely well received by the teachers, the school principal, and the schoolchildren. Many of these children do not have a lot of resources, human or material, in their lives, and they are thrilled at the interaction with and attention from young adults. Written evaluations each year by participating teachers and the principal have consistently been enthusiastic. I have been fortunate to have students who have done a lot of work with children and who really enjoy doing it. As a result, they have had a great deal of talent and energy to contribute to the school.

## Learning

Robert Coles (1989) has suggested that service is a mutual thing. It is not only helping others; it is being helped. Because we learn, we affirm ourselves in certain important ways, I think, both psychologically and morally. We have everything to gain by doing this as human beings and as citizens and as people who are trying to learn about the world. My students have been affirmed and empowered by their success in being helpful, and by the admiration and respect of the schoolchildren. One student who came to the course without much previous academic success was prompted by his experience to take himself more seriously and to assume more responsibility for himself and others. He wrote:

*The way the children acted toward me made me feel successful. . . . The children made me feel happy when they asked so many questions. It seemed that they looked up to us so much, and looked forward to our visits. It also impressed me that the children remembered our names. It made*

*me feel like we really made a difference, and it changed my negative view
that there is little we can do to help the underprivileged — I realize now
that we can leave impressions on these young lives, and maybe help them
see hope and change.*

The psychological and moral self-affirmation experienced by students has
contributed both to what they learned and to the moral energy and commitment they brought to looking for solutions to problems they saw.
Students have learned enough about the world so that they can address policy issues about poverty without being simplistic or uninformed. They have
gained a sense of the importance of theory to decisions about and moral
evaluation of practice. They have become familiar with central features of
some important recent philosophical theories. They have looked closely and
critically at a range of current policy proposals.

Overall I have been impressed with the high level of student enthusiasm
and high level of work by students in this course. I am convinced, and the
students have agreed, that the service-learning experience at the Hamilton
School is crucial to their intellectual accomplishments throughout the
course. All students have had a new vantage point from which to assess policy — the interests of the children with whom they worked, and their families. Many of them have been impelled by their experience with these children to develop exceptionally thoughtful proposals for solving problems the
children face. Students make specific normative philosophical theories
"their own" and use them to support their policy conclusions. It is difficult to
illustrate these accomplishments in short excerpts from student work, and
I will not try to do so in any thorough way. I do want to comment on some
important developments to give the students some voice here and to convey
some sense of their experience.

## Seminal Moments

Good service experiences such as this one that involve direct contact with
recipients offer possibilities to learn things quickly that might be passed over
in weeks of reading. An example: On her first day in a kindergarten classroom,
one student was assigned to help a child with reading readiness. He was looking at block letters for the word *house*, in an effort to recognize the word. When
he got stuck, as a hint, she asked him where he lived. "The projects," he replied.
Although the student had been thinking about and sensitive to the impact of
poverty on this child's life, she had not before understood the extent to which
his life experiences affected her efforts to teach him.

One regular theme in many students' reflections on the children they
work with is the impact of poverty in other arenas of the children's lives on
their experience at school, of which the house story is a striking example.
Perhaps the most important learning moment for another group of students

came when they listened to a different group of kindergartners discuss violence and death as an ordinary part of the fabric of their lives. On subsequent visits, teachers told us that many of the children went home to neighborhoods so unsafe that they were unable to go out and play after school. Deprived of the chance to play, they brought their "outside" energy to school, often finding it difficult to settle down and stay on task. Despite impressive and sympathetic teachers, one of whom had her second graders playing dodge ball in the classroom to help them settle down during the rest of the day, unsettled behavior was an obstacle to learning that had an impact on the whole class.

Seeing "discipline problems" in this context enabled my students to get beyond simple solutions such as heavier discipline. They proposed more adults in the classroom to work with children during the day, so that everyone's work time would not be disrupted by the need for the teacher to settle children down. (They felt they were helping in this way, and volunteers could serve that purpose.) They proposed after-school programs with organized sports activities and suggested that schools open many more hours for community use.

## Equity

The Hamilton School is an old school, unrenovated presumably due to tight budgets; it lacks material resources my students expected all schools to have. One student wrote:

> During one recess we were playing basketball with a "flat" ball and throwing it against a piece of wood on the wall, which took the place of a basket. Another day I wanted to play soccer with the children but the only grass was "hilly" and had rocks all over it. We ended up kicking the ball around on the pavement, which isn't good for the already beat-up ball. They also have the remains of what looks like a swing set on the side of the building. It's amazing to compare my grammar school facilities with theirs. We had two full-size softball fields, three or four basketball courts, swing sets, jungle gyms, and a full-size soccer field. It is depressing to think of how unfair this fact is.

Students generally have seen this situation as unfair and damaging to poor children. Another student wrote: "It is unfair that the middle- and upper-class children have so many advantages over the poor. Poor children who recognize that they are not afforded the same opportunities as other students often have a lower self-image . . . and feel cheated." Students generally agree that overall limits on funding and resources are relevant to opportunities and achievement over the long term. They ask whether and why they deserve more than the schoolchildren they help. Here is one journal comment:

*After visiting with these middle school children, it is sad to think of what the future has in store for them. Will the brightest student of this class have the same opportunities that I enjoyed even though I was only a mediocre student? A problem exists in the fact that most of them will not. Inequalities exist that make it easier for children who come from wealthy families to gain opportunities for advancement than children of poor families.*

Their experience and observations have led most students to support increases in funding for inner-city schools. In the last part of the course, we typically have animated discussions of the relative merits of equal funding, funding to a certain minimum, or tying funding level to system needs (e.g., increased funding to systems with more English-as-second-language and special-needs students). On this topic, the course's different components (theory, policy, texts, and service experience) have come together for the most useful discussions of policy.

## Deserving Versus Undeserving Poor

Toward the beginning of the course, before students have done any service work, we typically keep returning to the question of whether it is reasonable to talk about the deserving versus the undeserving poor, and what criteria might distinguish these groups. No one thinks that there are undeserving children, but some cling to the distinction as a way to sort out adults worthy of help from those who are not.

The service experience complicates my students' thinking tremendously. They really enjoy the children and often become passionate advocates for them. In his first journal entry, one student wrote:

*The most prominent thing that I learned overall after being assigned to a little boy named E is that nobody should ever judge anyone based on where they live, their background, or what they look like, because I have not met anyone in a long time that reminded me how innocent and pure we all were at one point in time. Granted I have not known any of them for a good amount of time yet, but it is like an old familiar feeling you get when you remember how being nice was second nature and all you wanted to do was play and have a good time.*

At the same time, students can see that some of the children, even the young ones, carry within them incredible pain and anger, which sometimes comes out in noncooperation and acting out, verbally and physically. If these children do not get more help now, my students feel, they might easily turn into the people whom some consider undeserving later in life. But could they be undeserving later if the problems originated from childhood circumstances for which they could hardly be to blame?

## Empathy and Obligation

The students' comments above speak eloquently to the empathetic identification that most of my students make with the children with whom they work. Without that identification, I doubt we would be able to have the kinds of discussions I have been describing above. This identification also has encouraged students to do more than I had anticipated in their work at the school. One student surprised himself by arranging to stay another hour and a half on our visits to work with a small group of children on peer mediation. Another group brought many kinds of portable sports equipment and turned the bare schoolyard into training stations for different sports during recess. Two years ago, when we found funding at Bentley, students invited the Hamilton School children and teachers to spend a day at Bentley and organized campus tours, a lunch, and sports and games.

In her important new book on caring, Joan Tronto suggests that an "ethic of care" takes as central "not — What, if anything, do I (we) owe to others? but rather — How can I (we) best meet my (our) caring responsibilities?" (1993: 137). I believe that over the course of their work at the Hamilton School, students shift from thinking about whether they have obligations to Tronto's kind of question. The issue of whether they or society should meet the needs of these children drops away, replaced with a focus on how we can best do what the children need.

# Final Thoughts

Community service by itself is an important expression of caring, initiative, and responsibility for what happens in our communities. It can improve the quality of life for those served. Service-learning of the kind I have been describing (community service in the context of courses that allow both extensive reflection on the experience and connections between that experience and social, institutional, and ethical issues) can be much more than this. Impelled by caring, informed through study, and empowered through the experience they have had, students can and might become socially responsible problem solvers. Coles (1989) suggests that the same can be true for involved faculty, and I can unequivocally agree. I accompanied students during their group time at the Hamilton School, acting as extra help and occasional problem solver or substitute for their individual assignments. I can easily pinpoint the kinds of gains my students have made through their involvement because I have experienced them too.

## References

Coles, Robert. (1989). "Learning by Doing Through Public Service. For Students and Faculty Alike: Interview With Arthur Levine." *Change* 21(5): 18-26.

Kotlowitz, Alex. (1991). *There Are No Children Here*. New York, NY: Nan A. Talese/Doubleday.

Kozol, Jonathan. (1991). *Savage Inequalities*. New York, NY: Crown Publishers.

Tronto, Joan. (1993). *Moral Boundaries: A Political Argument for an Ethic of Care*. New York, NY: Routledge.

**PH351: PERSPECTIVES ON POVERTY**
**Professor Carolyn Magid**
**Fall 1995**

# SYLLABUS

## PART I: INTRODUCTORY DISCUSSIONS

**Class 1:** Introduction to the course -- Topics, issues, requirements; introduction of course participants; exercise on defining poverty (handout). Prepare <u>writing assignment</u> for class 2: Based on your background knowledge and reading of short texts for class 2, answer the following questions: Is poverty a problem in the U.S. today? Why? Whose problem is it? Why? (Write about 500 words typed.)

**Class 2:** Is poverty a problem in the U.S. today? <u>Texts:</u> short selections distributed in class. Prepare <u>writing assignment</u> for class 3: Present and defend your own ideas about the topic questions for class 3 (listed immediately below). (Write about 500 words typed.)

**Class 3:** Ethical issues: What, if anything, are we morally obligated to do for poor people, and why? what do poor people have a right to, and from whom? What does justice require of our government? Introductory discussion. <u>Video in class:</u> *Ethics in America, Part 1* (excerpt on giving to people who beg in the street). <u>Texts:</u> Start reading for class 4 ff.

## PART II: PHILOSOPHICAL THEORIES OF OBLIGATION, RIGHTS, AND JUSTICE

**Class 4:** <u>Texts:</u> "United Nations Universal Declaration of Human Rights," National Conference of Catholic Bishops, *Economic Justice for All* (selections).

**Class 5:** <u>Texts:</u> Garrett Hardin, "Lifeboat Ethics: the Case Against Helping the Poor" and Peter Singer, "Rich and Poor".

**Class 6:** <u>Text:</u> John Rawls, "Justice as Rational Choice Behind a Veil of Ignorance."

**Class 7:** <u>Text:</u> Robert Nozick, *Anarchy, State and Utopia* (selections).

**Class 8:** <u>Text:</u> Kai Neilson, "Radical Egalitarianism."

**Class 9:** <u>Text:</u> Joan Tronto, *Moral Boundaries: A Political Argument for an Ethics of Care* (selections).

\*\*\*An essay assignment covering theories from Part II will be due in class 12--questions assigned.


## PART III: THERE ARE NO CHILDREN HERE

**Classes 10, 11, 12:** Reading and discussion of *There Are No Children Here,* by Alex Kotlowitz.


## PART IV:  PUBLIC EDUCATION IN POOR COMMUNITIES

For next  9 classes:

(1) <u>Service-Learning Assignment</u> at the Hamilton School, Brighton: The whole class will make 4 visits (on Wednesdays, leaving 11:20, returning by 2 p.m.)  You will be assigned to a specific classroom and project.  More on this in class. (2) <u>Texts:</u>  Jonathan Kozol, *Savage Inequalities* ; other texts may be announced.

(3) <u>Journal entries:</u> You will have 2 specific journal entry assignments due during this segment of the course.  Questions will focus on your service-learning experience and on the Kozol and Kotlowitz texts.


## PART V: EVALUATING POLICY PROPOSALS

For last 5 classes: In this part of the course, we will integrate philosophical theories, your knowledge of the lives of some poor children and of education in poor communities, your service experiences and your reflections on them.  Our goal will be to evaluate specific current policy proposals about ways to deal with poverty in the U.S.  We will focus on proposals about welfare and education.

<u>Topics:</u> (1) Kozol's proposals on funding public education; (2) welfare reform bills moving through Congress; (2) welfare reforms now in effect in Massachusetts; (3)  Cambridge proposal to consider income as well as race in assigning students to Cambridge elementary schools.

<u>Texts:</u> Current reporting on the above topics and short opinion pieces about them. (Most articles are from the *Boston Globe* and *The New York Times).*

<u>Assignments:</u> A short speech in the last class defending a specific proposal for change; a final essay either assessing a specific policy or policy proposal or addressing and assessing proposals for change at the Hamilton School .

---

**COURSE EVALUATION CRITERIA:**

Your course grade will be based on the following work:

(1) Essays on philosophical theories due in class 12 (see below) : 25%

(2) 4 journal entries due classes 2, 3, (see syllabus) and classes 16 and 21 (see below): 25%

(3) Final essay due at the end of term (see below): 25%

(4) Class participation in discussions, the service-learning project and last day speeches: 25%.

**PH351: PERSPECTIVES ON POVERTY**

### Essay Assignment
### Due in class Wednesday, October 18

**INSTRUCTIONS:**

(1) Write TWO of the following three short essays.

(2) Each essay should be approximately 800-1000 words, typed and double-spaced.

(3) Be sure to answer all parts of the topics you choose.

(4) If you quote from a course text, please give author and page in parentheses. If you quote from or take ideas from an outside source, please provide full footnote information.

**TOPICS:  (DO TWO)**

**Topic 1:**

We have studied a wide range of philosophical theories of justice, rights, obligation, and caring which have applications to the issue of poverty. Pick one of these theories with which you disagree and explain as fully and persuasively as possible the reasons for your disagreement. Your discussion must include some explicit discussion of the theory's approach to poverty, but feel free to consider other issues in your critical discussion.

**Topic 2:**

This essay asks you to connect our discussions of philosophical theories with the experience of the family whose life is chronicled in *There are No Children Here*. Pick the theory we have studied which seems to you most plausible and (1) explain **how** it would propose that we deal (individually and collectively) with the specific circumstances of the family in the text; (2) explain **what reasons it would give to support these conclusions**; (3) Say why you think this theory is a good one to use here. Be sure to consider the family's circumstances and to explain the theory's and your own reasoning in detail. (If you are writing on topics 2 and 3, do not use Tronto for both.)

**Topic 3:**

Tronto asks us to look at 4 ethical elements of care (attentiveness, responsibility, competence, and responsiveness), and their integration into an appropriate whole.  According to Tronto, we should do what is best "to maintain, continue and repair the world so we can live in it as well as possible."  (p.145)

Consider the government system of social services (and its representatives) as the "caretaker" for LaJoe and her family.  How would Tronto assess the adequacy of caretaking in this case?  (Be specific about problems and/or successes.)  Do you agree?  Why?

**PH351: PERSPECTIVES ON POVERTY**

### Instructions for Journal Entries

You have TWO journal entries due (Wednesday November 8 and Monday November 20). The journal entries are intended to allow you to reflect on your service experiences and on specific issues about poverty and education, and to connect your thinking to course issues and texts. Your journal entries should answer questions listed for each date.

**(1) Wednesday November 8 (based on first two visits):**

(a) Do the school and children experience problems because of poverty and being a school in a poor community? What problems? Are any problems and experiences similar to those in *Savage Inequalities* and/or *There Are No Children Here* ? (Explain similarities and differences you see.) (b) What was your most important observation/insight/learning experience about poverty/inner city schools during these visits? Why?

**(2) Monday November 20 (after 4 visits):**

Based on your own experience at the Hamilton School, the Kozol text, and other texts if relevant, what ideas do you have for improvements at the Hamilton School? (Try to focus primarily on improvements which will have some impact on poverty/poor people.) Why would these improvements be desirable?

Entries should be at least 500 words, and can be more. Please type them double-spaced with room for comments in margins. It is important that you submit entries on time, because we will take up topics you write on in classes where entries are due.

I'll read and comment on journals. Journals will be "graded" acceptable, acceptable+, distinguished, or unacceptable. Work that fits the specifications indicated in the assignment will be considered to be acceptable, acceptable+ or distinguished. To be judged distinguished, work will need to be exceptionally thoughtful. Consistently acceptable work will get a B-range grade. Consistently distinguished work will get an A. (Note that your grade will be based on these two journal entries and entries done at the beginning of this course.)

**PH351: PERSPECTIVES ON POVERTY**

### Final Speech Assignment
### Due for last class

COME TO CLASS PREPARED TO GIVE A 2-3 MINUTE SPEECH.
Your speech should state and defend one concrete proposal about how government, other institutions and/or individuals should act to deal with some aspect of poverty. Pick a proposal which is: (1) morally defensible (according to you), (2) capable of having real impact on the lives of poor people, and (3) practical (could conceivably be accomplished). Your speech should explain how the proposal meets these conditions.

## PH351: PERSPECTIVES ON POVERTY

### Final Essay Assignment
### Due at the scheduled exam time

Write an essay of about 1300-1500 words, typed double-spaced, on one of the following topics:

### (I) PROPOSALS FOR THE HAMILTON SCHOOL

Student journals have advocated a range of kinds of proposals for change at the Hamilton School, including: (1) more government money/spending (for facilities upgrades, new equipment and curricular materials, increased staffing, raising teacher salaries, decreasing class sizes, and training teachers and other staff); (2) increasing parent involvement; (3) adding human resources and role models through increasing college-school links, both with service-learning and student work programs; also adding high school mentor programs linking high school students with Hamilton School kids; (4) increasing business involvement (in contributions, aid to schools); (5) increasing volunteer efforts from the broader community (clean-ups, contributions, classroom volunteers, motivational speakers).

(i) which of the above if any are **required** for Hamilton School children to have the same opportunity to succeed in life as children from more advantaged student populations? Why?

(ii) Which do you think should be implemented, and by whom? Why?

(iii )If you needed to prioritize due to limited human and financial resources, which specific proposals do you think are most important? Why? (Explain why you pick the ones you pick, and why you don't pick the ones you don't pick.)

(As you answer these questions, try to bring out the moral principles concerning justice, rights, and obligation on which your approach is based.)

### (II) FEDERAL AND/OR STATE WELFARE REFORM

Evaluate either the welfare reform legislative proposal recently passed by the U.S. Senate (see *Boston Globe* article of 9/20/95 and other texts attached) or Massachusetts' welfare reform law which took effect 11/1/95 (see *Boston Globe* article of 10/31/95 and other texts attached) or both. Your essay should answer the following questions:

(1) what is being proposed, including how it is to be implemented, and with what expected effects?

(2) how would the policy/ies proposed affect the lives of poor people?

(3) should the government adopt these proposals? Why? As you argue for your position, try to bring out the moral principles about justice, rights, and/or obligation on which your approach is based. Also try to anticipate and answer objections of those who might disagree with you.

Describe proposals briefly enough to spend most of your essay on questions (2) and (3).

### (III) SHOULD INCOME LEVEL BE A FACTOR IN SCHOOL ASSIGNMENT CHOICES? (PROPOSAL FOR CAMBRIDGE PUBLIC SCHOOLS)

Answer the following questions with reference to the summary and article distributed in class:

(1) what is being proposed and how would it be implemented?

(2) how would the policy proposed affect the lives of poor children?

(3) Should the city adopt these proposals? Why? As you argue for your position, try to bring out the moral principles about justice, rights, and or/obligation on which your approach is based? Also try to anticipate and reply to objections of those who might disagree with you.

Describe proposals briefly enough so that you spend most of your essay on questions (2) and (3).

# Service-Learning in Ethics:
# A New Pedagogical Approach to the Old Theory-vs.-Practice Challenge

by Sally J. Scholz

Community projects and similar service-learning experiences can make an ethics course a more meaningful endeavor and encourage lasting value formation. This paper presents a case study of a community project from an ethics class at Villanova University. I begin with a discussion of the motivation for the course service requirement, a detailed course description, project planning, and some perceived outcomes. I end with a sample course syllabus.

It goes without saying that ethics courses challenge students to examine their beliefs and actions. But for many students, that challenge is merely a mental exercise and does not affect their daily lives. This is the teacher's challenge: to find some way to encourage students to make the transition from thought to action, i.e., to allow students the opportunity to discover how and why ethics courses are important to their experience. This must be accomplished without proclaiming a set of doctrines for students to uncritically accept. Rather, educators should strive to ensure that students continually examine the important problems that confront society and humanity in general.

Aside from teaching students about moral theory, a course in ethics should assist them in becoming ethical persons by developing a sense of self-awareness. Self-awareness is the capacity to see ourselves as part of a larger community both in how we treat one another and in how our actions affect the quality of life for others. If the students can see how they are part of a larger community, how each person's actions affect others both positively and negatively, then perhaps they will reflect a bit more critically on their use of resources, responsibility to others, and personal integrity — the traditional subject matter of ethics courses.

In addition, a well-developed moral imagination will allow the students the ability to feel sympathy and empathy for those who suffer, and compassion for near and distant people, etc. David Annis (1992) identifies stimulating moral sensitivity and imagination among the goals of teaching ethics. Students must be able to feel compassion, empathy, care, indignation over injustice, and a range of other moral sentiments in order to both think about what an ethical response would be and respond in an ethical manner.

One important way to develop a moral imagination, gain a sense of self-awareness, and challenge the intellectualism and insularity of theoretical or traditional practical ethics courses is to participate in a service-learning experience (cf. Groarke and Scholz 1996). In the case under discussion, the initial motivation for the service was to provide an opportunity for the students to see themselves as part of a larger moral community, one that extended beyond both the walls of the classroom and the boundaries of the campus. I wanted the students to know whom they were talking about when we spent class time discussing such things as our obligation to the poor. And I wanted them to participate in real-life attempts to create a just society rather than settle for talking about such attempts in the classroom.

Ethical Traditions and Contemporary Life is an intermediate ethics course (see page 192) that incorporates both moral theory and practical ethical issues. In teaching this course, I generally teach such standard theories as virtue theory, deontology, utilitarianism, Natural Law, and the ethics of care. In addition, we read selected articles from an applied ethics textbook. Throughout the semester, students respond to a thematic question. Thematic questions help them find a focus in their readings and also serve as a good basis from which to begin critiquing normative theories. For the particular semester in question, the thematic question was, Do we have an obligation to the poor and others in need? Variations on this question included, What is the extent of obligation to distant peoples? Who are the poor? What counts as service? What is the difference between an obligation to serve and a desire to serve? Must our stance on life-and-death issues (e.g., abortion and euthanasia) be consistent with our stance on obligations to the poor or needy (and how so)? Does our level of aid to the poor reveal a society-wide position of discrimination? What do hunger and pornography have in common? Should we enforce environmental standards on third-world countries receiving international aid? Is sustainable development possible and desirable ethically, economically, and environmentally? How do we avoid cultural imperialism in giving aid? And, of course, What are the reasons behind our answers to these questions?

Students were evaluated on the basis of class participation, three essay exams on the course reading and lecture material, and two papers. The first was on a research topic of their choice. For this assignment, students turned in a rough draft and met with me to discuss the draft. Only the final draft was graded. For the second paper, students could opt to write an intellectual journal or single paper, either of which was to focus on their service experience in relation to the course material. The service experience itself was not graded (though failure to complete the requisite service was figured into the final grade). Instead, the second paper, which made use of the service experience as well as the course material, was graded according to quality of argumentation, presentation, and content.

The class began with lectures on and discussions of obligation and the nature of ethics facilitated by Plato's *Euthyphro, Crito and the Apology*. Then, through the Natural Law tradition articulated by Aquinas, deontology represented by Kant, utilitarianism as presented by Mill, and the ethics of care found in the writings of Nel Noddings and Rita Manning, we reassessed our obligations to others.[1] The normative theories present the arguments for how our obligations are determined, measured, and evaluated. The service project, which is discussed further below, adds context to these arguments, thereby facilitating the move of ethics from classroom discussion to everyday life.

For the service-learning component of the course, the students were required to perform 15 hours of community service, subject to my approval. Some of them decided to fulfill the requirement by doing two different service projects to better address their specific interests. The goal was to expose them to people of different socioeconomic backgrounds, thereby better enabling them to reason about moral obligations to others in their immediate community as well as in the wider global community. Most chose to participate in a group project that I arranged as part of the class. This project culminated in a weekend at Caritas Mission in Appalachia,[2] a mission that serves the people of western Pennsylvania by providing whatever is necessary — food, clothing, social support, transportation to medical appointments, etc. The mission broadly defines "the poor" as anyone who has an unmet need.[3]

Prior to embarking on the weekend of work, the class gathered materials for the mission. We broke up into teams to collect donations of tools, hygiene products, food, baby supplies, and other miscellaneous supplies. Students collected these items from their peers in residence halls, and from churches, parents, and friends. We also solicited university faculty and staff for donations. When we arrived at the mission, we unloaded our van load of supplies and prepared for our work assignments. The mission staff divided us into a number of groups and sent us to work sites up to 30 miles away. We spent the day visiting the lonely and mentally ill, cleaning houses, doing heavy yard work, accompanying people on daily chores, and just getting to know some of the people of Appalachia in western Pennsylvania. In the evening, a number of students joined the mission staff in delivering meals and other supplies to area residents. Some of the supplies they delivered they had collected during the previous weeks, thereby allowing all of us to see the effects of our actions and witness a linking of two communities. The work was challenging and the results were often intangible. Nonetheless, we all benefited from the day, both individually and as a class. As one student declared, "When I first heard what we would be doing, I don't think that I recognized the important role that I was going to play in someone's life. I thought of our job as just cleaning. However, in one short day we all made an impact on someone's life."

I now turn to an examination of some of the results of the service component and, especially through the voices of the students, focus on the impact of the experience on course content and methodology. Clearly, the service project assisted the students in their attempts to understand ethical theory, and using that theory to reflect on their service helped them process the reality they witnessed.

*Being able to have a time to share our individual experiences with the class was very beneficial and helped to add insight into the meaning of the trip. I think that there is a very important reason to do something like this in an ethics course. Throughout the semester we have learned a number of normative theories; however, oftentimes the examples provided in class are not sufficient to allow us to go beyond understanding them by incorporating them into our daily life. All of the theories we have discussed have the notion of some sort of human dignity; however, they do not put them into practice.*

Upon completion of the service-learning project, students described the experience as "putting a face to the theory," and the people they worked with in Appalachia as the most memorable and influential teachers of their college careers. One rather important and unexpected result of the service experience was its effect on class unity. Although the students had consistently and respectfully dialogued together from the very beginning, after their experience they stated that they viewed one another and our class discussions in a different light. There was a greater sense of responsibility for one another and our common learning endeavor. The experience of doing service also gave us an additional basis for generating knowledge and discussion. Although we each performed a different task and offered our own impressions, the experience, coupled with our common knowledge of ethical theory, provided fertile ground for analysis and decision making. Some representative quotations from the students include:

*It also brought about a sense of unity to the class [that] makes it all the more comfortable to discuss and debate issues in class. I think it was a wonderful idea to be able to incorporate the theories and issues [that] we have discussed in class to actual realistic situations and conditions in life.*

*The group project is also beneficial because it gave the students an opportunity to get to know their classmates in a more personal way. This is important in recognizing our ethical responsibility to others as well, recognizing our interdependence and relationships with others around us, both those we know and those we have never met.*

*Through sharing our experiences, we learned more about each other, not as classmates but as caring individuals who are trying to make a difference.*

The service component assisted the students (and me) in gaining a heightened sense of self-awareness. Many students described the experience as "breaking out of the bubble" of their everyday campus life. For most, the service component of this class was their first serious experience with people from different cultural, socioeconomic, and educational backgrounds. In addition to highlighting our own place in the social structure, the experience added credibility to the notion that each individual, through the actions that she or he performs, may affect the justness of society in general:

> *By helping others I also helped myself to see my place in society. I realized that I was not insignificant to society as a whole and that one person can make a difference.*
>
> *Putting into practice the ideals and theories learned about in class discussion makes the overall effect of the course more tangible and more personal.*

At the time of the class, many students declared that the experience was a life-altering event. Two years later, one could see that for many of them, this declaration still held true. For example, one of the class participants decided to spend two years after college serving in the Peace Corps, other students participated in or organized volunteer trip experiences for other students at Villanova, and one woman used the service experience from our class as a model for a campus proposal to combat rising alcohol abuse on campus. According to her argument, service requirements in class (1) give students something interesting to do on the weekend, (2) add to the value of the educational experience, and (3) illustrate our interconnectedness to the wider community/society. While these results cannot be attributed solely to the class, linking the theoretical with practical experiences might be seen as providing a more solid foundation for service and lead to more lasting social involvement. As one student wrote:

> *Volunteering at Caritas was one of the most worthwhile experiences I have had while at college. The opportunity to serve some of America's most underprivileged citizens, coupled with a chance to truly get to know some of my classmates, will remain with me forever. The type of work that is done at Caritas is essential in helping to reform the problems that exist in American society.*

This case shows that ethics courses can make a difference. However, as ethics educators, we first have to make a difference in how we traditionally teach such classes. Students must see, understand, and feel the reasons philosophy, and ethics specifically, is valuable. Using a service-learning experience is one effective way to accomplish this. One student summed this up nicely:

> Much of what I have learned during the past two years will quickly be forgotten once I leave Villanova's classrooms to enter the "real world." Ironically, some of the most valuable lessons that I will carry with me were not taught in a classroom but rather on a weekend trip to Caritas Mission in Pennsylvania's rural Appalachia. These were lessons about life and love, about simplicity and optimism, joy and faith. Her [the woman she worked with] needs were not as tangible as the ones I set out to fulfill that weekend, yet they were just as real. It was not necessary to build a house that day, for we built a friendship instead. This service component became so much more than a class requirement; it served as a connection between ethical theory and the "real world." Through practice, we are able to see the morality and the inherent good in helping others. The lessons I learned that weekend will always remain close to my heart. I expected to be giving of myself in Appalachia, but I never expected to receive so much in return. When I reflect on my experiences at Villanova years from now, I will count Betty [the woman in Appalachia] among my most influential professors. She has had a terrific impact on my life.[4]

## Notes

1. Students read all primary sources in their entirety for the normative theories (see syllabus) with the exception of the ethics of care. Rosemarie Tong's *Feminine and Feminist Ethics* presented the care arguments.

2. Caritas Mission, Frenchville, PA.

3. A few students were unable to participate in the weekend mission experience and instead participated in alternative community service experiences. One worked with Habitat for Humanity, another tutored at an inner-city school, and another worked at an antiabortion support network.

4. Special thanks to Betsy Burk, Erica Calton, Megan Clancy, Margie Clemens, Denise Decell, Jenny Jacobs, Johanna Keely, Kate Kennedy, Christie Lehner, Stacey McArdle, Alieen McGuirk, Erin Neville, Gita Timmerman, and Lynnette Uhrin. They participated in this class and allowed me to quote them here. Their generosity and openness made this service-learning enterprise successful.

## References

Annis, David. (January/April 1992). "The Philosopher as Teacher. Teaching Ethics in Higher Education: Goals and the Implications of the Empirical Research on Moral Development." *Metaphilosophy* 23(1-2): 187-202.

Groarke, Leo, and Sally J. Scholz. (December 1996). "Seven Principles for Better Practical Ethics." *Teaching Philosophy* 19(4): 337-355.

# ETHICAL TRADITIONS AND CONTEMPORARY LIFE

## COURSE DESCRIPTION

Ethical Traditions and Contemporary Life is an exploration of a variety of major ethical theories in western philosophy as well as an examination of their application for some current personal and social moral problems. This course is designed to provide an environment that fosters cooperative learning thereby allowing students the opportunity to develop personal skills in critical thinking and evaluation, and respectful dialogue concerning difficult moral issues.

## REQUIRED TEXTS

Plato, *The Trial and Death of Socrates* (Indianapolis: Hackett, 1975)
Thomas Aquinas, *Treatise on Law* (Washington, D.C.: Gateway, 1992)
Immanuel Kant, *Grounding for the Metaphysics of Morals* (Indianapolis: Hackett, 1981)
John Stuart Mill, *Utilitarianism* (Indianapolis: Hackett, 1979)
Thomas Mappes and Jane Zembaty, *Social Ethics: Morality and Social Policy* (New York: McGraw-Hill, 1992)
Rosemarie Tong, *Feminine and Feminist Ethics* (Belmont: Wadsworth Publishing, 1993)

## COURSE OUTLINE

| | |
|---|---|
| Week 1: | Introduction, Community Service Discussion, Plato |
| Week 2: | Plato |
| Week 3: | Aquinas |
| Week 4: | Kant |
| Week 5: | Kant, Community Service Discussion |
| Week 6: | Mill |
| Week 7: | Mill, Feminist Ethics |
| Week 8: | Feminist Ethics |
| Week 9 & 10: | Alternative Perspectives: African American Ethics (Alain Locke), Liberation Theology Ethics (Gustavo Gutierrez), Native American Ethics |
| Week 11: | ISSUE: World Hunger: Singer, pp. 406-413, Hardin, pp. 413-420, Presidential Commission, pp. 403-406. |
| Week 12: | ISSUE: Euthanasia: Rachels, pp. 110- 115, Sullivan, pp. 115-121, Rachels, pp. 121-132, Rehnquist, pp. 140-146. |
| Week 13: | ISSUE: Discrimination and Preferential Treatment: Rowe, pp. 296-306, Murray, pp. 325-333, Bok, pp. 333-336. |
| Week 14: | ISSUE: Environment: Wenz, pp. 499-505, Russow, pp. 505-513, Guha, pp. 513-522. |
| Week 15: | ISSUE: Pornography: Longino, pp. 274-282, Wicclair, pp. 282-288, Attorney General, pp. 267-274. |

# The Power of Service-Learning in Developing Critical-Thinking Skills

by Mary Esther Schnaubelt

When I first taught the Community College of Aurora's critical-thinking class (identified in our catalog as Applied Thinking Strategies), I discovered what I considered to be a fundamental problem with the course. Service-learning turned out to be the solution to this problem as well as a way to expand the scope and depth of the class.

The course's purpose is to help students learn how to develop and enhance their thinking abilities for all aspects of life. In other words, it is concerned not with philosophical inquiry into the cognitive process but rather with skills development. This being the case, it suffered from the unique difficulty of trying to explore how to think without having any specific topic to think about or to use in applying and developing thinking skills.

The text most of our critical-thinking classes use contains a selection of excellent essays and excerpts from writing in the disciplines students are likely to encounter in college. These pieces are designed to serve as tools in developing specific thinking skills and as a focus for class assignments. While not all critical-thinking classes use this text, the general class approach is to use material in a text or texts as the basis for class activities. The difficulty I found in teaching critical thinking in this manner was twofold.

The first difficulty was classroom continuity. A critical-thinking class must examine the specific elements involved in thinking and practice utilization of those elements. By depending on a variety of readings as the tools for practice, the class lacks focus. This problem arises because one cannot think about particular ideas without engaging those ideas in all their complexity and depth. Using essays and excerpts simply as tools for thinking while not focusing on the complexity a particular idea demands results in a shallow activity. Learning in this manner scatters class concentration and leads to a lack of depth that contradicts the process of truly thinking critically.

Service-learning solved this problem by providing the class with a focused content, aside from developing basic thinking skills. This content gave the class continuity and the ability to engage in the process of fully developing ideas. This, in turn, provided depth without dramatically increasing the course workload. Since the students would be engaged outside of the classroom on community projects, the concepts and issues of community could be developed and explored throughout the semester, with the students supplying the necessary background information. The basic readings and homework for the course could then be focused on the specific critical-thinking skills being developed. The theme of community and the application of this theme to the specific projects the students were engaged in provided the class with topics perfectly suited to the application of critical-thinking skills.

A second difficulty with this course stemmed from the type of material it legitimized as significant. Traditionally, only the written word was presented as material on which to think and reflect. In order to improve students' thinking skills for academia and their careers, it is indeed essential to develop their skill in analyzing writing in a variety of fields. This, however, still represents a limited approach to thinking. Many areas in which people should and do engage in critical thinking exist outside of written works. Thus, the class now aims to develop thinking skills in students not only so that they may engage in reflection on the written word but also so that they may critically evaluate and understand the world around them. Essays on a text, while reflective of experiences in the world, are not the same as the opportunity to process lived experience.

Service-learning provided a shared real-world experience for all members of the class to work with and reflect upon. This commonality created a community within the class that would not have existed otherwise. It gave a shared focus for discussion and the application of emerging skills. Focusing on the service work in class also provided the benefit of putting students on more or less equal ground in terms of relevant experience.

We still, of course, dealt with many readings over the course of the semester. The majority of them, however, connected somehow to ideas of community. In this way, students in the class encountered four levels of experience. The foundational level was the development of critical-thinking skills. Immediately above this was the focus on community, achieved through readings, discussion, and shared experience. Next came the students' service project, a required learning experience but performed outside of class time. Finally, each student, using critical-thinking skills, had to synthesize all these different levels into his or her own articulation of a relationship with the community.

From a pedagogical perspective, this was a very interesting process to facilitate and witness. The students were initially skeptical about the value of doing a service project and were unclear as to how it could be important to the class as a whole. This perception changed as we began to work on the first skill covered in the class — problem solving. As the students had not yet begun their service work, we focused on the Aurora community as a whole. Each student was asked to identify what he or she perceived as the most significant problem facing Aurora. I then grouped people by identifying similar problems and tasked each group with solving a community issue. Each group presented its solution to the class, and the entire group discussed the viability of the proposal. While this was a very basic thinking exercise, it had an amazing effect on the class. Suddenly solutions to the issues of the community were accessible and within their grasp. While none of the students ended up working at an agency that addressed his or her specific issue, the activity still illustrated for them the power their creative thought had and gave them the inspiration to seek out and perform the service work they had previously questioned.

The final project brought together all the elements of the semester. The challenge of this project was that students had to take their specific service work and connect it to larger social problems. They then had to evaluate whether, given this larger framework, their work and the work of the agency they had worked with were an appropriate response. We had a week of in-class work to aid the students in developing their papers and presentations. This was valuable not only for peer feedback on the challenges of accomplishing such tasks; but, more important, it allowed other class members to work through the process of identifying social problems and solutions in areas in which the students had not previously worked.

Although the students had initially been reluctant, they gave the class a glowing evaluation and said the service-learning had been a valuable tool in learning critical thinking. Student comments included the following:

> *Working with children, I found several connections with the material the text covered. Many thinking skills and objectives used in class were carried over into my volunteer work.*

> *It helped me think from other perspectives. Before, I only thought of my [own] opinion. Now, I try to listen to other opinions openly, then respond with a thought-out answer. I became more tuned into what was really happening in people's situations instead of making a preconceived judgment.*

The majority of students planned to continue working in the community.

I would highly recommend that anyone who teaches critical thinking use some element of service-learning in his or her class. It is a powerful tool that all students can access and that provides the full depth of material needed to train and improve thinking skills.

# Sojourning in the Art World:
## Service-Learning in Philosophy of Art

by Dan Lloyd[1]

Not too long ago the trustees of my college decided to update the artistic holdings of our campus, and to this end they set out to acquire a contemporary work of art for permanent display in the college art museum. Not being timid, the trustees wanted a challenging, cutting-edge work, preferably from the West Coast, but they felt they lacked the expertise to find and buy the right piece. As it happened, a few of them had heard of my interest in modernism and its philosophical challenges, and so I found myself with an unusual assignment: I was to fly to Los Angeles with a $10,000 check and bring back something distinguished, a unique object to be discussed and appreciated for years to come.

I relished my task, but for the wrong reasons. I have good friends in L.A., and I used my official trip to spend time doing some unofficial socializing. Too much time, as it turned out. I put off my foray into the L.A. art world until suddenly it was my last day, and I had done nothing to complete my commission. My flight was barely two hours away as I rushed into one of the top galleries. The folks there, however, were very helpful. Yes, they told me, they had just the work for me, at exactly the price I could afford. It was a small recent sculpture by "J," a dynamic postmodernist with degrees from Yale and NYU and a considerable resume of solo and group shows, mainly in California. This particular untitled work was small and light — carry-on baggage. Indeed, they had just received it from J's studio and had not even unpacked it from its crate. Would I like to see it? My cab was waiting. Without even looking at the work, I told them I'd take it. I hastily signed the check over to the gallery, slipped my acquisition, still in its crate, in a duffel, and caught my flight with minutes to spare.

I was pleased. What I had heard of J reassured me that he had the status and ability to execute something notable, controversial, even brilliant. I returned to my office with the duffel bag and called my contact among the trustees, who set out immediately to see the work and congratulate me on a job well done. I cleared off my desk, and popped open the crate, eagerly unwinding the bubble wrap around J's magnum opus. But when I pulled off the last wrapper, I found not a sculpture but a joke. The "work" was nothing but a package of Twinkies, direct from a convenience store, complete with its 69¢ price tag. With alarm and confusion, I called the L.A. gallery that had sold me the piece. Yes, they said, that's the work — a package of Twinkies. No, J had not executed a brilliant copy of a package of Twinkies; he had, as I feared, simply gone out and bought the Twinkies and declared them to be his latest untitled work. No, I would not be entitled to a refund of $9,999.31. I had, after all, purchased a work by the famous artist J.

I hung up the phone and stared at the Twinkies in heart-pounding disbelief. A trustee of my college — my employer — would be arriving at any moment. My only hope, desperate as it was, would be to convince her that this very package of Twinkies was a work of art, indeed an interesting, even a good, work of art. At my door I heard a knock. What could I say? What would I say?

* * *

With this thought experiment I open my version of a philosophy of art course, also known as Art/Hartford (see pages 203-204). My students' immediate task, prior to any other exposure to the philosophy of art, is to save my job by constructing their best case for J's untitled work of art. To this end, I divide the class into groups of three or four and allow about 20 minutes of undirected conversation within each group. To help them, I unwind J's work from its bubble wrap and carefully place it before them. Then I reach into a paper bag for an ordinary package of Twinkies — they can confirm that the two are indistinguishable. The students regard J's "work" with disdain, but they soon warm to the job of distinguishing it from its ordinary counterpart: It is, first, ridiculously expensive — perhaps this makes it art. It was certified as art by the gallery from which I bought it. In the most relevant sense, it was created by a "real" artist, with training and credentials. It was destined for a pedestal here at the college, and would have a little bronze plaque installed at its base and a good theft alarm. With a little more discussion, they begin to recognize that J's work has very different content from the ordinary Twinkies. The work is ironic, humorous. By exalting a piece of junk food, the work underscores the extremes of our consumerist, mass-produced, disposable, and ultimately trashy culture. It invites our reflection on the internal contradictions of the package, with its jaunty, garish graphics, versus its dismal nutritional values, versus the list of chemicals from which a Twinkie is made (or extruded). None of this reflective content is present in the ordinary Twinkie, which is, after all, a mere 69¢ snack. Its "content," if it has any, is simply "Eat me!" But unlike J's work, it actively discourages the reflective consideration that J's piece actively provokes. The two could not be more different.

This example, and my students' interpretation of it, quickly immerses them in the philosophical challenge posed by modern art. Modernism, especially Pop Art, made it a mission to push on the boundaries of artworks and ordinary things, leading eventually to cases very similar to my imagined

Twinkies — Warhol's Brillo boxes and soup cans, for example. Modernism makes the point, in various ways, that there need be no discernible difference between a work of art and an ordinary thing.

This perspective on art reflects the theoretical perspective championed by Arthur Danto, one of the wittiest and most provocative contemporary writers on art. "J" is a favorite artist of Danto's, too, often invoked to highlight intuitions about the nature of art. "The Tales of J" develops the theory that artworks are products of an Art World, constituted essentially by a network of relations among artists, galleries, critics, and audiences. And it is this conception of art that opens the way toward a meaningful service-learning component in a philosophy of art course. The Art World has its outposts in the various arts in every city and town. At every art institution, daily discourse and decision contribute to the overall creation of the boundaries of art, and to community standards for good art. As it happens, most art institutions run on small budgets and can use the services of students. In return, students can listen to, or perhaps even contribute to, the street-level and streetwise discussions and daily system of artistic production.

In Art/Hartford, student placements are as various as the students' interests. In general, the students work at the less-well-funded and -established institutions — a small theater, a senior citizens craft center, a cultural center, an avant-garde gallery. Their work tends to be rather incidental to the welfare of the organizations they work for, owing to the limited hours they spend at their placements, as well as to the limited energies available for their training and supervision. But these constraints actually seem to enhance the experience, giving the students a chance to observe and, most important, to converse. The rickety outposts of the Art World we encounter in Art/Hartford impress the students with the realities of artistic production in this time and place.

To perceive the everyday activities of the Community Cultural Center, the local Repertory Theater, the Senior Citizens' Craft Center, the Downtown Gallery, or the Civic Ballet as constituting and creating the Art World requires a reflective reconsideration of those activities. In Art/Hartford, the first and most essential engine of reflection is the course itself. In the classroom, students read and discuss a number of "greatest hits" in the philosophy of art. They include Plato on imitation, Aristotle on tragedy, Kant on the beautiful, Tolstoy, Bell, Langer, Danto, and other contemporary thinkers, as well as genre-specific writers, such as Clement Greenberg, who raise specific philosophical issues for the various fine arts. In the first part of the course, we focus on the nature of art in general. In the second part, we turn to genres, following the interests of the students, interests also reflected in their community placements. At some point in every class, I can raise a question about how the issues in the reading are reflected in students' ongoing community experience. The connection is always there.

The first part of the course is historically ordered, and so we begin with an opposition between Plato (*Republic,* Books III and X) and Aristotle (*Poetics*) on the value of art and the specific desiderata of good art. Not surprisingly, these issues loom large in students' community experiences as well. First and foremost, the students see real contemporary art in a societal context, deeply conditioned by capitalism and politics. These extra-aesthetic forces can be usefully contrasted with the theoretical standards of Plato and Aristotle, and this theme is prominent again with Tolstoy ("What Is Art?") and through its conspicuous absence in Clive Bell's discussion of art as Significant Form. Institutional theories of art such as Danto's (1981) and Dickie's (1971) come later in the historical sequence, but to good effect. The course is then ripe for a thorough look at the contexts of artworks, and the students are certainly alert to the issue after some weeks in the Art World themselves.

A secondary theme running through the course is the distinction between art and craft. This too emerges first with Plato, but finds its fullest development in Collingwood. In the real Art World outposts of student experience, the distinction is often fuzzy. The students see beautiful and powerful works by outsiders to the official Art World, as well as insider works of dubious value. They wonder whether they themselves could make art or, by some sort of declaration of intent, become "real" artists. (As a course project, I encourage students to create their own works in the spirit of J and interpret them for the class.)

Every service-learning experience I've overseen (or engaged in myself) has led to a questioning of assumptions, and the experiences of Art/Hartford are no exception. Students come to the course with a romantic conception of the artist as a solitary genius at work in isolation from the mundane world, a special person with a mystical designation and calling. This lofty conception of high art informs much of the official history of art, and it is not explicitly challenged in the canon of aesthetics. But in the communities of Hartford no artist is an island, and the production of art is subject no less than other productions to social forces.

This has led the participants in Art/Hartford to a vivid realization of the interplay between art and social justice. That is, the question "what is art?" rapidly becomes transformed into a series of "who" questions: *Who* makes art? In our society, who *can* make art — who has the resources, the credentials, the sanction? For *whom* is the work made? *Who* can appreciate it? *Who* is allowed in the gallery door — with the education, the interests, and the time to appreciate art? And with each of these questions, we raise the possibility that many institutions and practices of the Art World are systematically and invisibly elitist. Feminist and Marxist critics, among others, have long observed that the official High Art World is often elitist and that writing about art often ignores the plurality of art worlds in a society. But that critique is beautifully realized in the experience of students sojourning in the Art World.

At the same time, the diversity of service-learning placements in the course illuminates the multiplicity of art worlds. Quite apart from the valorized New York Art World are all the individuals and groups making art out of their own experiences. Two students, for example, worked with a textile art workshop at a senior center located in the North End of Hartford, in the African-American community. The artists there, some making art for the first time, worked in blissful ignorance of the rise and fall of -isms in the world of high art. Nor was the value of such artworks in any way diminished by their distance from the romance of solitary genius.

In short, encounters with art animate every classroom discussion and all student writing. As I mentioned above, the primary engine of reflection is our class discussions of the readings and our explicit consideration of them in relation to Art/Hartford site work. However, reflection can be encouraged through other means as well:

**1. Reflective Writing.** Service-learning is of marginal value without careful thought about the interaction of community experience with classroom learning. Discussion facilitates this interaction, but, of course, writing is no less important. In my opinion, every sort of writing is improved if it is done in public — that is, if student essays are circulated to the class. Accordingly, in most of my classes students converse with one another electronically, usually in some sort of chat room format, but also through an exchange of drafts of longer essays.

**2. Reflection in the Community.** Research projects in the philosophy of art can draw on the expertise of local citizens of the Art World, including artists. These conversations illuminate another thread running throughout the philosophy of art, namely, theories of artistic creation and the psychology of the artist. This need not end with a student report or term paper. Rather, what students discover can be presented back to the community to foster the same reflective atmosphere that service-learning creates in the classroom. At Trinity, we have several means of integrating community voices in education and research, and returning the fruits of learning to the community. Artists can be interviewed and the interviews used to produce video documentaries, which are then aired on local cable TV (often in the schools). Or courses can culminate in public events — panels, debates, presentations — offered to both on-campus and off-campus audiences.

**3. The Professor in the Field.** For each type of service-learning I've introduced in my courses, I've found it very helpful to identify a way to participate in a project myself. Art/Hartford has led to an ongoing affiliation with the Connecticut Prison Association (recently renamed Community Partners in Action) and its Prison Arts Programs. Prison art is compelling outsider art, and raises many issues about alternative art worlds. It is also a vivid and concrete reflection of the diverse and specific lives of prisoners. As a philosopher, I am challenged in many ways — aesthetically, morally, and politically — by such art. My experience is thus like that of my students. It informs my teaching. No less important, it informs my life.

In conclusion, my experiments with service-learning in several philosophy courses, including Art/Hartford, suggest that service-learning is inherently philosophical. While it does contribute to the welfare of the community and also increases the civic engagement of students, neither of these outcomes is what I value most. Rather, it is the reflective connection students make between what they read and what they experience. The encounter is inevitably Socratic, as students discover the incompleteness and falsity of their assumptions, and it is equally Aristotelian, in the sense that their encounters lead them to a richer, more articulated description of the world around them. In the real world, a package of Twinkies might be art — or it might not be. But in the aftermath of service-learning in aesthetics, students never again see art as a cultural given, but instead begin to appreciate the diversity of voices and interests that intersect in its production.

## Note

1. I would like to thank the students of Art/Hartford for all their insight, and David Lisman for his helpful questions and advice.

## References

Danto, A. (1981). *The Transfiguration of the Commonplace*. Cambridge, MA: Harvard University Press.

Dickie, G. (1971). *Aesthetics: An Introduction*. Indianapolis, IN: Bobbs-Merrill.

# ART/HARTFORD
## Syllabus


## WELCOME

<>    **What is art?**

<>    **What makes a work of art good or bad?**

<>    **How do aesthetic values hook up with other kinds of values?**

<>    **How do artworks reflect the values and practices of the communities in which they are created?**

<>    **What is the nature of specific genres of art (e.g. painting, film, drama, performance art, photography...)?**

<>    **What is beauty?**

<>    **What can the city and people of Hartford teach us about these questions?**

These are the central questions of the philosophy of art, also known as aesthetics. In ART/HARTFORD we will discuss these central questions from the philosophy of art in the context of the contemporary art of area artists and performers. In our class meetings, we will read and discuss important works in the philosophy of art. These include classic philosophical writers (Plato, Aristotle, Kant, Tolstoy, Bell, Langer, Danto, and others) as well as genre-specific writers who raise specific philosophical issues for the various fine arts. Through our readings we will become fluent in the traditional frameworks of aesthetics, but we will also examine theoretical challenges to those frameworks, particularly the challenge raised by feminism and other new voices.

Outside of class we will look for artworks that challenge us. These works will be the case studies for the semester. Whenever possible, we will experience the works themselves through a variety of formal and informal "field trips." (We live in the field. Art is everywhere.)

In addition, students in the course will explore the nature of art at its point of origin, at the side of artists. To this end, a small part of extracurricular time each week will be spent in a "microinternship" at an area art institution. (You may also satisfy the out-of-class requirement through a separate one-credit internship under my supervision, with ART/HARTFORD (and an additional internship paper) as its academic component.)

## WHAT THIS CLASS WILL BE LIKE:

Fusion. Through discussion, we work together to enlarge our experience of art and to deepen our thought about it. No one, including the professor, is a final authority. The learning we achieve will be a communal project, built upon the commitment and effort of everyone in the course. The learning in this course will not be packaged. Be prepared for ART/HARTFORD insights/incites/in-sites to strike at any moment. Collaboration and community are key.

YOUR EFFORT:

1.  Class attendance is essential to keep the course coherent and to fulfill your role as teacher and colleague.

2.  The course readings are essential frameworks and common ground for all our discussions.

3.  Electronic discussion. ART/HARTFORD will have a bulletin board all to itself. That BB will be divided into topics. You will be contributing to the e-discussion twice a week (or more, if you feel like it), adding to any topic you choose. Here are the topics to start:
    <>  Great art. Your recommendations of shows/events/works that you think others will appreciate.
    <>  Puzzle cases. Shows/events/works that challenge the concept of art or other concepts discussed in the course. You'll describe and analyze your puzzle cases.
    <>  Reading and class discussion, continued. Issues that arise through the readings, in anticipation of or response to class discussion.
    <>  Your choice. The program allows you to create topics. Ultimately, the BB itself will become a student-designed work of electronic art.

4.  Collaborative work analysis. Shortly after reading week, you and a partner will analyze one work of art/? in terms of the authors read up to that point. This paper will be about five pages long.

5.  Micro-internship. You'll spend a few hours a week at an area art institution, doing what needs doing but, with luck, learning how art happens. I'll help you make initial contacts and get started. Plan to write a report on your experience at the end of the semester.

6.  Art work. Much of modern art tests the boundaries of art, and at the boundaries art is less a matter of skill or craft than it is of conception and idea. Your final work of the semester will be an art/? work, executed somehow on the Trinity campus. Plan to use only the materials you can scarf up for free.

7.  One-minute papers. We will often end class with these quick summaries of the day's important issues.

READINGS:

Readings are from Dickie, Sclafani, and Roblin, *Aesthetics, a Critical Anthology*.

# Philosophical Inquiry as Responsible Engagement

## by William M. Sullivan

Philosophers are at their best when they enable us to grasp the understandings and values embedded in human practices and institutions. The great concerns of philosophy during the 20th century have been of this kind: understanding the practice and implications of the natural sciences, for example, or trying to grasp the illusive relations between cognition and the largely tacit understandings involved in the use of language. The public contribution of philosophy has been its insistence that it is important to try to grasp these often hidden and unnoticed understandings of world, society, and self that silently shape our ways of living. Whether we are aware of them or not, philosophers have insisted, these assumptions are at work, enabling or disabling our thinking, etching the horizons of our expectations. Making tacit meanings explicit opens the possibility of freedom, of criticism and responsible engagement.

It must be said, however, that philosophers have not always been so ready to subject their own practices and beliefs to the sorts of critique that they have developed and applied to other areas. Happily, the philosophers writing here in *Beyond the Tower* represent a welcome countertrend. They are carrying the central philosophical task of critical inquiry into the emerging area of service-learning, which has recently become a focus of innovative academic practice in teaching, including philosophy courses that incorporate substantial components of experiential learning. These authors show how this movement, far from being peripheral to philosophical concerns, can give new urgency to important questions about the discipline of philosophy and the enterprise of higher education.

All the contributors are convinced of the importance of this movement. They bring to the topic conceptual rigor applied with infectious finesse. They explore and criticize the guiding assumptions of service-learning, both those explicitly proclaimed and what remains implicit in the pedagogy. However, this collection does not present a party line. The authors approach the subject from a variety of philosophical subfields and through a plurality of methods. They do not agree about a number of issues. They differ about how best to describe what service-learning in philosophy is — or ought to be — about. They are not agreed about the terminology to be employed for the approaches to knowledge that such courses involve; for example, whether or not service-learning represents a form of postmodernism. Nor are they unanimous in their understanding of how ethical reflection is related to questions of knowledge, though many of the contributors are concerned with this issue.

Despite these lively disagreements, a common theme emerges in these essays. This theme holds large implications for both the discipline of philosophy and higher education as a whole. The authors in this collection all conceive and practice philosophy as a discipline of self-reflective inquiry. But such a discipline, they argue, cannot be learned in any meaningful way aside from actually engaging the tacit understandings embedded in social life and expressed in culture. In order for philosophical education to take place, in other words, students must learn to actually practice the art of inquiry, thereby starting to make philosophy's critical techniques their own.

This view is consistent with the traditional rationale for including philosophy as a core discipline of the liberal arts: that is, the belief that developing the capacity for self-reflective inquiry importantly enhances both social and individual welfare. But how is this to be effectively done? Advocates of service-learning claim that carefully thought-out and monitored student engagement in service to the larger society provides a particularly effective way to develop students' capacities for reflective inquiry. At the same time, they argue, such service enables students to contribute to the common life the students share with their fellow citizens. The philosophers writing in this volume believe they can show how and why this is the case.

Their argument goes this way: Because philosophy as the practice of reflective inquiry cannot be effectively learned apart from examination of some cultural practices, it is important that students be engaged with issues that seem to them significant, that touch on their sense of identity and what they value. These issues may, of course, be encountered in texts, including historical texts, and in fact such texts are crucial to the enterprise. Advocates of service-learning need not claim that direct experience is the only way to promote critical self-reflection. Rather, they can claim that service-learning programs can be especially effective in enabling students to take a serious and critical perspective on their own previously unexamined beliefs.

Service-learning can do this, the argument continues, because it explicitly links inquiry to practices of democratic life. It involves students and faculty in social collaborations so that they connect with ongoing efforts of citizens to address common needs and problems. The context of service-learning makes it easier for students to see their own beliefs in relation to the larger social world and the perspectives of others who share that world. The inquiry comes alive, in other words, and is likely to become existentially real. Yet this is controlled inquiry. It remains grounded in the practices through which citizens cooperate to realize democratic purposes in problematic situations. Effective programs of service-learning, therefore, teach by example as well as precept that inquiry promotes responsible engagement.

This understanding of service-learning gives a clear priority to the notion that rationality is fundamentally practical in nature. Reason, on this understanding, is always rooted in the practices of a concrete social and cultural world. It is primarily exemplified in the efforts of participants to understand their world and its values. Several of the authors contrast this practical understanding of reason with the decontextualized, purely formal kind of rationality such as one finds in engineering or other technical pursuits where the aim is efficiency of action. Practical reason, for its part, aims at communication and mutual understanding. It is not surprising, then, that most of the contributors to *Beyond the Tower* embody philosophical styles that derive from the late Wittgenstein, Continental phenomenology and hermeneutics, and especially American pragmatism.

This affinity is worth thinking about. Since World War II, the preponderant conception of philosophy in American universities has been the notion of philosophy as a quintessentially technical field, defined by expertise, much as the natural sciences are. One important implication of installing this approach as the disciplinary orthodoxy has been to remove from discussion the way philosophers understand themselves and their role. Imitating the prestigious style of the natural sciences, philosophers have sought to define their role in terms of an elaborate, sometimes arcane, disciplinary specialization. From this perspective, teaching philosophy has ideally meant induction into this community of expert discourse. But just as the sciences have progressed by largely screening out contact with nonspecialists, the dominant model has sought to do the same. An unfortunate by-product has been a disciplinary insularity that has too often cut philosophers off from potentially fruitful collaboration beyond disciplinary boundaries.

Advocates of service-learning argue that this approach begs the question of philosophical method and identity. Serious consideration of service-learning, they imply, opens up some important questions that Anglo-American philosophical orthodoxy has arbitrarily bracketed and ignored. These questions are about the relationship between social conditions and epistemological categories, issues about how theory is to be understood in relation to practice, and finally the question of how philosophers should understand themselves and the nature of their enterprise. Indeed, if one grants that promoting reflection and deliberation among a wide segment of the population is at the core of the purpose of higher education, and of philosophy's historical aims, then partisans of philosophy as practical reason make a strong case against the way philosophy has constricted its disciplinary boundaries.

The contributors to *Beyond the Tower* are seeking to return to the teaching of philosophy an all-too-often-missing integrity. Developing the capacity for self-awareness cannot be separated, except artificially and at the risk of promoting a destructive sophism, from concerns about the ethical engagement of the person in life and society. If this is true for students, then it must also be the case, *a fortiori,* for academic professionals, academic disciplines, and institutions. Consequently, if service-learning's philosophical advocates can push their case that philosophy points beyond the dogmatic limitations of scientific empiricism toward a concern with the humanly formative processes of culture, this movement could have significant repercussions within philosophy as a field.

This emphasis upon the public referent and responsibility of philosophy may still be unfamiliar to many in the academy. However, it speaks directly to one of the central tensions in higher education today. In many quarters, controversy has been stirring around the issue of how to properly balance the academy's interest in specialized disciplinary inquiry with what is sometimes called its civic mission. This civic mission has been traditionally a primary concern of the humanities and, at least in their early days, of the social sciences. Furthermore, while this effort has sometimes taken highly restrictive, aristocratic forms, it has also been promoted in the name of democracy. It is noteworthy that in its democratic form it has had historically close links with the American pragmatist tradition.

Today, higher education and the academic profession have found themselves under increasing pressure from critics and patrons to measure up to standards of performance derived from the marketplace. Under these conditions another, very different kind of "pragmatism," the reduction of all values to means toward economic efficiency, threatens to undermine academic autonomy. In this context, the university is struggling to find a voice of authority, to speak self-confidently of its value in ways that carry conviction and yet are faithful to the institution's defining purposes. Here the long-standing tensions between disciplinary specialization and liberal or civic education cannot help but become more acute.

How should the academy understand itself, and why should the public support it with grants of autonomy as well as funds? The specialization model supposes that the real point of universities is to generate "useful knowledge," in the sense of products or techniques that deliver increased control over the processes of nature or society. On this model, education is a secondary outcome, aside from training up new specialists. By contrast, the alternative civic model insists that universities, including their functions of specialized research, exist to enable individuals and societies to understand themselves better, and so finally serve a practical purpose, construed in the moral rather than the technical sense.

A self-reflective service-learning movement could contribute importantly to making this case by showing why realizing such a conception of higher education is a public and not simply an academic concern. It would, moreover, be tragic if these efforts to reinvigorate a more engaged practice of learning were to be confused with the other, utilitarian sort of pragmatism that has become common coin in discussions of higher education as an "industry." For practical reasoning in its fuller sense is a crucial resource for enabling the academy to find its authentic voice in today's difficult environment. The editors and writers of *Beyond the Tower* have done us all real service in bringing these issues to clarity in an accessible, stimulating, and useful way. They point the way to a kind of philosophical education that can enable today's students to appreciate that independence of mind means not aloof superiority but self-confident and responsible social engagement.

# Appendix

# Annotated Bibliography:
## Service-Learning and Philosophy

Aristotle. (1980). *The Nicomachean Ethics,* translated with introduction by W.D. Ross, revised by J.L. Ackrill and J.O. Urmson. New York, NY: Oxford University Press.

> Aristotle, who flourished around 350 BC, is one of the founders of the Western philosophical tradition. He advocated a virtue ethics, and maintained that part of our ethical obligation is to be a good citizen.

Barber, B.R. (1984). *Strong Democracy.* Berkeley, CA: University of California Press.

> Building on the work of Rorty, Barber critiques the classical liberal tradition of political thought. He maintains that this tradition is due to epistemological foundationalism. He advocates for greater participatory democracy and a community pragmatic decision-making process.

Bellah, R.N., R. Madsen, W.M. Sullivan, A. Swidler, and S.M. Tipton. (1985). *Habits of the Heart: Individualism and Commitment in American Life.* New York, NY: Harper & Row.

> A seminal work in the tradition of civic republicanism, this book provides interviews with many people, illuminating their individualist orientation. This book provides an important analysis of the effects of procedural republicanism.

———. (1991). *The Good Society.* New York, NY: Alfred A. Knopf.

> This book builds upon the civic republican ideas of *Habits of the Heart,* and examines various institutions in our society in terms of their inadequacies and capability to contribute to the common good.

Boyte, H.C. (1989). *CommonWealth: A Return to Citizen Politics.* New York, NY: The Free Press.

> An early work defending citizen democracy, or commonwealth. Boyte provides some philosophical defense of this concept and then traces the United States's history of this public philosophy.

Clark, Septima. (1990). *Ready From Within: Septima Clark and the Civil Rights Movement,* edited by Cynthia Stokes Brown. Trenton, NJ: Africa World Press.

> Septima Clark was a leader in the American civil rights movement of

the 1950s and 1960s. She, along with Bernice Robinson, Esau Jenkins, and Myles Horton, founded the Citizenship Schools, where African-American citizens prepared themselves to participate in the political system.

Daly, M., ed. (1994). *Communitarianism: A New Public Ethics*. Belmont, CA: Wadsworth Publishers.
A good collection of essays pertaining to the debate between philosophical liberalism and communitarianism.

Danto, A. (1981). *The Transfiguration of the Commonplace*. Cambridge, MA: Harvard University Press.
Danto's theory of art, with many lovely thought experiments.

Day, Dorothy. (1952). *The Long Loneliness*. New York, NY: Harper & Brothers.
Dorothy Day was an American activist and leader in peace and social justice work in the middle years of this century. With Peter Maurin, she founded the Catholic Worker movement.

Dewey, J. (1927/1991). *The Public and Its Problems*. Athens, OH: Swallow Press.
Dewey is perhaps the most cited philosopher in connection with service-learning (see, for example, D.E. Giles, Jr., and J. Eyler, [1994], "The Theoretical Roots of Service-Learning in John Dewey: Toward a Theory of Service-Learning." *Michigan Journal of Community Service Learning* 1: 77-85). This is a frequently cited book in the service-learning movement. Here Dewey advocates for greater participatory democracy to create the great community.

———. (1963). *Liberalism and Social Action*. New York, NY: Capricorn.
In this small book, Dewey traces the development of liberalism from the strands of natural rights theory, romanticism, and idealism. These diverse strands, he argues, have left a tension within liberalism that has not been resolved. He thus articulates a vision of what liberalism needs to be and claims that this will be achieved primarily through education. He describes liberal education not merely as the acquisition of knowledge and skills but also as the development of moral character.

—————. (1993). "The Ethics of Democracy." In *The Political Writings*, edited by D. Morris and I. Shapiro, pp. 59-65. Indianapolis, IN: Hackett. (orig. published 1888)

>This essay contrasts democracy with aristocracy (as represented in Plato's *Republic*) and locates the superiority of democracy in its recognition of the importance of individuality.

Dickie, G. (1971). *Aesthetics: An Introduction*. Indianapolis, IN: Bobbs-Merrill.

>An overview of theories of art, with emphasis on the institutional theory.

—————, R. Sclafani, and R. Roblin. (1989). *Aesthetics: A Critical Anthology*. New York, NY: St. Martin's Press.

>The course anthology in Art/Hartford. It includes selections from all the authors mentioned in Lloyd's chapter.

Giroux, H.A. (1988). *Schooling and the Struggle for Public Life: Critical Pedagogy in the Modern Age*. Minneapolis, MN: University of Minnesota Press.

>An important early book by Giroux, who represents neo-Marxist public philosophy. Giroux maintains that equipping students with the critical skills to understand cultural hegemony is necessary to achieve social transformation.

Groarke, Leo, and Sally J. Scholz. (1996). "Seven Principles for Better Practical Ethics." *Teaching Philosophy* 19(4): 337-355.

>This article identifies seven problems with traditional approaches to teaching practical (or "applied") ethics. These problems are an overemphasis on theory, intellectualism, formalism, an emphasis on moral disagreement, overspecialization, insularity, and negativism. Alternative strategies for ethics courses are suggested, which include making theory subservient to practice, engaging students in nonintellectual ways, recognizing the limits of formalism, teaching in ways that emphasize agreements, integrating ethics into wider curriculum and public programming, and providing positive examples of moral behavior. These strategies are designed to better assist the student not only in understanding moral theory but also in being a moral person.

Gutmann, A. (1987). *Democratic Education*. Princeton, NJ: Princeton University Press.

>This is an important work for anyone interested in the issue of public education in a democracy. The author presents an account of the proper purpose of education — educating for citizenship — and of the

appropriate balance between state and parental authority over schools.

―――. (1992). "Communitarian Critics of Liberalism." In *Communitarianism and Individualism,* edited by S. Avineri and A. de-Shalit, pp. 120-136. Oxford, Eng.: Oxford University Press.

This essay discusses some of the major criticisms communitarians have leveled against liberalism. The author then makes the case that the liberal responses to these criticisms are adequate responses. Communitarian criticisms are not simply misguided, however; they point out important issues to which liberalism needs to pay attention. These critiques should be viewed as supplementing and strengthening liberalism rather than as refuting it.

Horton, Myles, and Paulo Freire. (1990). *We Make the Road by Walking: Conversations on Education and Social Change.* Philadelphia, PA: Temple University Press.

Myles Horton was an American educator who helped found the Highlander Folk School in 1930. Paulo Freire is a Brazilian educator who has done innovative work in education for literacy and empowerment of poor people in Brazil and around the world.

Kymlicka, W. (1989). "Liberal Individualism and Liberal Neutrality." *Ethics: An International Journal of Social, Political, and Legal Philosophy* 99: 883-905.

This essay responds to criticisms of liberal neutrality specifically based on the liberal conception of individualism. The author argues that each of the three criticisms he considers is based on a misunderstanding of the liberal view.

―――, and W. Norman. (1994). "Return of the Citizen: A Survey of Recent Work on Citizenship Theory." *Ethics: An International Journal of Social, Political, and Legal Philosophy* 104: 352-381.

As the title indicates, this is a survey of research concerned with citizenship. The essay summarizes the positions of several main approaches to citizenship and citizenship education, along with criticisms of each of these approaches. Includes an extensive bibliography.

Lisman, C.D. (1996). *The Curricular Integration of Ethics: Theory and Practice.* Westport, CT: Praeger.

This book provides a case study approach for integrating ethics discussion across the curriculum and suggests that critical reflection on ethical issues in the context of service-learning is one way to promote civic responsibility in the academic disciplines.

———. (1998). *Toward a Civil Society: Civic Literacy and Service Learning.* Westport, CT: Bergin & Garvey.

This book provides a defense of citizen democracy against procedural liberalism or procedural republicanism. It analyzes how different approaches to service-learning, such as voluntarism, experiential education, and justice, are problematic in their tendency to reinforce aspects of procedural republicanism. Lisman advocates a citizen democracy model of service-learning that includes community development efforts designed to promote sustainable democratic communities. He provides examples of such best practices of service-learning and a discussion of the civic virtues or skills required to help students become equipped to be citizen democrats. Lisman finally discusses the social responsibility of higher education.

Macedo, S. (1990). *Liberal Virtues: Citizenship, Virtue, and Community.* Oxford, Eng.: Oxford University Press.

This book makes the case that the communitarian criticisms of liberalism do not successfully refute liberalism. The author presents an account of liberal civic virtues that are not neutral or empty, such as self-critical reflectiveness, self-control, and active, autonomous self-development.

MacIntyre, A. (1981). *After Virtue.* Notre Dame, IN: University of Notre Dame Press.

A classic early presentation of a communitarian perspective. MacIntyre traces the development of moral theory to its current state, which he characterizes as a form of crisis; moral dialogue, he argues, has been stripped of all substance. He then seeks to re-create a meaningful form for moral thinking and speaking grounded in the concept of a tradition and the practices and accompanying virtues that support the tradition.

Marx, K. (1964). *Selected Writings in Sociology and Social Philosophy,* translated by T.B. Bottomore. New York, NY: McGraw-Hill.

A representative selection of Marx's writing useful for discussion of neo-Marxist public philosophy.

Nozick, R. (1974). *Anarchy, State, and Utopia*. New York, NY: Basic Books.
A libertarian public philosophy.

Palmer, P.J. (1996). *The Company of Strangers: Christians and the Renewal of America's Public Life*. New York, NY: Crossroad.
A useful book for discussion of the importance of promoting a sense of the public as an aspect of public philosophy.

Pratte, R. (1988). *The Civic Imperative: Examining the Need for Civic Education*. New York, NY: Teachers College Press.
An early work critiquing classical or philosophical liberalism and defending communitarianism or civic republicanism.

Rawls, J. (1971). *A Theory of Justice*. Cambridge, MA: The Belknap Press of Harvard University Press.
Rawls's seminal defense of contemporary liberalism.

————. (1993). *Political Liberalism*. New York, NY: Columbia University Press.
One of the defining texts of contemporary liberalism. The author presents an account of how a diverse society comprising many different, and often conflicting, views about the good can, and should, nonetheless engage in mutual discussion about the basic structures of society.

Rorty, R. (1979). *Philosophy and the Mirror of Nature*. Princeton, NJ: Princeton University Press.
A seminal work critiquing epistemological foundationalism. Rorty advocates a pragmatic decision-making process.

————. (1989/1997). *Contingency, Irony, and Solidarity*. Cambridge, Eng.: Cambridge University Press.
This represents an attempt to find a middle ground between liberalism and communitarian thinking. Rorty maintains that the self and society are contingent and that there is no foundational basis for ethics or public philosophy. He recommends that we must accommodate the need for people to live their lives as they please, even if they are a negative influence on society in some sense, as "ironist." He maintains that society should allow for the greatest amount of freedom of individuals to live their lives, and that in fact that is all the public philosophy we need. Finally, he maintains that ethics is constituted by the moral norms of particular societies, a version of cultural relativism, but still wants to maintain that there may be a common norm for ethics, solidarity.

Sandel, M. (1982). *Liberalism and the Limits of Justice.* Cambridge, Eng.: Cambridge University Press.

> Sandel provides his definitive critique of Rawlsian contemporary liberalism. He maintains that the Rawlsian concept of the socially unencumbered self is untrue. He also claims that Rawls's social contractarian argument is unsuccessful, partly because of the inadequacy of the atomistic view of the self implicit in Rawls's philosophy.

————. (1984). "Morality and the Liberal Ideal." In *Justice: Alternative Political Perspectives,* edited by J. Sterba, pp. 219-224. Belmont, CA: Wadsworth.

> Sandel is one of the major critics of liberalism from the communitarian perspective. In this essay, he argues that liberalism is untenable because it depends on an account of the self that is unrealistic. Liberalism gives priority to the right over the good because it claims that selves are prior to their ends. Sandel argues that selves simply cannot reasonably be conceived as being prior to their ends.

————. (1996). *Democracy's Discontent: America in Search of a Public Philosophy.* Cambridge, MA: The Belknap Press of Harvard University Press.

> Sandel provides a thorough historical discussion of the eclipse of civic republicanism by procedural republicanism (contemporary liberalism). He advocates for a restoration of civic republicanism by means of greater citizen democratic efforts, especially through strengthening local associational life.

Sullivan, W.M. (1982). *Reconstructing Public Philosophy.* Berkeley, CA: University of California Press.

> This is an early and influential work in defense of civic republicanism. This book formed the philosophical context for the work of *Habits of the Heart.*

Taylor, C. (1989). *Sources of the Self: The Making of the Modern Identity.* Cambridge, MA: Harvard University Press.

> A lengthy historical analysis of the historical and social construction of the modern concept of the liberal self. Taylor provides a basis for defending the concept of the socially encumbered self of communitarianism and a critique of the atomized self of classical liberalism.

———. (1991). *The Ethics of Authenticity*. Cambridge, MA: Harvard University Press.

> This is a brief synopsis of some of the ideas of *Sources of the Self*. Here Taylor provides a brief basis for understanding how, even though there may be no "core" self, the self becomes morally encumbered in dialogical relationships.

———. (1992). *Multiculturalism and the Politics of Recognition*. Princeton, NJ: Princeton University Press.

> An important effort of Taylor's to lay out the importance of the concept of community-developed concepts of the common good. He notes the challenge of promoting the common good in ways that are respectful of diversity.

# Contributors to This Volume

## Volume Editors

**Irene E. Harvey** is an associate professor at Penn State University. She has published a book entitled *Derrida and the Economy of Difference* and numerous articles on deconstruction, postmodernism, and contemporary French thought.

**C. David Lisman** is the director of the service-learning program at the University of Denver and a member of the editorial board of the *Michigan Journal of Community Service Learning*. His publications include *The Curricular Integration of Ethics* and *Toward a Civil Society: Civic Literacy and Civic Learning*.

## Authors

**Stephen L. Esquith** is professor of philosophy at Michigan State University. He is the author of *Intimacy and Spectacle: Liberal Theory as Political Education* (Cornell, 1994) as well as several edited collections on democratic theory.

**Judith M. Green** is the author of *Deep Democracy: Community, Diversity, and Transformation* (Rowman & Littlefield, 1999). She is associate professor of philosophy at Fordham University in New York City, where she teaches courses in democratic theory, American pragmatism, ethics, African-American philosophy, and Native American philosophy.

**Goodwin Liu** is a former program director of the Corporation for National Service. Having recently completed his law degree from Yale University, Goodwin currently is employed at the U.S. Department of Education.

**Cathy Ludlum Foos** is associate professor of philosophy at Indiana University East. Her research focuses on the ethical and political implications of service-learning.

**Hugh Lacey** is professor of philosophy at Swarthmore College, where he teaches philosophy of science and Latin American liberation theology. His most recent publication is *Is Science Value Free? Values and Scientific Understanding* (Routledge, 1999).

**Dan Lloyd** is associate philosophy professor at Trinity College, Hartford, Connecticut.

**Carolyn H. Magid,** associate professor of philosophy at Bentley College, is in her seventh year of organizing community service-learning projects in the Boston public schools. Her current research deals with social justice issues about public and institutional policies (especially policies about education and work).

**Mary Esther Schnaubelt** serves as the executive director of Parents for Public Schools (PPS) of Jackson, Mississippi. PPS is a grass-roots, nonprofit organization that works to recruit students, involve parents, and improve Jackson's public schools.

**Sally J. Scholz** is an assistant professor of philosophy at Villanova University. Containing articles on domestic violence, oppression, language, and solidarity and other topics in social philosophy, her book *On Beauvoir* was published in 1999 by Wadsworth Press.

**William M. Sullivan** is a senior scholar at the Carnegie Foundation for the Advancement of Teaching. He is coauthor of *Habits of the Heart: Individualism and Commitment in American Life* and *The Good Society* and author of *Reconstructing Public Philosophy* and *Work and Integrity: The Crisis and Promise of Professionalism in American Life*.

**Eugene J. Valentine** is associate professor of philosophy at Shawnee State University. He has taught approximately 900 students in service-learning courses over the past 10 years.

**John Wallace** is professor of philosophy at the University of Minnesota. He is a founder and a member of the steering committee of the Invisible College, a national organization of educators working with their students to build a more decent society. He is also a founder and a member of the Jane Addams School for Democracy in St. Paul, Minnesota.

# Series Editor

**Edward Zlotkowski** is professor of English at Bentley College. Founding director of the Bentley Service-Learning Project, he has published and spoken on a wide variety of service-learning topics. Currently, he is also a senior associate at the American Association for Higher Education.

## About AAHE

**AAHE's Vision** AAHE envisions a higher education enterprise that helps all Americans achieve the deep, lifelong learning they need to grow as individuals, participate in the democratic process, and succeed in a global economy.

**AAHE's Mission** AAHE is the individual membership organization that promotes the changes higher education must make to ensure its effectiveness in a complex, interconnected world. The association equips individuals and institutions committed to such changes with the knowledge they need to bring them about.

## About AAHE's Series on Service-Learning in the Disciplines

Consisting of 18 monographs, the Series goes beyond simple "how to" to provide a rigorous intellectual forum. *Theoretical essays* illuminate issues of general importance to educators interested in using a service-learning pedagogy. *Pedagogical essays* discuss the design, implementation, conceptual content, outcomes, advantages, and disadvantages of specific service-learning programs, courses, and projects. All essays are authored by teacher-scholars in that discipline.

Representative of a wide range of individual interests and approaches, the Series provides substantive discussions supported by research, course models in a rich conceptual context, annotated bibliographies, and program descriptions.

See the order form for the list of disciplines covered in the Series, pricing, and ordering information.

# Yes! Send me the following monographs as they are released.

| Price per vol. (includes shipping*): | List $28.50 ea | AAHE Member $24.50 ea |
|---|---|---|

**Bulk prices** (multiple copies of the *same* monograph only):
10-24 copies $22.50 ea; 25-99 copies $21.00 ea; 100+ copies $15.00 ea

| | Quantity | Price | Subtotal |
|---|---|---|---|
| Complete Series (all 18 vols.) | | $405 | |
| Accounting | | | |
| Biology | | | |
| Communication Studies | | | |
| Composition | | | |
| Engineering | | | |
| Environmental Studies | | | |
| History | | | |
| Management | | | |
| Medical Education | | | |
| Nursing | | | |
| Peace Studies | | | |
| Philosophy | | | |
| Political Science | | | |
| Psychology | | | |
| Sociology | | | |
| Spanish | | | |
| Teacher Education | | | |
| Women's Studies | | | |

**Total** _____

## Shipping*

Price includes shipping to U.S. destinations via UPS. Call AAHE's Publications Orders Desk at 202/293-6440 x780 if you need information about express and/or foreign delivery.

## Payment (F.I.D. #52-0891675)

All orders must be prepaid by check, credit card, or institutional purchase order/number, except AAHE members may ask to be billed.

❑ Bill me; I am an AAHE member. (Provide member # below)
❑ Check payable to "AAHE."
❑ Institutional Purchase Order/Number: #_____
❑ VISA ❑ MasterCard ❑ AmEx

Cardholder's Name (please print)

Cardholder's Signature

Card Number                                                         Exp. Date

**Bill This Order To** (if "Ship To" address is different, please provide on an attached sheet) :

Name                                          AAHE Member #  __ __ __ __ __

Institution                          Address

City                          State          Zip

Phone/Email                          Fax

**Mail/Fax this order to:** AAHE Publications, PO Box 98168, Washington, DC 20090-8168; fax 202/293-0073; www.aahe.org. Visit AAHE's website to read excerpts from other volumes in the Series. Need help with your order? Call 202/293-6440 x780.